NEW MEDIA

IN THE

MUSLIM WORLD

Indiana Series in Middle East Studies

MARK TESSLER, GENERAL EDITOR

NEW MEDIA

IN THE

MUSLIM WORLD

The Emerging Public Sphere

SECOND EDITION

Dale F. Eickelman
and
Jon W. Anderson

Editors

INDIANA
University Press
Bloomington and Indianapolis

This book is a publication of

Indiana University Press
601 North Morton Street
Bloomington, IN 47404-3797 USA

http://iupress.indiana.edu

Telephone orders   800-842-6796
Fax orders   812-855-7931
Orders by e-mail   iuporder@indiana.edu

Library of Congress Cataloging-in-Publication Data

New media in the Muslim world : the emerging public sphere /
Dale F. Eickelman and Jon W. Anderson, editors. — 2nd ed.
    p. cm. — (Indiana series in Middle East studies)
 Includes bibliographical references and index.
  ISBN 0-253-34252-X (alk. paper) — ISBN 0-253-21605-2
(pbk. : alk.paper)
 1. Communication—Religious aspects—Islam.
2. Communication—Social aspects—Islamic countries.
3. Communication policy—Islamic countries. 4. Discourse
analysis—Social aspects—Islamic countries. 5. Mass media
in Islam. I. Eickelman, Dale F., date II. Anderson, Jon W.
III. Series.
 BP185.7 .N48 2003
 302.23'0917'671—dc21

                                        2002153776

2 3 4 5 08 07 06 05

To
AMAL,
LILLIAN CLAIRE,
and
MIRIAM

CONTENTS

LIST OF FIGURES AND ILLUSTRATIONS

The events of September 11, 2001, and its aftermath brought home not only the significance of the events themselves but also of the rapidly evolving new media environment— for Europe and North America and for the Muslim world—and the increasing interconnectivity among producers, consumers, and subjects of all forms of media. A recruitment video, circulated since May 2001 by the terrorist al-Qaʿida organization, slickly combined clips from CNN, the BBC, and Saudi and Russian television with their own CNN-style footage from training camps and "seminars" in Afghanistan, which took on new significance after September 11.[1] The Arabic-language al-Jazeera Satellite Television, based in Qatar and styled after CNN, came under intense scrutiny and political pressure as its policy of airing "other" voices that had already vexed Arab governments became an issue for policymakers everywhere. For the first time, British Prime Minister Tony Blair used al-Jazeera rather than the BBC to make an original policy statement, and al-Jazeera became a sought-out venue for U.S. government spokespersons, including the president's national security advisor, as well as an object of widespread scrutiny (El-Nawawy and Iskander 2002). These actions highlight the multiple and often unpredictable combinations of new media and new publics, new people and new interpretations that are reshaping the public sphere in the Muslim world.

New media undermine the theatre of the state, which Salvatore (1998) has called "staging virtue," with the theatre of the "street," making evident the multiple connections of this expanding public sphere. Eight months after al-Jazeera's Kabul studio was hit twice by "smart bombs" during the U.S. campaign to rout al-Qaʿida from Afghanistan and Osama bin Laden from the international airwaves, CNN, whose coverage in the 1991 Gulf War provided a model for al-Jazeera, "adopted a formal policy to avoid use of videotaped statements by Palestinian suicide bombers" and sent its top news executive "for consultations with Israeli officials about covering the conflict," after Israeli carriers threatened to drop CNN and placed Fox News next to CNN on the dial to offer "an alternative at the touch of a button" (Carter 2002). In between, private "hactivists" were busily disrupting Internet service to sites that they sought to silence. These and other interventions, from complaints about media incitement to national security claims, involve more than rights to speak and to represent. They involve constructions of the public sphere that are made particularly problematic by the advent of new media and growing recognition of their role in a rapidly changing communications ecology.

The extended social infrastructure of public communication is the context, frame, and often the referent of new media. New media frequently, but not always, offer self-consciously alternative forums for alternative voices, from the emergence of Islamic themes in romance novels in Bangladesh (Maimuna Huq, this volume) to thinking about modernity (Armbrust, this volume) to activists' campaigns for a public role (Robert W. Hefner, this volume) to new habits of listening, reading, and watching (Abu-Lughod 1995, Salamandra 2000, Öncü 2000, Hirschkind 2001). While new media give access to messages and voices that existing, particularly mass, media restrict or relegate to less public channels, they are in time also colonized by existing media institutions (Anderson, this volume) and newly emerging orders of discourse about Islam (Öncü 1995, Christmann 1998, Salamandra 1998), as new channels for communication become increasingly significant. Initial Internet sites created by some newspapers in Lebanon and other Middle Eastern countries, for example, were little more than home pages without content or were simply mirrors of their print editions. Increasingly, however, some of these sites rapidly evolve in complex and diverse ways to reach different audiences than the print editions, facilitating the emergence of a new generation of journalists and information specialists, thus shifting the balance from newspapers' long and authoritative editorials to more diverse and immediate content (Gonzalez-Quijano, this volume).

What and to whom new media connect their users and producers pragmatically involves three layers or contexts of the social infrastructure of communication. One is the world of Muslim opinion, discourse, talk, and teaching focused by religion and concerning its doctrine, practice, and proper role in society. Spokespersons legitimized by conventional systems of learning and their means of production increasingly find themselves complemented and even challenged not just by locally rooted understandings of Islam, with which they are familiar, but with rival and alternative articulations of belief and practice. Also, rising levels of education create audiences for articulating and justifying religious practices that erode older distinctions between "high" and "low" forms of public religious expression (Öncü 2000, also Anderson, this volume). An important part of the dialogue with other Muslims involves new social capital that draws on contemporary intellectual styles and uses different communication technologies to circulate messages and views about what is properly Islamic. New media, from the Internet and audiocassettes to Islamic-themed novels and television dramas, add new performance genres to those of learned commentary and sermons that are already articulated in a range of works from scholarly treatises to chapbooks. As Armbrust and others in this volume explain, the new media draw in resources and skills of distinctly bourgeois character and settings. Far from limiting the potential audience, these resources and skills represent the expansion of Islamic public spheres that was set in motion by the spread of education, the essential social capital of new, growing middle classes, which are beginning to attract the notice of U.S. policymakers. "We must speak," said Deputy Secretary of Defense Paul Wolfowitz, who articulated a doctrine of permanent war on terrorism, "to the hundreds of millions of moderate and tolerant people in the Muslim world, regardless of where they live, who aspire to enjoy the blessings of freedom and democracy and free enterprise" (quoted in Schmitt 2002).

A second layer or context emerges in those Muslim-majority societies where many local religious ideas and practices, long taken for granted and understood as Islamic, come under increasing scrutiny with growing familiarity with other Islamic communities and ways of doing things. New media play a major role in this foregrounding and questioning of local practices (Bowen 1999) and in changing local balances of competing religious authorities (Hefner, this volume), criticisms of other views, and defenses of one's own in public.

A third context is found in the larger public spheres in which Muslims are minorities, sometimes as immigrants and sometimes as converts, for whom the dynamics of new media include forging and sustaining contact and continued interactions between diasporas and homelands, increasingly through media (Starrett, this volume). The significance of such ties has long been recognized, as in the role of overseas Lebanese in influencing village and national politics (Winder 1967), but may mean that expatriates and immigrants are called upon to explain or interpret—or to distance themselves from—politics of their former homelands. New communications technologies make such interaction immediate and interconnected. This may strengthen sectarian bonds; it also fosters keen attention to the fates of emigrants and Muslims in Western countries. In some contexts, it leads to a greater openness, as when women can more directly join public discussions about their role in society and public debate over such issues as family law; in other contexts, it may only reinforce entrenched views.

In all these contexts, new media blur boundaries and link public spheres that are Islamic with those that are technological, secular, and political, based on class as well as sect, on "cold" ties (such as bureaucracy and duty to the state) as well as the "warm" ones of family and immediate community (Eickelman and Salvatore 2002: 110–12). They provide channels for hate groups, too, but their very porousness offers little basis for exclusivity. One of the new media's chief empirical characteristics is a consistent, often insistent, outreach. An overriding feature of the contemporary communications ecology is that new media expand to shape the public sphere increasingly as a marketplace of ideas, identities, and discourses.

Responses to the attacks of September 11, 2001, provide a case in point. Muslims and Islamic spokespersons almost universally condemned the attacks as non-Islamic (typically on the Qur'anic injunction against attacking noncombatants) and as tragedies with which anyone could identify. By November 2001, however, in Muslim-majority countries from Egypt to Bangladesh, rhetorical themes had begun to develop against U.S. imperialism, which secular media attributed to "imperialist muscle-flexing" and Islamic media to Western fears of the rising power of Islam. Muslim communities in the West also directly registered fears in the U.S. and European media which were quickly communicated to the Middle East both through personal and public channels with coverage of anti-Muslim and anti-Arab incidents and official acknowledgments that "Islam is for peace." An important entailment of new media is this thickening not just of ties to diasporas but also horizontally with other communities, including non-Muslim ones, that inflect new senses of "Muslim" community in the Muslim media.

The marketplace of ideas, identities, and ties is more than a metaphor. It is a reality that decisively shifts forums and resources of such discourse and its practices in favor of middle-class actors. Huq (personal communication, April 21, 2002) reports a pattern of educated Islamist youth in the middle and upper classes in Bangladesh introducing the works of more moderate writers on hot-button issues such as gender—authors who are regarded with suspicion equally by conservative traditionalists and radical activists. Authors of works that inspire these youth, such as the influential Egyptian Shaykh Yusuf al-Qaradawi, have similar followings throughout the Middle East and reach a global audience through the Internet (Anderson 2001) as well as through translations.

Throughout the Middle East and Muslim-majority societies elsewhere, the increasing complexity of "local" settings is evident. Gonzales-Quijano (in this volume) opens his analysis of the reshaping of publication and the media in Lebanon with the arresting image of an Internet café that has supplanted Beirut's Permanent Book Exhibit. Together with the ubiquitous satellite dish, Internet cafés have become icons of new media consumption across the Middle East. Internet cafés are particularly venues for youth, and Gonzalez-Quijano notes that younger members of established publishing families increasingly go into digital publishing and Internet services from web-site design and hosting to connections for users.

Likewise, existing publications and commercial publishing expertise have been the initial base for Internet ventures in neighboring countries, and Internet cafés are popular at least partly for repackaging telecommunications service (Anderson 1997). "A family that doesn't have money for a computer and Internet account at home can afford a dinar for the child to have an hour at an Internet café," a proprietor in Amman noted of his clientele (interview with Jon Anderson, June 13, 2001). Thus, the domestication of new media goes hand-in-hand with fostering new public places and new publics. But does this use of the new media constitute a public sphere?

Not by itself, argues Robert W. Hefner (in this volume): "there is nothing inevitable about the transition from plurality to civic pluralism." Echoing Jenny B. White (1999), he finds amplification, not transformation, when looking at the larger communications repertoire of one of Indonesia's militant Islamic groups. That group marshaled a range of new communication technologies that became broadly available across Indonesia in the 1990s, "beginning with the fax machine and new software programs for desktop publishing, but quickly came to include the Internet, which was introduced into large Indonesian cities in late 1997 and early 1998," to project themselves into a public sphere dominated by Indonesia's larger and more moderate Muslim groups. Like the Daudi Bohras of Bombay (Blank 2001), who embraced information technology to unite their community, Indonesia's Lashkar Jihad use it to enhance their organization in the face of more established groups, but on its own terms.

In all, the evidence to date affirms the outcome of amplified extremist voices over the liberalizing one at the institutional level, but just the opposite at the individual level, where a clear enhancement of agency is commonly the gloss on, if not the outcome of, the new media discussed here. The novelties of the media discussed in this book lie in their incompleteness and in users' abilities to utilize them differently, for different purposes, and in different contexts. The Internet, teenage romance novels, popular cinema, fax and telephone for political networking, religious tracts and educational material all entail more participation by their users than has been associated with "media" viewed through the optics of broadcasting and the press. This, and not just the multiplication of channels, makes the control of state and religious authorities over what is printed or broadcast increasingly problematic (Teitelbaum 2002). Audiences are now defined by exponential rises of mass education since the mid-twentieth century in Muslim-majority countries and the much greater ease of communications and travel for religious goals, education, labor migration, and emigration.

New media and their contexts draw attention to the social organization of communication in which different media operate. They point to an emerging public sphere between the "masses," evoked by an earlier era of state authorities and political leaders, and face-to-face solidarities of family, neighborhood, and community. Desktop publishing, delivery by fax and other small media, and Internet activists—but even more, Internet users—engender formal responses in the censored or "directed" large media, just as do the reading habits of youth, which vex traditionalists and radicals equally, obliging them, even if unwillingly, to call attention to the messages contained in media of more limited circulation, thereby eroding social distance and providing a model for others. Texts from sources as disparate as South Asia, the Middle East, and Europe circulate to American society, where they are adapted for Islamic teaching and sermons alongside material from the non-Muslim American mass media; similar patterns with Bangla and Indonesian translations of writings by Arab preachers are beginning to appear in media spaces opened by other writings.

The new media analyzed in this book are sometimes limited in audience, modes of participation, content, and authority. However, the practical result is opening up interpretation and introducing "lay" interpreters (Bunt 2000), "other" voices, and the scrutiny of conventional religious and political authority. There are no guarantees that the results will match liberal expectations long attached to enhanced flows of communication and information. While these seem to occur at an individual level, that does not necessarily happen at the level of institutions: existing ones prove adept at grasping the opportunities in new media to amplify their presences and capabilities, too.

The role of new media in expanding the public spheres of Islam, in Muslim-majority societies and for extended transnational Muslim networks, is as complex and multi-dimensional as the connections of these spheres locally and internationally. If it is unpredictable, the consequences are not: eroding social distance and multiplying role models are reshaping the meanings of *local* and *global,* and new media are their means.

NOTE

1. Excerpts of the video with translations and commentary by Richard Bulliet, Fawaz Gerges, and John Voll are on-line at <http://www.ciaonet.org/cbr/cbr00/video/excerpts/excerpts_index.html>.

WORKS CITED

Abu-Lughod, Lila. 1995. "The Objects of Soap Opera: Egyptian Television and the Cultural Politics of Modernity." In *Worlds Apart: Modernity through the Prism of the Local,* ed. Daniel Miller, pp. 190–210. London: Routledge.

Anderson, Jon W. 1997. "The Internet in the Middle East: Commerce Brings Region On-Line." *Middle East Executive Reports* 20, no. 12 (December): 8, 11–16.

———. 2001. "Muslim Networks in Cyberspace: Islam in the Post-modern Public Sphere." Presented at "The Dynamism of Muslim Societies," a conference of the Islamic Area Studies Project, Tokyo, October 5–8.

Blank, Jonah. 2001. *Mullahs on the Mainframe: Islam and Modernity among the Daudi Bhoras.* Chicago: University of Chicago Press.

Bowen, John R. 1999. "Legal Reasoning and Public Discourse in Indonesian Islam." In *New Media in the Muslim World: The Emerging Public Sphere,* 1st ed., ed. Dale F. Eickelman and Jon W. Anderson, pp. 80–105. Bloomington: Indiana University Press.

Bunt, Gary. 2000. *Virtually Islamic: Computer-Mediated Communication and Cyber Islamic Environments.* Cardiff: University of Wales Press.

Carter, Bill. 2002. "CNN, Amid Criticism in Israel, Adopts Terror Report Policy." *New York Times,* June 21, sec. C, p. 6.

Christmann, Andreas. 1998. "Islamic Scholar and Religious Leader: A Portrait of Shaykh Muhammad Sa'id al-Buti." *Islam and Christian-Muslim Relations* 9, no. 2 (July): 149–69.

Eickelman, Dale F., and Armando Salvatore. 2002. "The Public Sphere and Muslim Identities." *European Journal of Sociology* 43, no. 1: 92–115.

El-Nawawy, Mohammed, and Adel Iskander. 2002. *Al-Jazeera: How the Free Arab News Network Scooped the World and Changed the Middle East.* Boulder: Westview Press.

Hirschkind, Charles. 2001. "The Ethics of Listening: Cassette-Sermon Audition in Contemporary Egypt." *American Ethnologist* 28, no. 3 (Fall): 623–49.

Öncü, Ayse. 1995. "Packaging Islam: Cultural Politics on the Landscape of Turkish Commercial Television." *Public Culture* 8, no. 1 (Fall): 51–71.

———. 2000. "The Banal and the Subversive: Politics of Language on Turkish Television." *European Journal of Cultural Studies* 3, no. 3 (September): 296–318.

Salamandra, Christa. 1998. "Moustache Hairs Lost: Ramadan Television Serials and the Construction of Identity in Damascus, Syria." *Visual Anthropology* 10, no. 2: 227–48.

———. 2000. "Consuming Damascus: Public Culture and the Construction of Social Identity." In *Mass Mediations: New Approaches to Popular Culture in the Middle East and Beyond,* ed. Walter Armbrust, pp. 182–202. Berkeley: University of California Press.

Salvatore, Armando. 1998. "Staging Virtue: The Disembodiment of Self-Correctness and the Making of Islam as a Public Norm." *Yearbook of the Sociology of Islam* 1: 87–119.

Schmitt, Eric. 2002. "Pentagon Official Seeks Support for Moderate Muslim Nations." *New York Times,* June 2, sec. A, p. 13.

Teitelbaum, Joshua. 2002. "Dueling for *Da'wa:* State vs. Society on the Saudi Internet." *Middle East Journal* 56, no. 2 (Spring): 222–39.

White, Jenny B. 1999. "Amplifying Trust: Community and Communication in Turkey." In *New Media in the Muslim World: The Emerging Public Sphere,* 1st ed., ed. Dale F. Eickelman and Jon W. Anderson, pp. 162–79. Bloomington: Indiana University Press.

Winder, R. Bayly. 1967. "The Lebanese in West Africa." In *Immigrants and Associations,* ed. Lloyd A. Fallers, pp. 103–53. The Hague: Mouton.

ACKNOWLEDGMENTS

This book draws on several lines of inquiry into civil society and new media and information technology. These have included workshops, conferences, and symposia at professional meetings since the mid-1990s: a symposium on the Information Revolution in the Arab World at Georgetown University, a workshop on new religious writings and their audiences at the Rockefeller Foundation's Bellagio Study Center, panels on civil pluralism and new media at successive annual meetings of the American Anthropological Association, and a two-year Euro-American Summer Institute on "Public Spheres and Muslim Identities" supported by the Alexander von Humboldt Foundation and the Wissenschaftskolleg zu Berlin. Along the way, we have benefited from advice and comments by colleagues—including Arjun Appadurai, Richard Bulliet, Michael Collins Dunn, Brian Larkin, Madawi al-Rasheed, Armando Salvatore, and Richard L. Tapper—which we gratefully acknowledge. Preparation of this volume was assisted by grants from the Claire Garber Goodman Fund at Dartmouth College and support from the Publication Fund of the Anthropology Department at the Catholic University of America. For the first edition, in 1997–1998 the Woodrow Wilson International Center for Scholars provided Dale F. Eickelman with an intellectual milieu that bridged academic and policy research and was appropriate for addressing issues of wide public concern. Christian Hummel, William F. P. Raynolds, and Allison L. Schumitsch provided critical and timely support for the second edition.

NOTE ON TRANSLITERATION

This book draws on source materials in Arabic, Bangla, Indonesian, Persian, Turkish, Urdu, transliteration conventions preferred by Muslims writing in English, and colloquial as well as literary uses in all these languages. As consistently as possible, we use the system adopted by the *International Journal of Middle East Studies,* except that we omit diacritics. Although religious terms often derive from Arabic—for example, the Arabic plural *'ulama* (men of learning) becomes *ulema* in Turkish—we decided not to impose the Arabic where it does not accurately reflect local or regional usage. When appropriate, the common origins of such terms are indicated in the glossary. Likewise, the plural of most foreign terms, especially those derived from Arabic, is indicated by the addition of an "s" to the singular.

NEW MEDIA
IN THE
MUSLIM WORLD

1 /

REDEFINING MUSLIM PUBLICS

Dale F. Eickelman and Jon W. Anderson

A new sense of public is emerging throughout Muslim-majority states and Muslim communities elsewhere. It is shaped by increasingly open contests over the authoritative use of the symbolic language of Islam. New and increasingly accessible modes of communication have made these contests increasingly global, so that even local disputes take on transnational dimensions. These increasingly open and accessible forms of communication play a significant role in fragmenting and contesting political and religious authority. Muslims, of course, act not just as Muslims but according to class interests, out of a sense of nationalism, on behalf of tribal or family networks, and from all the diverse motives that characterize human endeavor. Increasingly, however, large numbers of Muslims explain their goals in terms of the normative language of Islam. Muslim identity politics take many different forms that are not unitary or identical, but such politics have become a significant force in both Muslim-majority states and those in which Muslims form only a minority of the population. It is in this sense that one can speak of an emerging Muslim public sphere.

Situated outside formal state control, this distinctly Muslim public sphere exists at the intersections of religious, political, and social life. Facilitated by the proliferation of media in the modern world, the Muslim public can challenge or limit state and conventional religious authorities and contribute to the creation of civil society. With access to contemporary forms of communication that range from the press and broadcast media to fax machines and audio- and videocassettes and from the telephone to the Internet, Muslims, like members of Christian coalitions, Hindu revivalists (Juergens-meyer 1993), Jewish activists, Sikh militants, and protagonists of Asian and African values, have more rapid and flexible ways of building and sustain-ing contact with constituencies than was available in earlier decades. The asymmetries of the earlier mass media revolution are being reversed by new media in new hands. This combination of new media and new contributors to religious and political debates fosters an awareness on the part of all actors of the diverse ways in which Islam and Islamic values can be created and feeds into new senses of a public space that is discursive, performative, and participative, and not confined to formal institutions recognized by state authorities.

Public dialogue has long held a special place in the Muslim world. A religious public sphere of learned scholars, schools of jurisprudence, and their supporters was often autonomous from the official sphere of rulers in the early Islamic centuries. The precedent was set in the inquisition (*mihna*) of 833–848, in which four successive caliphs decreed that Muslims had to accept the belief that the Qur'an was created, in spite of intensely held popu-lar support for the traditionalist view that it always existed. This authori-tarian imposition of doctrine met fierce resistance, and the effort was aban-doned after fifteen years. The result was to strengthen the role of men of learning (*'ulama*) in the public sphere from the third Islamic century through the modern era. Subsequent caliphs and other temporal rulers intervened in this sphere only with caution, and in general left it alone (Hurvitz 1997: 6).

In more recent times, especially since the Second World War and the end of colonial rule in many parts of the world, state authorities have used modern means of communication and bureaucracy to craft, refashion, and promote a publicly expressed code of competencies that all citizens or sub-jects should assimilate and practice in order to achieve modernity. Since the 1970s, few citizens of Muslim-majority countries unabashedly accept the legitimacy of state claims to monopolize this task. Just as there is a general scholarly recognition that there are multiple paths to modernity (Eisenstadt 1996: 396–426), there is a practical awareness that there are multiple claim-ants to the task of staging virtue (Salvatore 1998a: 87–89), including a pub-lic engagement in the name of religion. In this respect, Muslim activists, at least in public discourse, come close to what Warner (1990: 42–43) has called the republican virtues of colonial America, in which print or other media are used to direct consciousness to and craft certain models of civil-ity, membership within a community, and citizenship within a nation, all resting on more or less mutual packages of commitments and expectations (Salvatore 1997: 55–56).

Publicly shared ideas of community, identity, and leadership take significantly new shapes in such engagements, even as many communities and authorities claim an unchanged continuity with the past. Mass education, so important in the development of nationalism in an earlier era (Gellner 1983: 28-29), and a proliferation of media and means of communication have multiplied the possibilities for creating communities and networks among them, dissolving prior barriers of space and distance and opening new grounds for interaction and mutual recognition.

States in this century have taken it upon themselves to control the broadcast and printed word to foster common, shared, and modern identities at least as much as to deny these means to potential opponents. The centralized, asymmetrical structure of mass media is a product of this; states see these media as vehicles of consolidation and standardization. The correspondingly piecemeal and sporadic impulses to control the small media of fax machines, desktop publishing, and video- and audiocassettes demonstrate how those media contribute to the fragmentation of political and religious authority by bypassing established channels. When recast as differences between senders and receivers, distinctions between center and periphery become far more ambiguous and porous as the senders become multiple and shifting.

Some new media seen as innovative even in the 1980s are now almost taken for granted. In countries such as Saudi Arabia, the same fax machines that rapidly disseminate criticisms of the regime are also essential to the conduct of business. The state is powerless to limit their use without disrupting the economy. Audiocassette tapes spread the sermons of Ayatollah Khomeni and others in the pre-revolutionary Iran of the 1970s, just as videotapes of anti-regime preachers and demonstrations today circulate in some countries of the Arabian peninsula. One such video, showing employees of the Saudi embassy in London videotaping masked demonstrators while the demonstrators videotape the embassy (CDLR 1994), indicates both how commonplace and how flexible the new media have become. Some of these media utilize existing formats, such as desktop-published newspapers. Others, such as Islamic law journals, create an innovative format in which readers from different walks of life—not just conventionally trained religious specialists—exchange views with editors and thus contribute to enlarging the ways in which legal interpretations are made and who can make them. Broadcast *fatwa*s, or religious rulings, have much the same effect: they convert a form of highly personalized interpretation that in an earlier era was provided to individual questioners into more generic messages for a mass audience (Messick 1996: 319–20), and, thereby, shift part of the burden of interpretation to the listener/reader.

Internationally circulated Islamic educational videos, CD-ROMs, booklets, and Internet communications ranging from e-mail to World Wide Web pages frequently borrow formats as new and innovative to Western audiences as they are in Muslim contexts. It is not just that they are new; they are impersonal in the sense that they may be fitted to multiple contexts, put to diverse uses, employed by different people. Place becomes less contextually important than use: Is Pat Robertson's Web page less innovative than that of the Muslim Students Association? Perhaps because of a Western tendency to distinguish between spiritual and technical matters, the use of high-tech communications for religious purposes continues to seem noteworthy to secularists when they initially encounter it, but from Indonesia to Morocco, e-mail and the Internet foster new and rapid forms of communication and coordination for the religiously minded. Indeed, recent scholarly work on globalization and localization in the creation of Muslim private and public spheres in Indonesia (Bowen 1993: 315–30, Hefner 1997, George 1997) has been incorporated into the ongoing discourse of Muslim intellectuals in Indonesia and elsewhere.

Messages also migrate from one medium to another. Novels and recently even comic books (Douglas and Malti-Douglas 1994) address questions of how to lead an Islamic life, a domain previously exclusive to religious scholars who gave advice in the form of religious decrees (*fatwa*s) or published booklets. The proliferation and privatization of television and radio, furthest advanced in Turkey and Lebanon among Muslim-majority countries although still subject to significant government restrictions (Kinzer 1997), includes a significant amount of religious discourse and subtle changes in what is deemed "religious" as broadcasters, competing for market share, reach beyond traditional religious figures to draw the widest audiences. These are counterparts in the public sphere of the earlier displacement of subversive or dissenting messages into more private channels, such as jokes or, in some cases, theater enjoyed primarily by the elite. Newer media reverse this flow and open channels to an expanding public space.

Two effects follow from the boundary crossings of these messages. First, asymmetries between senders and receivers, and between producers and consumers, are reduced as more people participate in religious and civil discourse. In this sense, the new media are more participatory, whether by the access they give for the uninitiated to join the conversation or by the implicit invitation to interpret that accompanies more generic, less personalized messages bound to particular contexts. This incompleteness that invites the further interpretation of messages is the mirror of more symmetrical, more interactive sender-receiver relations that characterize the newer media to which these messages migrate.

Second, boundaries between public and private communication that once seemed clear become blurred as telephones and faxes are used to cross frontiers once readily policed by censors, and conversations that were previously confined to people who knew each other move into a public of anonymous senders and recipients, and thus into a rhetoric of norms that transform the social imaginary and the idea of the public (Warner 1992: 378–79). Messages intended for one medium, such as print, may acquire significantly different meanings when broadcast or faxed, and in all media there are competing and fragmented voices. Thus a leading Arab secularist, Syria's

Sadeq Jalal al-ʿAzm, can debate Shaykh Yusuf al-Qaradawi, a leading preacher and conservative religious scholar, on a Qatar-based pan-Arab satellite channel (al-Jazira TV 1997). Even now, such a debate would be unlikely on the state-controlled broadcast media, which generally avoid religious controversy. However, the Qaradawi/al-ʿAzm debate took place in an alternative broadcast medium, satellite television, where the weighting of questions primarily toward a fundamentalist religious viewpoint provided cover for the more unconventional secularist view expressed by al-ʿAzm. Viewpoints suppressed in one medium almost inevitably find an outlet in others. Thus the newer small media give broader access to these messages and widen the base of their producers, erode the gap between producer and consumer, and create new standards of public rhetoric. They create public space.

In this respect, new media share some of the properties of ritual in that they are performative. Media do not merely convey messages; they are also part of the message. When Saudi traditionalist *ʿulama* opposed the introduction of radio broadcasting, Ibn Saud quelled their protests by inaugurating Saudi broadcasting with a Qurʾanic recitation, which has been a staple ever since. More recently, King Fahd used television in a major 1992 speech, a year after the end of the 1991 Gulf War, to reaffirm the kingdom's existing political values and contain growing dissent (Rasheed 1996: 359–63). Lacking access to this medium of legitimacy, opponents within Saudi Arabia and elsewhere replied primarily through the small media; but some, such as opponents within the religious establishment, replied through mosques and foreign newspapers. Although some of these media are prohibited or, in the case of mosques, not expressly authorized, the various protagonists are drawn together into an increasingly public sphere of performance with the enhanced accessibility of new media. As Taylor (1993: 220–21) argues, members of modern societies are deemed to meet in a common space through a variety of media and through face-to-face encounters, and "thus to be able to form a common mind about matters of shared concern."

ISLAM AND INFORMATION

The new technologies of communication facilitate distinctively modern senses of religious and political identity that, rooted in specific local contexts, are also systematized on a translocal horizon opened by new forms of communication. Notwithstanding modern claims that Islam as practiced is uniform and universal, religious identities are everywhere joined to ethnic, political, and linguistic ones, where heightened senses of Muslim identity traditionally figure in local, regional, national, and transnational agendas and claims for leadership. At a local level, Moro nationalism in the Philippines is fueled by appeals to common Muslim identity, but the appeal is to a distinct ethnolinguistic group. It took shape only with the emergence of a colonial elite educated under U.S. rule, and emerged as a viable popular movement only after Philippine independence (McKenna 1998). At a more global level, the Organization of the Islamic Conference, a truly international body, works through state organizations and copes with both national and international rivals. Such identities are set in relations to specific others. And, as times change, many would agree with conservative Muslim intellectuals like Pakistan's Zafar Ishaq Ansari (1997), who observes that there is no longer any hard and fast line between West and rest, either as ideal types or as functioning communities, as we become aware of contemporary flows of communication. Boundaries are no longer primarily territorial, although these still count, but much more complex and cross-cutting. Those thought of as religious and civilizational, as Huntington (1993) and others remind us, transcend locality, as do other, intermediate levels in which specific bonds of loyalty and trust are elaborated for the purposes of business, worship, and community (Fukuyama 1996).

The emergence of a public sphere in which precedence is given to those who can authoritatively articulate universal standards depends on print and other media to assert this alternative sense of identity. Even as spokespersons for some groups assert that they seek a return to past values, as do some ethnonationalists and Muslim fundamentalists, they do so in a distinctively modern way, oriented to the future and assimilating new technologies and communicative forms (Bayart 1996: 239–41). In an era of restructuring state sectors, advancing market economies, global media cultures—including the globalization of idealized ethnic, sectarian, and regional cultures—and rapid flows of people and money, attempts to speak of transnational cultures, religious traditions, civil societies, or public spheres must take into account a fluidity of identities in these contexts that rests on their essentially, and alternatively, mediated character.

As in earlier public spheres, challenges to authority revolve around rights to interpret. Consequently, Muslim politics is less an expression of a unitary voice (although many would claim this as the goal) than an engagement to argue over correct interpretations. What is new today is that these engagements spill out of a few specialized channels into many generalized ones. They do not necessarily become more public than in the past—mosque-universities were public places and legal writings were public documents, although few had access to them; they instead become public in different ways. Their characteristic feature is more, and new, interpreters and, from them, the engagement of a more diverse and wider public.

The conversations and statements that contribute to this public sphere involve trusted partners, channels, media, topics, genres, and other communicative conventions set within different social realities. The result can be seen as both complex and evanescent since more publicness does not inevitably lead to greater participation in associational life—but it is the foundation from which associations can begin to emerge. Some channels, topics, and genres that have risen to prominence appeal primarily to the middle-class Muslim educators, engineers, doctors, and accountants whose techniques of thought and analysis these conventions deploy. These new genres attract identifiable social segments just as a bureaucratized form of Sufism earlier in this century acquired a following in the burgeoning bureaucracy of Egypt (Gilsenan 1973). Others, such as the telephone and local, even neighborhood, television channels in Turkey, fit the personalized network structures and information-seeking behavior of proletarian migrants, whose own networks of kin and friends have become widely, even internationally, dispersed. Across the social scale, some appeals have gained international reach, such as those of the late Ali Shariati (Iran) and Sudan's Hasan al-Turabi, who cast traditional learning in a modern idiom to transcend traditional scholarship in style and substance. Syria's Muhammad Shahrur and Iran's Abdokarim Soroush have similarly attracted followers, interpreters, and translators disseminating their ideas.

The messages of these thinkers, as of more anonymous persons, are inseparable from their context not just in tone and style, but also in the means of communication that they and others choose. In an era of multiple and alternative channels of communication, issues of how various publics are reached, how messages with religious and political content are listened to in the new Middle East and Muslim world, and what the limits on form and content are in different channels of communication are as important as the overt content of their messages. Much attention has been paid to how institutions formally recognized by the state provide agreed-upon boundaries of civility. Less has been paid to means of communicating the "ties that bind" (Qur'an 31: 22), to use a Qur'anic phrase that suggests how submission to Islam relates to the overlapping ties of kinship, language, and nations that contribute equally to creating institutions and a healthy dispersion of authority. Such means range from the lowly telephone for mobilizing dispersed networks of migrants in Istanbul's working-class suburbs to the Internet for creating new networks in and to the Middle East's overseas populations; they include transformed genres from Islamic romances and political comic books to new law journals in Indonesia and imported religious education material for African-American Muslims. They extend to movie making and magazines as well as amateur cassettes and leaflets, all in multiple, overlapping, international conversations.

NEW PUBLICS AND NEW MEDIA

Throughout the Muslim world—South and Southeast Asia, the Middle East and Central Asia, Africa, and the Muslim communities of Europe, the United States, and elsewhere—increasingly vocal debates on what it means to be a Muslim and how to live a Muslim life frequently translate in highly divergent ways from one context to another. This means that the available publics are significantly expanded not just in numbers or reach, but also in diversity of opinion, over what was possible just a few decades earlier. Upon publication of Salman Rushdie's *Satanic Verses* in 1988, opposition press coverage in Pakistan emphasized how the government's heavy-handed censorship cut committed Pakistani Muslims off from discussions initiated by their counterparts elsewhere. Thus the editor of the mass circulation *Takbir* (Karachi) wrote of the tragedy that Muslims in Britain and the United States could have direct access to Rushdie's book, even if this pained their sensibilities, while censorship kept Muslims in Pakistan ignorant and unable to contribute to international debates (Salah ud-Din 1989).

Some of the new thinkers participating in debates within the Muslim-majority world are becoming better known, as boundaries both of debate and of channels in which debates flow shift. Ironically, however, while Arabic remains a universal medium at one level, language differences within the Muslim world significantly constrain the circulation of ideas. Some Indonesian religious intellectuals, often trained in the United States and Canada, interpret developments in the Arab world, but virtually no Arab intellectuals follow debates on Muslim intellectual and political life in Southeast Asia (Madjid 1997). To some Muslim intellectuals, English has emerged as a preferred medium to call attention to new ideas. One leading Arab religious intellectual recently observed that, even to spread ideas in the Arab world, it helps to have one's ideas known in the English-speaking world and taken seriously by speakers of English, Muslim and non-Muslim alike (personal communication, New York, March 22, 1997).

New media aid this process significantly. Minor and emergent channels of communication that have proliferated are not mass in the same sense as conventional print and broadcasting. They are composed and consumed within more specialized, often voluntarily entered fields where producers and consumers, senders and receivers, are far less distinguishable than broadcasters or the press and their audiences. Instead, they merge in a kind of transnational community that moves the center of discussion and its impetus off-shore or overseas because their technology is mobile or was first available there (Anderson 1997). At times these contributions are anonymous, as is the case with some Internet postings, a tactic that transforms the notion of the public toward participation, as might illicit leaflets. In colonial America and the early years of the American republic, anonymous pamphlets were a major factor in sustaining an emerging public space (Warner 1990). At times, the anonymous leaflet or Internet posting plays a similar role today, as do generic spokespersons in the conventional press; although in some new media such messages are hard to distinguish from those of crackpots or fringe elements, or from disinformation contributed by regional security services.

Except in Turkey and, until recently, in Lebanon, where privately owned broadcast media have become increasingly circumscribed since the end of the civil war in 1995 (Norton 1997), television and radio are the province of official, usually state, institutions or, in the case of the Saudi-owned Middle East Broadcast Center (MBC), establishment commercial interests that limit their range of editorial expression. Through these media, establishments articulate their visions for education, worship, social services, politics, and entertainment (Alterman 1998: 15–24). Emanating from a center, they provide an authorized, top-down pattern of communication, so that competing voices are more likely to emerge through the alternative small media. Audio- and videocassette tapes are ubiquitous in the Middle East, and most countries acknowledge their significance by conducting rigorous inspections at frontiers, where they are subject to special scrutiny. Arab Postal Union regulations ban the posting of video- and audiocassettes. Such tapes circulate sermons, religious instruction, chants, and occasionally subversive folk music, including North African *ra'i*, as well as other entertainments; they utilize accessible, affordable technologies and vernacular languages to get messages across borders and past official and self-appointed guardians. They extend the speech communities of mosque or locality and also, as Babb and Wadley (1995) have shown for India, homogenize and demarcate regions and localities. To such media as cassettes can now be added local and even neighborhood television and radio stations in Turkey, plus forms of narrowcasting that range from pamphlets to the telephone and Internet discussion groups. Such forms of media link religious identity and civic action to activities in daily life, family, neighborhood, education, dress, jurisprudence, and patterns of consumption.

New media refigure audiences as communities, because senders and receivers have far more in common, not just in interests but also in cultural style and social position. While not nearly as widespread as the production and consumption of cassette tapes and pamphlets, the Internet reproduces many of these features at the opposite end of the social scale. As is characteristic of all these new media, the social and cultural distance on the Internet between producer and consumer is radically reduced. Similarly, with small but influential magazines in Egypt or law reviews in Indonesia, the size of audience is sometimes less significant than the quality and nature of the audience reached for a given purpose.

Another characteristic of the new media is that they occupy an interstitial space between the super-literacy of traditional religious specialists and mass sub-literacy or illiteracy. Their natural home is the emerging middle, bourgeois classes of the Muslim world. They draw—dangerously, in the view of traditionalists—on the techniques of multiple media domains, producing a creolized discourse that is not authorized anywhere but instead links others in an intermediate discourse (Anderson 1995). To the enthusiasts of such forms of communications, the eclecticism they permit is attractive. They are set in contexts of a generation-long rise in the level of mass education in Muslim countries and a relentless urbanization that has filled cities with both a work-seeking proletariat and career-seeking professionals whose mobility is international. Labor migration that puts Sri Lankan and Filipina maids and Pakistani construction workers in the Arab Gulf also facilitates the emigration of Egyptian, Palestinian, and Pakistani doctors, engineers, teachers, and administrators. Most labor migrants in the Muslim world are likely to be Muslims, which reinforces the international, or creole, character of their public space as an intermediate rather than merely disconnected or diasporic one. It is they who first consume and produce the new media, from *ra'i* music to Internet newsgroups.

The publics that emerge around these forms of communication create a globalization from below that complements and draws on techniques of globalization known in finance and mass marketing. While globalization from above is driven by multi-national corporations, globalization from below is traditionally associated with labor migration. Both constitute incorporation in an increasingly technological world. At their core are professional classes who are at least partly at home with the multiplying media of communication and the skills to operate them and more proletarian counterparts who use new media to incorporate expanding networks of otherwise traditional relations. Among the technicians of globalization as well as its participants, these professionals are both producers and consumers, forming communities on their own scale: interstitial, fluid, and resting on shared communications, a minimal definition of what constitutes a public space.

NEW PEOPLE

By new people, we mean those who have emerged and have benefited from the huge increase in modern mass education, especially higher education. Circles of literacy have been vastly widened and enhanced, creating a dense continuum between mass non-literacy and elite super-literacy. A generation of state-sponsored and, increasingly, private religious schools independent of state support spread the techniques of literacy and the demand for its products, along with a sense of the right to interpret religious texts or to choose interpretations attuned to immediate practical needs and aspirations. The transnational peak of this population takes the form of mobile professionals—a Tunisian Muslim psychotherapist in St. Louis or a Somali Muslim gynecologist in Toronto or an Egyptian Muslim computer programmer in Silicon Valley. But more modest examples of the beneficiaries of mass higher education are equally significant, as are those with less, but still some, education who move from rural village to working-class suburbs of Istanbul or Cairo or Dhaka.

The widening circle of those affected by the new media rests on this foundation of expanded education constituting a market for new mixes of ideas. In principle, traditional mosque-universities (*madrasa*s) in the Muslim world were open to all members of the community; in practice, they empowered a narrow elite to interpret traditions and communicate authoritative interpretive techniques to others (Eickelman 1992: 106–10). Modern mass education means not only more widely spread skills, but also wider, competing repertoires of intellectual techniques and authorities and the erosion of exclusivities that previously defined communities of discourse.

These transformations increase the range of participants in discussions about Islamic values and practice. Women and minorities find their way into arenas of political and religious discourse. Women in Iran may formally acknowledge the male interpreters of Islamic discourse, but this acknowledgment is often marked with barely concealed irony and skepticism, the weapons of the weak in the face of arbitrary authority (Torab 1996: 241-44). Educated people who are not religious scholars increasingly contribute to the discussion of legal issues and create alternative sites for religious discourse and representation. Many of them claim legitimacy on the basis of simplified, systematized, and down-market interpretations of basic texts. Criticism from the shrinking numbers of traditionally educated scholars does not obscure the fact that the new media engage wider and more public communities with claims to interpret and to provide additional techniques of interpretation.

In book publishing, the work of the Syrian civil engineer Muhammad Shahrur is a case in point. His approach to rethinking the meaning of the Qur'an entails a Kantian notion of public enlightenment by ideas, independent of the writer's status and thus to be evaluated on their persuasiveness alone. Despite the length of Shahrur's first book (over 800 pages) and its cost (half a month's salary for a government engineer in Egypt), it sold over 25,000 copies in authorized printings in Syria and many more in pirate and photocopy editions throughout the Arab Middle East, even though formally banned in many of the countries of the region (Eickelman 1993; interview, Eickelman with Muhammad Shahrur, Hanover, N.H., November 27, 1998).

At the other end of the spectrum, government-paid preachers (*khatib*s) appear on television from Morocco to Pakistan. Some preachers, such as Egypt's Muhammad Sha'rawi and Syria's Sa'id Ramadan al-Buti, achieve media fame. Most, however, have difficulty extending their reach beyond the Friday sermon and the mosque-university. Shahrur, by comparison, joins an ever-widening cadre of interpreters of Islam who link vernacular expression, modern education, and Islamic themes. Few *madrasa*s are yet on-line, with curricula and faculty profiles, although the International Islamic University of Malaysia, and a counterpart in Herndon, Virginia, target modern (and international) audiences through the Internet, as do branches of major Sufi orders, followers of the work of the Iranian thinker Abdolkarim Soroush, some *da'wa* (outreach) organizations, some of the theological schools in Qom, and at least one religious training school in Pakistan.

NEW THINKING

One feature of the new public sphere is a reintellectualization of Islamic discourse. Jeremiads against Western thought are still common, but critiques of Islamic micro-intellectuals or *lumpenintelligentsia*—to use Olivier Roy's (1992: 72) term—miss the point that such thinkers successfully join global and local communities of discourse and reach wider audiences than their predecessors.

By reintellectualization, we mean presenting Islamic doctrine and discourse in accessible, vernacular terms, even if this contributes to basic reconfigurations of doctrine and practice. Reintellectualization has sometimes been thought of as the province of folk or local Islam, a category that has been criticized for deflecting attention from the presence of the global in the local throughout the Muslim world. But more is involved with new media and new people: Islamic discourse has not only moved to the vernacular and become accessible to significantly wider publics, it has also become framed in styles of reasoning and forms of argument that draw on wider, less exclusive or erudite bodies of knowledge, including those of applied science and engineering. Shahrur draws his images from the Qur'an and civil engineering, as well as from the linguistics of de Saussure, Sapir, and Whorf. In an intellectual world of systems and subjects, Islam becomes approachable in different ways, one system in a world of systems. It has long been the case that Islam is recognized as an alternative among competing systems of religious belief and practice, and susceptible to multiple interpretive techniques. This in itself is not new—one thinks of the Andalusian 'Ali ibn Hazm (994–1064), author of extensive writings on various Muslim sects as well as the creeds of Jews and Christians, and of Christian missionaries in thirteenth-century Andalusia who learned Arabic in order to persuade Muslims of the error of their faith and the truth of Christianity—but now the available contrasts range beyond religious systems, so that some believers view Islam as competing with scientific disciplines, on the one hand, and secular political philosophies, on the other (for example, Ahmed 1992).

It is problematic to assert that the interpretation of Islamic precepts (*ijtihad*) was ever closed (Eickelman and Piscatori 1996: 26). Instead, the modern period in Egypt and Iran and parts of North Africa and South Asia compartmentalized Islamic practice into distinct institutions under colonial or secular governments. But even defensive accommodations, starting with Islamic responses to imperialism in northern India in the second half of the nineteenth century, have been accompanied by continuous reinterpretation. In its older conventional form as jurisprudence interpreted by traditionally educated scholars, the *shari'a* had become increasingly marginalized and irrelevant to social life, of interest to religious scholars only. In its new form as a set of normative rules avidly discussed in the public sphere, not only are elements of it implemented, often in novel circumstances, but it becomes a significant element of the political agenda (Brown 1997: 374, Eickelman 1998: 258, Nauimi 1996, Salvatore 1998b). One trend has been toward the *de facto* privatization of religious faith. Another trend has been toward radical doctrines, such as Khomeni's principle of *wilayat-i faqih*, which asserts the sovereignty of jurists over the texts they interpret. However, even among jurists in Iran, there has been vigorous debate over whether Khomeni's doctrine oversteps the appropriate role for the Shi'i religious establishment (Mir-Hosseini 1999). These two positions, however, merely define the ends of a continuum, the intermediate points of which acknowledge in practice a vigorous and growing religious public sphere and vigorous debate and diversity within it.

The reintellectualization of Islam is anchored less in long-standing conventions of interpretation than in the current experiences of believers. In this respect, Islamic discourse and practice is rapidly shifting from the boundary-minded forms it assumed after the advent of European imperial expansion into Muslim lands to a more confident and differentiated internal and external dialogue. The internal element of this reintellectualization engages many more believers in explicitly articulating Islamic beliefs than did its predecessors. As Gaffney (1994) relates in his detailed analysis of provincial Egyptian sermons, those identified as Islamists build their authority not only on personal reputation and knowledge of texts but, increasingly, from a demonstrated practical grasp of society and an ability to share with their audiences a grasp of their daily challenges. Similarly in Indonesia, the most politically influential religious intellectuals are those able to communicate their beliefs to large numbers of Muslims, delicately balancing state exigencies against the constantly growing religious public sphere (Hefner 1997). As Aswab Mahasin, an Indonesian human rights activist, remarked, the growing influence of Muslim social styles in the public sphere made many people who were previously embarrassed about their faith, because it looked backward and unmodern, proud to act like Muslims (cited in Hefner 1997: 111). Likewise, the relationship between Shi'i religious authority (*marja'*) and follower has always been two-way. Ambitious *ayatollah*s adjust their *fatwa*s to accommodate popular opinion, just as reformist *ayatollah*s often have to give in to the wishes of their followers. The major post-revolutionary development in Iranian religious thought is the challenge to the seminary-trained clerics of Qom by Muslim intellectuals educated outside the seminary, such as the London-educated Abdokarim Soroush (Mir-Hosseini 1999). At all times, believers have sought *fatwa*s from religious authorities to guide them on specific issues. In turn, *fatwa*s have conventionally responded to unique instances and have not been meant as generic pronouncements of doctrine or practice. When published or broadcast and thus widely distributed, however, they fill different, more anonymous and "public," functions.

A NEW RELIGIOUS PUBLIC SPHERE

The conjuncture of new media, new people, and the reintellec-tualization of Islamic discourse has broad implications. The first is that the translation or movement of messages from one medium to another changes the balance of what gets into circulation and who introduces new ideas. The proliferation of actors able to assert a public role leads to a fragmenta-tion of authority, and it increases the numbers of persons involved in creat-ing and sustaining a religious-civil public sphere. Even sloganeering—whether through graffiti, anonymous photocopied leaflets, or pamphlets—qualita-tively changes the sum of Islamic discourse, even more so as many such documents are anonymous. The transposition of religious (and political) issues to new media also changes the associative ecology of Islamic dis-course, juxtaposing religious issues in innovative ways with commerce, en-tertainment, and the professions, and contributing to the greater perva-siveness of religious themes in an increasingly redefined public life.

Issues such as who gets on national television and publishes mass-circu-lation books and newspapers and who gets confined to the small media contribute to the shaping of a new public sphere. Such channeling—who gets to speak in certain media or deflected to others—has always involved complex interlocking factors, such as official and unofficial censorship, avail-able infrastructure, and gatekeepers who control access to newsprint, stu-dios, and other required resources, including the training needed to use cer-tain media. Messages are the complex products of many actors and factors, and when some actors and their messages are deflected from the major me-dia into the smaller ones, the intermediaries between producers and audi-ences diminish, along with the ability of state and religious gatekeepers to influence what is said; and the sense of community correspondingly grows with senses of threat or insecurity. The determinant is not, however, the technological consequences of certain media. Media merely enable. Avail-able technologies have a bearing on the messages communicated and the means of doing so, but equally important are the rising levels of education and the growing cultural understanding among the beneficiaries of mass education of politics and religion as embedded in contingent social rela-tions, actions, and representations (Warner 1990: 6).

The second set of implications arising from the proliferation of new media is the emergence of new public spheres in which religious norms, practices, and values play a significant and sustained role that is not neces-sarily coterminous with civil society but that can offer powerful support to it (Hefner 1997: 110–16). In most Western contexts, religion has been for-mally consigned to the private sphere, although many observers comment that this may be due more to specific Western political reaction since the sixteenth century to a centralized and politicized church hierarchy than to anything inherent in civil society itself. Muslim-majority countries have never had such a centralized church structure against which to react, and the basis for regime legitimacy in most Muslim states is more tenuous than that for many of their Western counterparts. The boundary between public and private in most Muslim-majority states has never been clear or fixed. Thus religious speeches at weddings in Damascus, attended by hundreds of guests, including prominent political authorities, are formally private events. Nonetheless, they are tolerated, guests spread word of what was said, and videotapes of the talk circulate after the event. A speech at a different wedding several days later may provide a sharp rejoinder that is equally communicated to a wide and diverse public through word of mouth and videotape. Neither speech is mentioned in the authorized state media, yet the talks and the fact of their circulation are known to state authorities, some of whom listened to the talks when initially given (Eickelman field notes, Damascus, August 16, 1997). Neither public in an official sense nor private in a personal one, this space is nevertheless a privileged one, with its own formalities and well-understood scope.

Such blurring of lines—or, as we put it here, such intermediate, connective spaces—remind us of the impossibility of distinguishing sharply between public and private and point to more important continuities between one sphere and another that make them public between the private, on the one hand, and the political, on the other. We believe that it is more useful to see such events as giving wedding speeches in Damascus, publishing texts on the Internet, opening law journals to debates about Islamic requirements, or moving those into the genre of romance novels as elements of a public sphere in which cultural entrepreneurs adapt existing cultural practices to new communicative environments. The result, of course, is to develop and promote new understandings of the role of religion in society. As media command attention to it, the emergence of this new public sphere in turn promotes changes in the orientation and style of official discourse, which at least indirectly is obliged to take account of what is said (as in the case of denunciations faxed to Saudi Arabia) or to be perceived as ignoring or tolerating it (as in the case of Damascene wedding speeches). It also has a significant effect on the everyday practices embedded in social relations, where religious or political authority is a matter of face-to-face biographical familiarity rather than the more formal credentials or structural position that is its equivalent in the large media.

These new publics emerge along a continuum between mass communication aimed at everyone and direct personal communications to specific others with whom one already has a personal relationship. This expanding space of public dealings with those whom Alfred Schutz called contemporaries beyond one's face-to-face consociates (Schutz 1967: 15–19)—indeed doing everything possible to turn the anonymous or unknown contemporary into a consociate working under common assumptions of civility and morality—is an important part of developing a public sphere in which religion plays a vital role. It contributes to the recognition that such a public is not mass and anonymous, but defined by mutual participation—indeed, by performance. In this sense, which Benedict Anderson (1991: 37–46) refers to as a growing sense of reading together, the public sphere emerges less from associations, more strictly the domain of civil society, than from ways of dealing confidently with others in an expanding social universe of shared communication.

We suggest that by looking at the intricate multiplicity of horizontal relationships, especially among the rapidly increasing numbers of beneficiaries of mass education, new messages, and new communication media, one discovers alternative ways of thinking about Islam, acting on Islamic principles, and creating senses of community and public space. Such a realization among large numbers of people is a measure of the potential for a rapidly emerging public sphere and a civil society that plays a vital role within it.

WORKS CITED

Ahmed, Akbar S. 1992. *Postmodernism and Islam: Predicament and Promise.* London: Routledge.

Alterman, Jon B. 1998. *New Media, New Politics? From Satellite Television to the Internet in the Arab World.* Washington, D.C.: Washington Institute for Near East Policy.

Anderson, Benedict. 1991. *Imagined Communities: Reflections on the Origin and Spread of Nationalism.* London: Verso.

Anderson, Jon. 1995. "Cybarites, Knowledge Workers and New Creoles on the Information Superhighway." *Anthropology Today* 11, no. 4 (August): 13–15.

———. 1997. "Globalizing Politics and Religion in the Muslim World." *Journal of Electronic Publishing* 3, no. 1 (September). <http://www.press.umich.edu:80/jep/03–01/Anderson.html>

Ansari, Zafar Ishaq. 1997. Comments made at the International Symposium, The Islamic World and Global Co-operation: Preparing for the 21st Century, Kuala Lumpur, April 26, 1997.

Babb, Lawrence, and Susan S. Wadley, eds. 1995. *Media and the Transformation of Religion in South Asia.* Philadelphia: University of Pennsylvania Press.

Bayart, Jean-François. 1996. *L'illusion identitaire.* Paris: Fayard.

Bowen, John. 1993. *Muslims through Discourse.* Princeton: Princeton University Press.

Brown, Nathan J. 1997. "*Shari'a* and the State in the Modern Middle East." *International Journal of Middle East Studies* 29, no. 3 (April): 359–76.

Chazan, Robert. 1989. *Daggers of Faith: Thirteenth-Century Christian Missionizing and Jewish Response.* Berkeley and Los Angeles: University of California Press.

Committee for the Defence of Legitimate Rights (CDLR, Lajnat al-Difa' 'an al-Hurur al-Shar'iyya). c. 1994. *Intifadat Burayda* (The Burayda Uprising). Videotape. Publisher and place not mentioned. (Videotape of a demonstration that took place on September 18, 1994.)

Douglas, Allen, and Fedwa Malti-Douglas. 1994. *Arab Comic Strips: Politics of an Emerging Mass Culture.* Bloomington: Indiana University Press.

Eickelman, Dale F. 1992. "The Art of Memory: Islamic Education and Its Social Reproduction." In *Comparing Muslim Societies: Knowledge and the State in a World Civilization,* ed. Juan R. I. Cole, pp. 97–132. Ann Arbor: University of Michigan Press.

———.1993. "Islamic Liberalism Strikes Back." *Middle East Studies Association Bulletin* 27, no. 2 (December): 163–68.

———. 1998. *The Middle East and Central Asia: An Anthropological Approach,* 3rd ed. Upper Saddle River, N.J.: Prentice Hall.

Eickelman, Dale F., and James Piscatori. 1996. *Muslim Politics.* Princeton: Princeton University Press.

Eisenstadt, Shmuel. 1996. *Japanese Civilization: A Comparative View.* Chicago: University of Chicago Press.

Fukuyama, Francis. 1996. *Trust: The Social Virtues and the Creation of Prosperity.* New York: Free Press.

Gaffney, Patrick D. 1994. *The Prophet's Pulpit: Islamic Preaching in Contemporary Egypt.* Berkeley and Los Angeles: University of California Press.

Gellner, Ernest. 1983. *Nations and Nationalism.* Ithaca and London: Cornell University Press.

George, Kenneth M. 1997. "Some Things That Have Happened to *The Sun After September 1965:* Politics and the Interpretation of an Indonesian Painting." *Comparative Studies in Society and History* 39, no. 4 (October): 603–34.

Gilsenan, Michael. 1973. *Saint and Sufi in Modern Egypt.* Oxford: Oxford University Press.

Hefner, Robert W. 1997. "Islamization and Democratization in Indonesia." In *Islam in an Era of Nation-States,* ed. Robert W. Hefner and Patricia Horvatich, pp. 75–127. Honolulu: University of Hawaii Press.

Huntington, Samuel. 1993. "The Clash of Civilizations?" *Foreign Affairs* 72, no. 3 (Summer): 22–49.

Hurvitz, Nimrod. 1997. "The *Mihna* (Inquisition) and the Public Sphere." Paper presented at the International Workshop, The Public Sphere in Muslim Societies, at the Van Leer Jerusalem Institute, October 6–7, 1997.

al-Jazira Satellite Television. 1997. Debate between Sadiq Jalal al-ʿAzm and Yusuf al-Qaradawi, moderated by Faysal al-Qasim, broadcast in the series *The Opposite Direction (al-Ittijah al-Muʿakis),* May 27, 1997.

Juergensmeyer, Mark. 1993. *The New Cold War? Religious Nationalism Confronts the Modern State.* Berkeley and Los Angeles: University of California Press.

Kinzer, Stephen. 1997. "A Terror to Journalists, He Sniffs Out Terrorists." *New York Times,* September 1, p. A4.

McKenna, Thomas. 1998. *Muslim Rulers and Rebels: Islamic Authority and Armed Separatism in the Southern Philippines.* Berkeley and Los Angeles: University of California Press.

Madjid, Nurcholish. 1997. "The Resurgence of Islam in Indonesia: Challenges and Opportunities." Middle East Studies Association Distinguished Visiting Scholar lecture, San Francisco, November 23.

Masud, Muhammad Khalid, Brinkley Messick, and David S. Powers, eds. 1996. *Islamic Legal Interpretation: Muftis and Their Fatwas.* Cambridge: Harvard University Press.

Messick, Brinkley. 1996. "Media Muftis: Radio Fatwas in Yemen." In *Islamic Legal Interpretation: Muftis and Their Fatwas,* ed. Muhammad Khalid Masud, Brinkley Messick, and David S. Powers, pp. 311–20. Cambridge: Harvard University Press.

Mir-Hosseini, Ziba. 1999. *Islam and Gender: The Religious Debate in Contemporary Iran.* Princeton: Princeton University Press.

al-Nauimi, Najeeb bin Mohamed. 1996. "Qatar's Purse Strings" (letter). *The Economist* (London), October 5, p. 8.

Norton, Augustus Richard. 1997. Personal communication, September 13, 1997.

al-Rasheed, Madawi. 1996. "God, the King and the Nation: Political Rhetoric in Saudi Arabia in the 1990s." *Middle East Journal* 50, no. 3 (Summer): 359-71.

Roy, Olivier. 1992. *L'échec de l'Islam politique* (The Failure of Political Islam). Paris: Éditions du Seuil. (English translation, *The Failure of Political Islam.* Cambridge: Harvard University Press, 1994.)

Salah ud-Din. 1989. Editorial in *Takbir* (Karachi), February 9. (DFE is grateful to Khalid Masud for translating the editorial from Urdu.)

Salvatore, Armando. 1997. *Islam and the Political Discourse of Modernity.* Reading (UK): Ithaca Press.

———. 1998a. "Staging Virtue: The Disembodiment of Self-Correctness and the Making of Islam as a Public Norm." *Yearbook of the Sociology of Islam* 1: 87–119.

———. 1998b. "Discursive Contentions in Islamic Terms: Fundamentalism vs. Liberalism?" In *Islamic Fundamentalisms: Myths and Realities,* ed. Ahmad Moussalli, pp. 75–102. Reading, UK: Ithaca Press.

Schutz, Alfred. 1967. *Collected Papers I: The Problem of Social Reality,* ed. Maurice Natanson. The Hague: Martinus Nijhoff.

Taylor, Charles. 1993. "Modernity and the Rise of the Public Sphere." *The Tanner Lectures on Human Values* 14: 203–60.

Torab, Azam. 1996. "Piety as Gendered Agency: A Study of *Jalaseh* Ritual Discourse in an Urban Neighbourhood in Iran." *Journal of the Royal Anthropological Institute* (N.S.) 2, no. 2 (June): 235–52.

Warner, Michael. 1990. *The Letters of the Republic.* Cambridge: Harvard University Press.

———. 1992. "The Mass Public and the Mass Subject." In *Habermas and the Public Sphere*, ed. Craig Calhoun, pp. 377–401. Cambridge: MIT Press.

2 /

The New Media, Civic Pluralism, and the Struggle for Political Reform

Augustus Richard Norton

When the al-Aqsa intifada began in the autumn of 2000, images of a terrified boy and his equally terrified father transfixed television viewers in the Middle East and beyond. As Muhammad al-Durra and his father were caught in the crossfire between Israelis and Palestinian demonstrators, the father futilely attempted to protect his son, edging him behind his back as they crouched against a wall and behind a large drum marking a checkpoint. In one moment the boy is alive with fear, in the next he slumps dead across his father's lap. His father, devastated, looks blankly into space. Within minutes, images of young Muhammad's death were beamed worldwide by satellite television, al-Jazeera, Future Television, LBC, BBC, CNN, and others. Images of the boy's final seconds were quickly posted on the Internet, spawning debate, accusations, and counter-accusations, official denials of responsibility by Israel, and, of course, web sites (for example, <http://www.fortunecity.com/marina/commodity/1089/id147.htm>). In reaction to the images, massive demonstrations erupted in Arab capitals, and citizens castigated their governments for impotence in the face of Israeli oppression of the Palestinians. Even where enthusiasm had faded for the cause of Palestinian nationalism, as in Kuwait, the issue became newly politicized. A mere five years earlier, certainly a decade before, more reliable but also more sedate foreign media would have marginalized the event, and the regional state media—television featuring soporific news readers detailing quotidian events in the ruler's life and banal government newspapers—would not wish to rile the masses.

In October 2002, two years into the al-Aqsa intifada, as the United States attacked targets in Afghanistan in retaliation for the horrendous attacks of September 11, Osama bin Laden and his associates appeared on al-Jazeera, the wildly successful Qatari-based news channel that is in part an Arabic-language answer to CNN. Bin Laden appeared in a shrewdly choreographed videotape and spoke eloquently to the Arab viewers, evoking twentieth-century political manipulation of the Arab world, the fate of Palestinians, the plight of Iraq, and threats to the sacred sites of the Arabian Peninsula. In the United States, official spokespeople and countless talking heads cried "foul." Bin Laden did not really care about Palestine and Palestinians, it was avowed; he was only trying to exploit the confrontations between Israelis and the Palestinians to gain a broader constituency.

A search for bin Laden's "true" beliefs misses the point entirely. Whether in his heart of hearts bin Laden mourned for the fate of Jerusalem was far less important than the fact that he was able to bypass governments and capitalize on widespread discontent by speaking resonantly to the public. If few Muslims approved of the terrorism that he employed, far more took his critique of the existing power structure to heart. U.S. National Security Advisor Condoleezza Rice soon pressured U.S. networks to deny bin Laden and al-Qaʿida a place on their broadcasts, arguing unpersuasively that the messages could contain hidden codes. The problem was not hidden code, but the power of propaganda and the fact that bin Laden's television visage reinforced his importance and gave context to the killing that he spawned. U.S. media executives quickly acquiesced to the government request, and after pressure was applied on the Qatari government, al-Jazeera subsequently adopted a more cautious approach to broadcasting unedited statements from al-Qaʿida.

As the discomfort of the U.S. government revealed, the phenomenon of new media challenges existing governments, confronts American hegemony, and presents themes of disharmony, discord, discontent, and even vicious violence. Halcyon forecasts of a globalized market, universal values, and the seduction of yuppie culture are belied by the headlines that define the dawn of the new century. Yet, unpacked and contextualized, there is considerable promise for improvement in the human condition in the Muslim world precisely because contentious issues of government accountability, individual rights, and not least, religion have become topics of broad debate.

Much of what is happening is hidden from Western view not just by barriers of language and distance, but also by metaphors that betray stereotypes rather than reveal reality. An example is the use of "the street" to refer to mass public opinion in Muslim countries, especially Arab countries. Not only does the term imply a formless mass of people swayed by the sentiments of the moment and manipulated by autocrats, a modern parallel to "the mob" in revolutionary France or "the crowd" in nineteenth-century England, but also few nuances of opinion and no need to stratify points of view by class, gender, age, or regional or occupational distinctions. "The street thinks . . ." intone sage-sounding television performers, as though talking about tidal movements. A rough equivalent for the United States would be "the mall thinks . . ." But that is not used, because closer to home it is well understood that there are different points of view, different regions to hear from, and that no single group speaks authentically for the United States.

The Muslim world has not been immune to international travel and migration, increasingly globalized trade, and the penetration of all but the most remote geographic nooks and crannies by radio, television, cellular telephones, fax machines, and computers, as well as inexpensive means of printing and reproduction. Why should Islamabad be less susceptible than Cleveland to the pace of global change? Members of Muslim societies at the dawn of the twenty-first century use land-line telephones or cellular models (sometimes several at once), read pulp novels, go to the beach, operate fax machines, and debate their religion. Thankfully, there is more to the story. The focus of new media overlaps with a heightened interest in civic pluralism in the Muslim world.

Pluralism has always been more marked in Muslim societies than prevailing essentialist stereotypes suggest; but, even so, the diversity of Muslim-majority societies and awareness in them of intra-Muslim differences are increasing rapidly. From the lowly telephone to the latest Pentium computer, electronic communications permit both conventional and virtual neighborhoods to become sites for identifying, addressing, and solving shared concerns and complaints. Accessible, cheap communication technologies and mass education feed the appetite for new media.

Authoritative interpretations of Islam, long the preserve of learned men (*'ulama*), are now in many hands. Indeed, some of the most creative thinking on Islam in recent years has been done by Muslim men and women with little or no formal training in Islamic jurisprudence (*fiqh*) or other specialties of the conventionally trained *'ulama*. At the same time, Islamically correct pulp novels and popularized interpretations of Muslim ideals and norms enjoy a wide readership. The authority of the *'ulama* of a generation ago is now contested. The competition for Islamic authority is booming in the variety of tapes, inexpensive books, pamphlets, and kitsch that fill the marketplace.

In Saudi Arabia, the Committee for the Defense of Legitimate Rights (CDLR) challenged the regime's authority in the 1990s. The London-based group exploited the telephone and the fax machine to publicize its Islamist program and to report on the purported misdeeds of and corruption in the ruling family. One leader of the committee asserts that "Khomeini's was a cassette revolution, ours will be a fax revolution" (al-Rasheed 1996: 16). By decade's end, the kingdom addressed the challenge by co-opting the leading figures in the CDLR, and buttressed its Islamic credentials by lending tacit and active encouragement to the most conservative tendencies in Saudi society.

As elsewhere in the Muslim world, the Saudi *'ulama,* paid or subsidized by the government, have no obvious advantage in the contest for popular support. In most settings they suffer severe disadvantages by their association with the government, which is often perceived with suspicion and fear. Bin Laden has certainly been a beneficiary of *'ulama* failings, just as he and al-Qaʿida were beneficiaries of official Saudi efforts to propagate the particularly conservative and often intolerant variant of Islam that dominates society.

The structural context of growing diversity in large parts of the Muslim world raises important questions for the political evolution of Muslim societies at the dawn of the twenty-first century. In particular, what are the prospects for the transformations of authoritarian governments and what role will the new media and civic pluralism play in inspiring or shaping political reform?

Certainly it is wishful thinking to presume that new media are in themselves an antidote to authoritarianism. The discursive voices of the new media are fascinating, but their political importance has yet to be demonstrated. It is by no means clear how civic pluralism translates into political power, if at all. They may provide a fortuitous rationale for the political class to attempt to maintain its grip on power instead of to loosen it. Authoritarian governments enjoy support in the West, where the status quo is usually viewed as preferable to the potential turmoil of transition. Change is often perceived as jeopardizing Western links to stable authoritarian governments, especially in the Muslim world. One only need ponder the examples of Egypt, Pakistan, or Saudi Arabia. In each case, major Western powers preferred the predictable comfort of autocratic rule to the uncertainties of change, notwithstanding eloquent avowals of support for human rights and democracy.

So, it is ironic that the horrors of September 11 led the U.S. government to "discover" political reform in the Muslim world. It is ironic because American opposition has often stymied reform. A good example is the Palestinian authority that emerged from the Oslo Accords. Faced with evidence of a lively, well-educated Palestinian society with arguable potential for democratic development, the United States, in league with Israel, preferred a Palestinian dictatorship to guarantee order. When, in 1993, I asked Yossi Bellin, the Israeli deputy foreign minister who played a leading role in the Oslo Accords, whether Israel would be better served by an institutionalized, participant political system than by the creation of a fragile structure of peace resting on the power of a dictator (Yasir Arafat), he replied: "My friend, the Palestinian state is going to be a dictatorship just like all the other Arab states." Now with the Oslo framework in shambles, the United States and Israel may embrace reform less as a vehicle for the actualization of democratic potential by the Palestinians than in order to find a more pliant, more effectual strongman.

Despite caveats about the persistence of authoritarian government in the Muslim world, social developments that point to the emergence of alternative voices and even a modest weakening of governmental control deserve attention. The quest for government hegemony in the post-colonial Muslim world has often centered on the reproduction of social values and the fostering of national solidarity, particularly in authoritarian republics such as Egypt, Iran, and Turkey; but this quest has largely failed. Instead, government is simply one of many competing sites, albeit a powerful one, in which values and ideals are adapted, debated, reshaped, or nourished. Although government efforts to shape, if not control, the dissemination of political communications persist, censorship is less effective than in the recent past, and sometimes it only serves to parody the abuse of power. While newspapers, radio, and television are relatively susceptible to control through licensing, restricted access to supplies of newsprint, and sweeping libel and press laws, newer media, such as the mass production of audiocassette tapes, are typically unlicensed and anonymous. Ubiquitous ministries of information, established on the premise that information flows downward, find their relevance steadily eroded by the new media, which spread laterally. The horizontal proliferation of information undermines vertical lines of control. Day by day, it seems, the ministry of information becomes more important as a source of employment than as a means of control.

Even so, the post-independence Muslim-majority state has proven remarkably durable and resistant to reform. Despite widespread sentiment in the Muslim-majority world for more accountable, less autocratic governance, the state continues to impose political structures and institutions with remarkably little resistance from society. Many Muslim-majority states have persistently crushed autonomous forms of association, and the legacy of authoritarianism in the Muslim world is stunted civil society. This is not a cultural artifact but a direct result of the policies of the twentieth-century state, with its penchant for a single political party and suspicion of independent voices. Thinking them not to be independent, government policies have tended to privilege populist Islamist forces, sometimes by design, but often as a side effect of the suppression of potential opponents among the secular opposition.

Government intolerance of dissent stems from several factors, chief among which is the political economy of the state, which has, in many instances, been able to draw upon a variety of natural resources and geopolitical rents (for example, cash infusions such as oil income and foreign aid) rather than rely upon a system of taxation. Taxation requires the active participation of citizens. It is no accident that political reforms have been pursued most seriously when straitened resources have forced reductions in subsidies and increased taxes. Consider the contrasting cases of Jordan and Egypt. In Jordan, by the late 1980s, the state was bereft of external subsidies and faced insolvency. In Egypt, despite the awesome economic challenges the country faces, donors have not been shy about picking up the tab for a bloated public sector while underwriting myriad developmental and adjustment projects that have staved off economic ruin.

As the state has proven to be not only durable but also embedded, it is remarkable that the missing player is the state, especially since the behavior and fate of the state will substantially effect the further development of civic pluralism. The state still casts a large shadow even as a parallel global system of non-sovereign actors emerges (Rosenau 1990). The usual examples of these actors include groups such as Amnesty International and Human Rights Watch, which adroitly adopt the new media; but Jon W. Anderson's work on "virtual Islamic communities" (this volume) suggests a more novel example in oppositional groups finding a place on the Internet. The contemporary state must not only contend with growing domestic efforts to shape social values; it also faces an international milieu in which the state is increasingly susceptible to critique and opprobrium. There the transnationality of media (for example, the Saudi opposition's faxes, Islamic sermons on cassettes, CNN, al-Jazeera, and other satellite channels) undermines the state's control by providing alternative sources of information that people can use, whether they are displaced as refugees or labor migrants, members of a diaspora, creolized, or none of the above.

Perhaps we should be grateful that the state is constrained but not endangered. As Hann and Dunn (1996: 7) note, "Despite much heady talk of 'world civil society' in the context of globalisation, there is as yet no sign of any plausible alternative to the state as the primary institutional framework within which security and solidarity can be established in late twentieth-century social conditions." The state remains indispensable, especially for the maintenance of public order. Unfortunately, some governments construe public order in self-serving and capricious ways.

THE RISE AND FALL OF EGYPT'S LAW 93

On May 27, 1995, the People's Assembly of Egypt passed a comprehensive press law (Law 93/95) to curtail even mild allusions to official misbehavior and corruption. It included harsh punishments for libel (defined in the vaguest of terms): mandatory imprisonment, fines, and preventive detention. The law was widely viewed by Cairenes as a response to the increasing attention being paid by the press to incidents of corruption around President Husni Mubarak. The law held journalists responsible for the veracity of their reports, even if they were merely reprinting reports first published abroad. The assembly speaker Fathi Srour pushed the law through the house, permitting no serious debate, and Law 93 seemed destined to be a *fait accompli*. However, the professional press syndicate reacted strongly to what was quickly branded the "Press Assassination Law." In response, Mubarak agreed to the creation of a "semi-government" committee with a mandate to recommend amendments to the law. After several months of meetings, months in which journalists were aggressively prosecuted for violating Law 93, the prospects for modification of the law dimmed. In March 1996, the committee's modestly amended law was submitted to the Shura Council, the upper house of parliament. Despite outspoken efforts by leading journalists to gain modification of the law, the Shura Council refused to permit any additional changes, and the draft law was referred to the People's Assembly for passage in June 1996.

During this period, the leadership of the press syndicate led a carefully orchestrated campaign against Law 93. Their strategy included mass resignations by senior syndicate members, coupled with relentless confirmations of their loyalty to the state. Throughout the crisis, the syndicate was at pains to keep it a "family" dispute to insure that the government did not see its opposition as a source of insecurity. To the surprise of many observers, President Mubarak lent his support to the press syndicate, and Law 93 was abrogated. This was an impressive victory for the journalists, especially in the face of heavy opposition from government hard-liners. One participant in the crisis was struck by the careful strategic calculations that were made, the most decisive of which was enlisting the president as an arbiter, thereby neutralizing his earlier tacit support for the tough press law. Equally important, the president of the syndicate, Ibrahim Nafaʿ, who is close to Mubarak and trusted by the president, played a key role in successfully ending the crisis. Despite his connections—Nafaʿ is a member of the political elite in Egypt and accustomed to being taken seriously—he apparently had no advance warning of Law 93 and was angry that he had not been consulted. Nonetheless, Nafaʿ understood that escalation would play into the hands of the regime's hard-liners and impair negotiations. In effect, he wanted to avoid a sense of threat to the government or Mubarak. As one insider noted, "We did not want polarization."

In contrast, Egypt's university professors were flummoxed in 1993 by the government's decision to appoint university deans rather than elect them, as had been the custom. In that case, the government was responding to the growing Islamist presence on campus and seeking to deny them high-profile leadership positions. But where the university professors were unsuccessful in getting the change rescinded, the journalists' unified response was made easier by the small size of their syndicate and by its liberal tradition. Furthermore, since Islamists do not control the press syndicate, there was no risk of lending momentum to the most significant opposition force in Egypt. Had hard-liners prevailed, the syndicate might have been vulnerable to radicalization. As one close observer noted,

> For the first time in a long while a strong professional movement appeared, with popular backing, without initiative for the Islamist forces. The journalists' movement brought together a national consensus between numerous factions of liberal, leftist, and government forces, and

> the Islamic factions joined in, but not as leader or most important player. This indicates the natural root of Islamist strength—it grows in the absence of alternative forces!!

Also noteworthy is the fact that 700 members of the syndicate work for the establishment daily, *al-Ahram* (of which Nafaʿ is chairman of the board), and the syndicate was able to draw upon its considerable resources. Many of the key working papers were drafted by an *al-Ahram* working group created by Nafaʿ. Several leading rights-oriented groups were also instrumental in preparing thoughtful critiques of Law 93, especially the Legal Center for Human Rights, which organized a workshop in June 1995 to study press legislation.

While the defeat of Law 93 was celebrated as a victory for a free press and for civil society, the circumstances that defined the crisis were unusual. The case illustrates how reform can take place in Egypt's authoritarian political system, but it also underlines the low likelihood that other syndicates, most of them quite large, could emulate the success of the journalists. The case highlights the real locus of power in Egypt and the specificity of the power structure. The rise and fall of Law 93 illustrates just how deeply embedded is authoritarian rule in Egypt. Most associations lack the solidarity and the connections necessary to reverse major government decisions.

There is, however, strong sentiment in Egypt, as elsewhere in the Muslim world, for political reform. One member of the political elite, a reformer, argues,

> Now there are at least two generations among the youth of Egypt in the workforce and active population [whose political consciousness awakened during the mid-seventies], their age being between 25 and 35, who support political freedom and freedom of expression as an absolute value. They are born with rights and live with them, and they won't give them up. Those that do not take rights seriously cannot remember the previous era of oppression, to say nothing about the important values of freedom and human rights in the international context.

The writer's claims are not so much wrong as that they misconstrue politics. Politics is not merely a product of sentiments and moods but a contest of organized interests. Therefore we turn now to the question of how civic pluralism translates into political influence, and whether civic pluralism leads to political pluralism.

THE IMPORTANCE OF CIVIL SOCIETY

Civic pluralism meets the state in the realms where norms are contested and where the boundaries of state and society overlap. It is in civil society that contemporary citizenship is being redefined and public space is negotiated. In civil society, sentiments and moods crystallize as formal and informal efforts to promote self-interest. If the rise of civic pluralism creates greater opportunity for individual action, the site for agency to be realized is civil society.

Although we should be justifiably skeptical of tropes of civil society that confuse the ideal-typical with the empirical, we should not ignore the fact that themes of civil society—translated, mutated, reinterpreted—have become part of the political discourse of the Muslim world. As Robert Hefner notes, "Much of the theoretical writing on civil democracy has been more concerned with summarizing technical debates among professional philosophers than it has in demonstrating whether those ideas inform actual people's political actions in real human societies" (1998: 7). Rather than focusing on competing theoretical perspectives, it is much more relevant, as Hefner implies, to look at what is actually happening.

The "discovery" of civil society as a topic of debate in the Muslim world is neither an example of ideological imperialism nor a Western liberal's fantasy. The reason that civil society has attracted serious attention is because it evokes crucial questions: How may people peacefully organize outside of government control? How is citizenship engendered and strengthened? What role should the state play as a referee or rule-setter? How should people's needs be met in the wake of the retreating state?

The civil society construct has suffered from several weaknesses when it has been addressed in the West. Some proponents, as well as many critics, have tended to conflate the concept with democracy or democratization, which has led to wishful thinking about political reform and has implicated writing on civil society with problematic U.S. government programs for promoting democracy. The result is either blind endorsement of civil society or disdainful rejection of the construct, depending upon one's biases, and both mask the significant value of much recent discussion.

It is widely claimed that civil society checks the power of government, that it is the natural opponent of autocracy. This is a claim extracted from the observation of mature democracies in the West, and it is even problematic there. One can argue that civil society in some Western societies has been undermined by the full-blown development of the modern state, which provides many of the services and protections originally available within the framework of civil society. It is a bit naïve to expect that authoritarian government will be routinely challenged by groups of citizens who lack effective legal frameworks to resist, to protest, or to demonstrate. Moreover, civil society is not locked into a zero-sum game with the state. A more differentiated view of state–society relations is necessary, one that recognizes the opportunities for a dialogue at arm's length with a powerful state. Where government revenue derives largely from rents rather than the extraction of taxes, the purpose of the dialogue will often be rent-seeking.

Historically, civil society emerged as a bourgeois phenomenon and a reaction to expanding extraction by the state. Subsequently, the project of bourgeois civil society was liberalism, not democracy. In the contemporary Muslim world, where the middle class is anxious to preserve its access to state largesse (rents), it is often palpably unenthusiastic about democracy as well. As G. White (1995: 77–78) suggests,

> There is historical evidence to suggest that the bourgeoisie—and many of its subalterns in the middle strata—are more interested in the liberal than the democratic component of liberal democracy, in negative rather than positive freedoms, and in a more strictly political than a socio-economic definition of democracy. Other sections of civil society, poorer segments of the population, the industrial working class, groups representing socially subordinated or politically marginalized groups such as women, neglected regions, and ethnic, racial, and religious groups— have an interest not merely in the liberal but also in the democratic potential of liberal democracy, in the sense that it opens up new channels for articulating their grievances and pressuring the state to do something about them.

Several examples from recent scholarship on civil society illustrate that the bourgeoisie's disincentives for promoting democracy are clear. In Syria, until the regime launched economic reforms in the 1980s, the predominantly Sunni merchant class—the entrepreneurial heart of the country—was purposefully disadvantaged by the state's strategy of development that promoted state-owned industrialization and restricted private enterprise, as well as land reform. The legitimacy formula of the Ba'athist state was predicated on the building of a broader base in the urban lower class and the rural peasantry and suppressing the merchants, who were viewed as the core of support for the *ancien régime*. Now that the merchants are back in favor, their interests lie in improving their access to information, insuring the mobility of capital, and enjoying the consistent protection of law. They have little interest in democratizing Syria, which would have the effect of granting a larger voice to employees of public-sector companies or to the peasantry; to do so would jeopardize their newly privileged economic relationship with the state (Hinnebusch 1995).

The clearest illustration of the importance of distinguishing between the project of liberalism and the project of democracy is arguably Turkey. Turkey's encounter with democracy is only a half-century old, and throughout this period significant segments of the middle class have been extremely skeptical of democracy, never more obviously than in the 1950s, when the Democratic Party, led by Adnan Menderes, won power and kept it by building a populist base of support in the urban lower class and among the peasantry. Under Menderes, Kemalist laicism was relaxed, and, for the first time in the republic's history, Islamic institutions were actually promoted by the state. The army, for whom laicism often seems a political fetish, intervened to end the excursion into populist democracy and hanged Menderes in the process. The coup found enthusiastic support among the middle class, including many of Turkey's professional and other associations. One sees a similar pattern in Turkey in the 1990s, after the rise to power of Refah Partisi, the pro-Islam party. Self-proclaimed members of civil society proclaim regularly that they count on the army to intervene "to save democracy"—a strange conception of democracy, to be sure.

In Egypt, the government has met the challenge of reform by suppressing civil society. Stymied by refreshingly independent judges in applying new legislation to regulate external funding and generally tighten the control on non-governmental organizations, a signal example was chosen to chill opposition voices. The target was Professor Saad Eddin Ibrahim, an internationally known and respected sociologist and a leading advocate of democratic reform and human rights in Egypt. After Ibrahim played an organizing role in monitoring parliamentary elections and in revealing considerable vote fraud, as well as examining discrimination against Coptic Christian Egyptians, he was prosecuted for accepting foreign funding (although for technical reasons his research center fell outside the scope of the law that the state applied), defaming Egypt, and embezzling funds. He was convicted in very sloppy court proceedings in 2001 and sentenced to jail for seven years. After an appeal on substantive and procedural grounds, Ibrahim was released for retrial in 2002.

In July 2002, Ibrahim and eighteen of his colleagues were re-convicted of the same crimes and four defendants were sentenced to prison terms. The longest sentence meted out was to Ibrahim, who received a seven-year term for "tarnishing Egypt's reputation abroad," among a variety of other crimes, including fraud and illegally receiving funds from the European Union for monitoring parliamentary elections and reporting on discrimination suffered by the Coptic minority. The court went beyond the prosecutor's charges, and alluded to funding that Ibrahim received from the Swiss Human Rights Organization, al-Jazeera Satellite TV, and from Haifa University (for a subscription to an Ibn Khaldoun Center publication), among other organizations. Predictably, the chilling effect has been palpable in Egypt's NGO sector, where many activists now shiver at the thought of accepting foreign funding. Ibrahim's young, idealistic colleagues have been stigmatized by the charges leveled against them and will find the going very tough as they attempt to pursue professional careers.[1]

Oddly, although Ibrahim was well known for his advocacy of democracy in the Arab world (he had been honored by Freedom House, among other U.S.-based organizations), the initial reaction from the Bush administration was relatively muted. (In fairness, so was the response of the Middle East Studies Association, the leading professional organization of its kind in North America, and the very organization that honored Ibrahim with its

Academic Freedom Award in 2001.) Government spokespeople expressed "disappointment" at the convictions, but were reluctant to level sharp criticism of the Mubarak government. The U.S. government's silence punctuated the basic contradiction between rhetorical advocacy of democracy and freedom in the Arab world, and realpolitic calculation.

Democracy and reform have been central motifs of U.S. commentary, within and without government circles, following the terrorist attacks of September 2001, but the Ibrahim case illustrates that other interests heavily condition U.S. support for democracy. Egypt, after all, is an important American friend in the Middle East. Following a surge of supporting statements from politicians, commentators, and academics (for example, Friedman 2002, Diehl 2002, Norton 2002), the Bush administration announced on August 15, 2002, that as a result of the persecution of Ibrahim it would not extend further aid to Egypt over and above the annual allocation of two billion dollars. In a sense, this was an empty threat, since neither Congress nor the administration was contemplating further aid. The belated U.S. action met a recalcitrant response in Cairo, including from President Mubarak and his major political advisor 'Usama al-Baz.

As a tactical matter, by focusing its criticism solely on the Ibrahim case, the U.S. government played right into the hands of the anti-Ibrahim slander campaign in Egypt by highlighting Ibrahim's dual nationality and feeding the accusation—by now common in the Egyptian press—that Ibrahim's activism served foreign masters, not Egyptian interests. Had the United States focused its complaints more broadly on the arbitrary legal procedures associated with the Emergency Law that has been in effect in Egypt since Anwar Sadat's assassination in 1981, and which facilitated the state's persecution of Ibrahim and his co-defendants, opinion leaders in Egypt may have been less inclined to rally around Mubarak. However, the U.S. response was calibrated to be as narrow and as palatable as possible, so as not to upset the geopolitical apple cart. Thus, President Bush was wont to reassure Mubarak that his stance did not jeopardize the generous annual stream of U.S. aid.

Unfortunately, in the aftermath of September 11, 2001, conditions for reform are even worse across the Muslim world. Leaders like Husni Mubarak have used the "war against terrorism" to deny any space to the opposition and deny any exercise of basic human rights to whomever they choose. Mubarak offered the view that "terrorists have no human rights"; so for opponents classified as terrorists, the gloves are off. Militant opposition groups, including Islamist groups bent on replacing the state, are major beneficiaries of these policies, which only serve to validate their critique of government oppression and corruption.

Of course, the formal associations of bourgeois civil society, such as Egyptian NGOs, are only part of the picture. Comparatively less attention has been paid to networks of informal civic associations, which have filled the void left by governments' failure to meet the needs of the urban lower classes and the rural poor. Perhaps the most attention has focused on the impressive array of service organizations created by Islamist opposition movements. What the reformist-oriented Islamists have accomplished is impressive and should be seen as an important step toward a more inclusive civil society. Nonetheless, the Islamists' efforts are only one segment of an array of informal networks that crisscross the urbanscapes of the Muslim world (Singerman 1995, J. B. White 1996). It appears that their success has been less in creating networks of informal association than in exploiting patterns of association based on reciprocal relationships. Only when these informal forms of civic pluralism have been politicized—which is to say, only when the participants believe that there are political solutions to their problems—will political movements emerge. In this regard, the importance of the new media is to help sensitize heretofore economically marginalized people to the prospect that life chances can be improved.

We should not expect creative thinking about reform and political change to come from the regimes in the Muslim world. They are too embedded in privilege and too insecure in their power to think deeply about fundamental political or economic reform. The discourses that will give shape to change must emerge from society, and new media are some of its channels. New media are central to expanding the public space. Some of the examples provided in this book hint that growing civic pluralism in the Muslim world will result increasingly in organized demands on governments. Even if progress is slowed by the developments of 2001 and 2002, the slow retreat of authoritarianism in the Muslim world remains likely.

NOTES

This section is based on fieldwork conducted in Cairo with Farhad Kazemi in 1995 and 1996.

1. Egypt's highest appeals court overturned Ibrahim's conviction on December 3, 2002, ordering a third retrial.

WORKS CITED

Diehl, Jackson. 2002. "The Silence Signal," *Washington Post,* August 4, sec. A, p. 15.

Friedman, Thomas L. 2002. "Bush's Shame," *New York Times,* August 4, sec. 4, p. 13.

Hann, Chris, and Elizabeth Dunn, eds. 1996. *Civil Society: Challenging Western Models.* London and New York: Routledge.

Hefner, Robert W. 1998. "On the History and Cross-Cultural Possibility of a Democratic Political Ideal." In *Democratic Civility: The History and Cross-Cultural Possibility of a Modern Political Ideal,* ed. Robert W. Hefner, pp. 3–44. New Brunswick, N.J.: Transaction Books.

Hinnebusch, Raymond A. 1995. "State, Civil Society, and Political Change in Syria." In *Civil Society in the Middle East,* ed. Augustus Richard Norton, vol. 1, pp. 214–42. Leiden: E.J. Brill.

Kazemi, Farhad, and Augustus Richard Norton. 1996. "Civil Society, Political Reform, and Authoritarianism in the Middle East." *Contention* 5, no. 2 (Winter): 107–19.

Norton, Augustus Richard. 2002. "As Egypt Smothers Reform, U.S. Looks On," *Los Angeles Times,* August 12, p. 11.

al-Rasheed, Madawi. 1996. "Saudi Arabia's Islamic Opposition." *Current History* 995, no. 597: 16–22.

Rosenau, James. 1990. *Global Turbulence and World Politics.* Princeton: Princeton University Press.

Singerman, Diane. 1995. *Avenues of Participation: Family, Politics and Networks in Urban Quarters of Cairo.* Princeton: Princeton University Press.

White, Gordon. 1995. "Civil Society, Democratization and Development (II): Two Country Cases." *Democratization* 2, no. 2 (Summer): 56–84.

White, Jenny B. 1996. "Civic Culture and Islam in Urban Turkey." In *Civil Society: Challenging Western Models,* ed. Chris Hann and Elizabeth Dunn, pp. 143–54. New York: Routledge.

3 /

COMMUNICATION AND CONTROL IN
THE MIDDLE EAST:
PUBLICATION AND ITS DISCONTENTS

Dale F. Eickelman

Authority to suppress or "guide" the printed and spoken word in the Middle East has become inherently vitiated by social and technological developments that are reaching full force in the 1990s. In Gamal al-Ghitani's *Zayni Barakat* (1988: 200–201), a historical allegory written in the early 1970s satirizing Nasser's rule, a chief spy in Mamluk Egypt dreams of a world in which everyone is numbered and agents of authority can intervene in a conversation and move it in a particular direction. Sadly only for the censors, mass education and new communications technologies have rendered that dream impossible. Desktop publishing makes the expensive, vulnerable printing presses of older technologies obsolete; satellite dishes, even when heavily taxed and regulated, evade effective government control; and Internet and computer links are rapidly eroding control of what is said (Alterman 1998: 45–72).

The frontier between banned words and images and those that are tolerated in the Middle East has never been fixed, but access to new technologies has multiplied the channels through which ideas and information can be circulated and has enlarged the scope of what can be said and to whom. It has eroded the ability of authorities to censor and repress, to project an uncontested "central" message defining political and religious issues for large numbers of people. In other words, the lines between the "official" and "hidden" transcripts (Scott 1990: 3–4) have become increasingly blurred. Censors may still restrict what is said in the mainstream press and broadcast media, but these media have lost the exclusivity they once had. Mass education and the availability of alternative media have irrevocably altered how "authoritative" discourse is read and heard.

State efforts to gain control of one medium—the press, the broadcast media, or even music—lead only to the proliferation of other means of communication and foster, albeit inadvertently, a "civil society" of dissent. The Iranian example is well known. From 1958 until 1969, Iran had only commercial television, but this ceased with the advent of National Iranian Radio and Television (NIRT). Ostensibly independent when founded in 1969, NIRT lost its credibility in the early 1970s when, in the midst of an urban guerrilla movement, viewers were offered long lectures by Parviz Sabeti, a SAVAK (state security) official in charge of ideological matters, on the sinister intentions of "subversive" groups. Subsequent broadcast "confessions" by captured guerrillas further discredited the state-controlled medium (Sreberny-Mohammadi and Mohammadi 1994: 69). When the Shah exiled key members of the religious opposition, leaflets and audiocassettes smuggled into Iran or taped from international telephone calls and passed from hand to hand—creating bonds of complicity and trust among those involved— became a primary vehicle of communication.

A more recent example is contemporary Saudi Arabia, where the fax and photocopy machine make bans on the printed word impossible to enforce without alienating regime supporters. Threats in the Saudi-controlled media (for example, *al-Sharq al-Awsat* 1994) to make those who distribute or comment on leaflets that defame or slander the "legitimate rulers" (*wila' al-umur*) as guilty as their creators make public implicit circles of complicity and draw attention to the inability of authorities to control such communications. Newspapers, dependent on their presses, imported newsprint, and formal distribution networks, are easy to control. The "small media"— cassettes, photocopies, desktop publications, and electronic mail—are not. Such technologies, combined with the wider audiences created by mass education, create an irreversible trend toward a freer market in religious, political, and social ideas and foster a pluralism often resisted and poorly understood both by states and by religious authorities. These new technologies challenge those who seek authoritatively to demarcate the lines between the licit and the illicit.

In earlier eras, control and censorship were more predictable. The bookplate of Egypt's King Farouk (reproduced in Mitchell 1988: 91) foregrounds a turbaned man of learning next to a printing press. He is handing a book to a peasant, alongside his water buffalo and plough, who has stopped work in his field. In the background is a silhouette of Cairo's citadel and Farouk's name in calligraphy, topped by a crown. The image exemplifies the top-down notion of communication, where those in authority control what is printed and how it is disseminated.

It was easier to control the public word with older communications technologies. Printing presses could be confiscated, sequestered, or destroyed. More subtle techniques have emerged since the 1960s—manipulation of newsprint prices and supplies, direct or indirect publication subsidies, and control of distribution channels—strategies in which countries such as Morocco have excelled. Under such circumstances, a self-censorship more pervasive than any imposed by state security officials also constrained what was said.

When full literacy was restricted, for all practical purposes, to an elite, the print media—pamphlets, newspapers, periodicals, and books—addressed the elite and thus authority directly. From the late nineteenth century onward, however, the multiplication of printed religious texts, at first controlled by religious authorities, "struck right at the heart of person-to-person transmission of knowledge" and significantly enlarged audiences (Robinson 1993: 239). Print initially enabled religious scholars, the 'ulama, to expand their influence in public affairs because they sponsored and controlled religious publications. Yet the ironic consequence of printing reduced their authority because of the rapidly increasing number of educated persons and the shift to a more accessible, popular language (Robinson 1993: 245).

The frontier between the banned and the tolerated has become more uncertain in the past few decades with the advent of mass education, particularly mass higher education, throughout the Middle East because it has increased dramatically the audience for the printed word and the publicly spoken political and religious words of the broadcast media, audiocassettes, and videos. Although the onset of the commitment to mass education varies throughout the Middle East—1952 for Egypt, 1956 for Morocco, and 1970 for the Sultanate of Oman, for example—its growth in all cases was exponential. The combination of mass education and the "intellectual technology" of communication innovations has also changed what is said and not said, radically altering audiences, concepts, and practices (see Eickelman 1992).

Although the broadcast media and cassettes have become important means of communication, the printed word retains a special place in "authoritative" communications. Even if only a minority of the population read books, a much larger number hear them spoken about—and books, following the paradigm of the Qur'an—remain central to the cultural imagination (Atiyeh 1995). The most rapid growth for the printed word is in what Yves Gonzalez-Quijano (1998) calls "Islamic books"—inexpensive, attractively printed texts that are accessible to a readership who lack the literary skills of the educated cadres of an earlier era and that take advantage of new printing technologies. Such books and pamphlets have also captured an increasing market share in Muslim majority countries outside the Arab world. As Huq (this volume) explains, teenage romance novels, once a specialty distributed in "secular" bookstores, now have Islamic counterparts, which are distributed through religious bookstores (Fig. 3.1). In Pakistan, the types of religious books that sell in Islamabad, Karachi, and Lahore differ some-

Figure 3.1. Secular and Islamic books are generally sold in separate bookstores in Dhaka, but the cover art for these novels suggests a competition for audiences also characteristic of publications elsewhere in South Asia and the Middle East. Budhdhodeb Guho, *Pardeshia* (The Foreigner) (Dhaka: Shameem Ahmed, 1985), above, is generally considered a "secular" novel; while Kasem Bin Abubakar, *Basar Rat* (Wedding Night) (Dhaka: Kakoli Prokashoni, 1993), right, is an "Islamic" one (Courtesy Maimuna Huq).

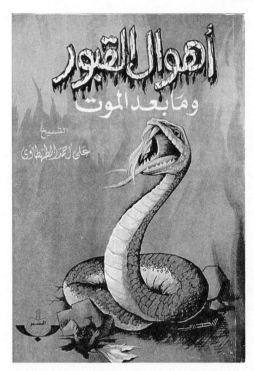

Figure 3.2. The eye-catching cover and theme of Shaykh ʿAli Ahmad al-Tahtawi's *Ahwal al-qubur wa-ma baʿd al-mawt* (Terrors of the Grave and What Follows Death) (Cairo: Dar al-Bashir, 1987) typifies the inexpensive, widely circulated "Islamic" book, the fastest growing segment of Egyptian and Middle Eastern publishing.

what in each city, but in all cities religious titles far outsell other titles (Eickelman and Anderson 1997: 54–55). In Morocco, *Muʾtamar sahafi mʿa jinn Muslim* (Press Conference with a Muslim Jinn), generally available only in pirated photocopies, is a best-seller, with students at the nation's thirteen public universities among the major consumers.

Since the late 1970s, religious books have eclipsed other types of publications, often bypassing bookstores and being sold on sidewalks, in kiosks, and in general-goods stores (Starrett 1995). The style of these books is usually a breezy mix of literary and colloquial diction; the covers are eye-catching. Some of the books deal with religious themes and the afterlife or answer questions on how to be Muslim in the modern world (Fig. 3.2); others deal directly with the political questions of the day, such as a Saudi pamphlet that argues that democracy is incompatible with Islam because Islam offers governance by the Creator (*al-khaliq*)—as understood by a properly instructed religious elite—whereas "democracy," derided as a non-Arabic term, implies rule by the created (*al-makhluqin*), where unbelievers and the ignorant have an equal say in governance and usurp God's rule (Sharif 1992:16–18).

In many parts of the Muslim world, including North Africa, the style of argument is sometimes regarded with amusement, but it is more accessible

to recent beneficiaries of mass education and appeals more to their perceived interests and needs than books written by the established literary,
religious, and political elite. Advertisers too have begun to notice such books:
on the inside cover of some of Shaykh Sha'rawi's books in Egypt, for example, are advertisements for consumer goods—in decorative script and
citing Qur'anic verses.[1]

These "Islamic" books point to the changing nature of religious—and
political—discourse. Many take the form of practical manuals on how
women ought to conduct themselves in modern societies, children's religious education (Starrett 1996), death and the hereafter, and reconciling
Islam with science. At one level, they indicate how religious and political
beliefs are increasingly transformed into a conscious system. At another
level, they encourage and mirror the growing fragmentation of religious
and political authority. The net result of these changes—the growing tendency to think of religious belief and practice as a self-contained system and
the fragmentation of authority—is to reconfigure the symbolic production
of politics.

The accessibility of such writing to new audiences is an important theme
that has parallels with the broadcast media. Unfortunately, few studies concern audience response to Middle Eastern media.[2] One of the first, conducted in Iran in the 1970s, revealed that a large portion of the population
did not understand the language of broadcasting, "especially news programming" (Sreberny-Mohammadi and Mohammadi 1994: 69). In the late 1960s,
when newscasts were in "standard" Arabic, I had the dubious honor in a
rural area of western Morocco of "translating" the formal Arabic of radio
newscasts into colloquial Moroccan. Programming in Moroccan Arabic and
in the Berber languages expanded significantly only after Colonel Qadhdhafi
allowed Moroccan dissidents to broadcast in colloquial Arabic from Libya
in the early 1970s.

The gap between broadcast production and audiences has narrowed in
recent years, but it remains significant. A former minister of information in
an Arab country commented on the decision to build a second television
network: "We didn't need any opinion polls. I knew what the public
wanted."[3] The commercial film industry in Egypt may have a better sense of
popular taste: the Egyptian film *al-Irhabi* (The Terrorist) (Galal 1994) may
seem crude in its portrayal of Islamic activists. Starring 'Adil Imam, one of
Egypt's best-known actors, the film portrays Islamists as violent, naive, and
boorish, manipulated by authoritarian leaders. Bourgeois life, in contrast,
is depicted as cosmopolitan, comfortable, and tolerant. Egyptian commercial film-makers, unhappy with the Islamist project in Egypt, did not require instruction in the propaganda potential of mass communications—
particularly in the video version of the film, which could be viewed in the
privacy of homes in case some viewers were reluctant to see it in public

cinemas. Some Arab intellectuals laugh at the film's crude portrayals, but a village-born Egyptian political scientist explains that the producers had a finely honed sense of the primary audience for whom the film was intended.[4] Similarly, many creators of more "highbrow" publications have yet to adjust to the "market economy" of popular religious and political writing.

In electoral politics as well, politicians only incrementally acquire the skills needed to communicate to audiences through print and the mass media. The 1992-1993 Moroccan local and parliamentary elections were more open than earlier ones, with candidates given access to television for the first time, and even more access was permitted for the 1997 local and parliamentary elections. Unfortunately, most presentations took the form of speeches to party followers, so their impact on the elections was negligible.

In general, censorship and control of print and other media has had to become more multidimensional and nuanced. It shows a greater sophistication on the part of state gatekeepers about which media make a significant impact on the population. Thus small intellectual magazines in Tehran publish on a latitude of subjects, as the authorities—who retain tight control on radio, television, and the content of Friday sermons—know that their political impact is minimal and that the costs of repression outweigh those of turning a blind eye. Nonetheless, Islamic texts that few people read are published in profusion in post-revolutionary Iran, although what people buy is the more scarce "secular" magazine or book. In Morocco, censorship is frequently selective. In 1992, the arrest and trial of Hajj Muhammad Mustafa Tabit, a senior Moroccan police official convicted of raping over 300 women—activities he preserved in a personal videotape archive—went unreported by the Moroccan broadcast media. In contrast, newspapers, with the exception of one semi-official publication, carried daily accounts of the trial, which took place during Ramadan, the month of fasting. The timing was important, for the trial doubled as a morality play. Newspaper circulation soared as a result, and papers were rented out by the hour at some kiosks in Rabat and Casablanca. In Morocco, where most people get their news from the broadcast media, state-controlled except for a private radio station in which a holding company related to the palace has a significant interest, newspaper coverage—which reaches a much smaller number of people—offered a safety valve sufficient to control rumors and give the appearance of a relatively unfettered press.[5] Likewise, cassettes of Berber and Arabic songs commenting on the case circulated freely, although they were never mentioned in the broadcast or print media (Lakhsassi 1998).

Political and religious communications that are banned take on a new significance. The words of a hand-copied leaflet concerning how one can earn sufficient "credit" to enter paradise may be politically innocuous, but the risk a sailor in the Moroccan navy took to copy it and the bonds of complicity created in passing it to trusted mates parallels the circulation of leaflets in Afghanistan's Islamic Youth Organization in the 1960s (Edwards 1995) and the now common distribution of photocopied leaflets.

On a technologically more sophisticated level, the "fax wars" in Saudi Arabia successfully evade government efforts to restrict criticism of the regime, which is virtually powerless to control the incursions of the "small media." Prohibitions against circulating such documents only draw further attention to them (for example, *al-Sharq al-Awsat* 1994). Efforts to ban books can also be easily circumvented. In 1991, Saudi Arabia banned Muhammad Shahrur's *al-Kitab wa-l-Qur'an* (The Book and the Qur'an). Nonetheless, an estimated 10,000 photocopies circulated within the kingdom ("Prophetic" 1993). Although also banned in Egypt, large numbers of photocopies of the book circulated there as well, and for several years after the 1992 assassination of journalist Farag Fuda, for which Islamists claimed responsibility, *al-Kitab* was published in Egypt in a pirated edition, which reached its third printing in mid-1995.[6] Even mainstream newspapers can escape state disapproval and build readership by publishing articles that attack Islamist doctrine, although readers sympathetic to such views can read the summaries of Islamist arguments differently (for example, Anonymous 1992).

Technology is supposedly neutral, but technological innovations subtly alter the structure and content of disseminated messages. Print and other technologies create new forms of community and transform authority and social boundaries. Thus an Egyptian newspaper reported that a raid on a software import firm yielded computer discs that disclosed the structure of the clandestine wing of the Muslim Brotherhood and potential targets for political action and infiltration into the police, judiciary, press, medical, and other professions. Omani security uncovered a similar use of computers in a sweep of Islamists that resulted in more than 300 arrests beginning in June 1994 ("Up to 70 Suspects" 1994; Abdullah 1995).

In some regions, audiocassettes have begun to supplement or replace pamphlets as a vehicle for religious debate. A pamphlet has the advantage of greater anonymity for the author—voices on cassette can often disclose authorship—but cassettes have other advantages. Inexpensive, easy to smuggle, and readily reproduced, they may be played in the home, automobile, mosque, or other meeting places. The sermons of Lebanon's Shaykh Husayn Fadlallah and Egypt's Shaykh 'Abd al-Hamid Kishk are available throughout the Middle East and wherever Arabic-speaking Muslims are found in Europe and America. Cassettes, like the other "small" media, make it easier for Muslims to keep abreast of developments elsewhere in the Muslim world and to feel as if they participate in them. "Voiced Islam" (*al-Islam al-sawti*) has thus become a force rivaling "print Islam."

Recent developments in communication technologies also empower protest groups within societies. Conscious that Islamic groups elsewhere bear similarities to their own situation and influenced by transformations in the Islamic political vocabulary, hitherto isolated protest movements or individuals acquire a bolder voice and are encouraged to act more decisively. The recent rapid expansion of Islamic publishing and the emergence of television channels controlled by religiously oriented groups in Turkey is a case in point (see Yavuz, this volume; also Gazeteciler ve Yazarlar Vakfi 1994). Even repressive states have to take uncontrolled messages into account. Concerned about waning youth audiences for Iranian state television, a small interministerial group in Tehran called the "Optimal Image" (*Simay-i-Matlub*) committee considered adopting programs that could rival Western music videos for audience appeal.[7]

The content of Friday sermons also shows the influence of a wide range of print and broadcast media, and preachers now assume that the audience has been so influenced. They incorporate references and allusions to a wide range of texts and events (Gaffney 1994: 50, 215; Eickelman 1990). Preachers cite contemporary Muslim intellectuals such as Sayyid Qutb, Mawdudi, Kishk, and Shaykh Ibn Baz of Saudi Arabia as well as Western writers and publications. In Saudi sermons distributed via cassettes during the 1990-1991 Gulf crisis, preachers invoked such sources as the memoirs of Richard Nixon, the Voice of America, the *Financial Times*, CNN, the writings of George Bush, and contemporary Arab periodicals like *al-Hayat* and *al-Watan al-ʿArabi*. Criticism is often indirect. For example, an approving reference to the probity of the "rightly guided" caliphs of early Islamic history would not be lost on the audience as a veiled attack on the injustice and immorality of present-day leaders.

Dissident and subversive messages are also communicated through *nashid*s, martial chants that rival *raʿi* or even rap music in popularity. The importance of the *nashid*s and rap music is that they represent the ways in which popular cultural forms can be mobilized to foster claims and counterclaims in Muslim politics. The insistent rhythms, assertive refrains, and often mocking tones are especially effective in articulating protest. Humor serves a similar function. Although Morocco's Ahmed Sanoussi is no longer allowed access to the stadiums that once drew up to 40,000 people to hear his performances, his cassettes and appearances in small theaters consistently draw capacity crowds who appreciate his political satire (Hedges 1995). Comic strips often have the same effect (Douglas and Malti-Douglas 1994). Hannah Arendt (1986: 65) reminds us: "To remain in authority requires respect for the person or the office. The greatest enemy of authority, therefore, is contempt." Music, poster art, and graffiti can also be subversive and indirectly indicate rival claims to authority. They are popular representations of symbolic politics, but, as we would expect, they may be ambiguous in their political message.

In conclusion, the "migration" of messages, media, writers, and styles of discourse is part of an increasing fragmentation of authority. It also multiplies the ways in which authority can be represented and by whom. "Islamic" books and cassette sermons set aside the long tradition of authoritative discourse by religious scholars, so that chemists, medical doctors, journalists, and even garage mechanics, for example, can interpret "Islamic" principles as equals with scholars who have graduated from the schools of the *'ulama*. This multiplication of voices in public discussion of religious and political belief further erodes the boundaries between kinds or sources of authoritative speech.

In addition, new forms of communication and their increased rapidity allow "peripheries" and audiences to talk back and can infuse new life to local and regional traditions. When states shut down one form of communication, others take its place, or diasporas sustain voices that otherwise would be silenced or muted. New technologies of communication and publication also enable those who hold minority views, including extremists, to join forces with like-minded people elsewhere to accomplish common goals. The new political geography of communications may actually facilitate pluralism. Finally, in the sense that symbolic and political connections across national and other political boundaries are encouraged, conventional understandings of "external" and "internal" become increasingly blurred.

Through fragmenting authority and discourse, the new technologies of communication, combined with the multiplication of agency facilitated by rising educational levels, contribute significantly to re-imagining Middle Eastern politics and religion. Understanding the dynamics of these new voices and the media through which they are disseminated entails listening to the many voices of the region, not merely to those of a Westernized elite. This fragmentation may contribute to political volatility in the short run, but in the long run, it may become one of the major factors leading to a more civil society throughout the Middle East and elsewhere in the Muslim world.

NOTES

1. I am grateful to Yves Gonzalez-Quijano (personal communication, September 12, 1994) for drawing my attention to advertisements in religious books and pamphlets, an issue further discussed by Starrett (this volume).

2. See, however, Pollock and el Assal (1995) and Claeson and el Assal (1996). Kamalipour and Mowlana (1994) provide a country-by-country inventory of press and broadcast laws and facilities. For television in Morocco, see Poindexter (1991).

3. Interview, New York, October 18, 1993.

4. Ibrahim Karawan (personal communication, Bellagio, Italy, March 23, 1995).

5. For a summary of the Tabit affair, see Rocco (1993).

6. As of mid-1996, the book had again been withdrawn from circulation in Egypt (personal communication, Nasr Hamid Abu Zaid, Leiden, March 26, 1997).

7. Majid Tehranian, personal communication, February 2, 1995.

WORKS CITED

Abdullah, Salem. 1995. *Oman Islamism: An Unexpected Confrontation with the Government.* Annandale, Va.: United Association for Studies and Research.

Abubakar, Kasem Bin. 1993. *Basar Rat* (Wedding Night). Dhakar: Kakoli Prokashoni.

Alterman, Jon B. 1998. *New Media, New Politics? From Satellite Television to the Internet in the Arab World.* Washington, D.C.: Washington Institute for Near East Policy.

Anonymous. 1992. "Shra'it al-tatarruf 'ala l-rasif: Jins, wa-fitna wa-tahrid" (Extremist Cassettes on the Sidewalk: Sex, Rebellion, and Incitement). *al-Ishtiraki* (Casablanca), June 21, pp. 2–3.

Arendt, Hannah. 1986 (1969). "Communicative Power." In *Power,* ed. Steven Lukes, pp. 2–3. Oxford: Blackwell.

Atiyeh, George N., ed. 1995. *The Book in the Islamic World: The Written Word and Communication in the Middle East.* Albany: State University of New York Press.

Claeson, Matthew, and Elaine el Assal, eds. 1996. *Global Information Resources: Where Audiences around the World Turn for News and Information.* Washington: United States Information Agency, Office of Research and Media Reaction.

Douglas, Allen, and Fadwa Malti-Douglas. 1994. *Arab Comic Strips: Politics of an Emerging Mass Culture.* Bloomington: Indiana University Press.

Edwards, David B. 1995. "Print Islam: Media and Religious Revolution in Afghanistan." *Anthropological Quarterly* 68, no. 3 (July): 171–84.

Eickelman, Dale F. 1990. "Identité nationale et discours religieux en Oman" (National Discourse and Religious Identity in Oman). In *Intellectuels et militants de l'Islam contemporain,* ed. Gilles Kepel and Yann Richard, pp. 103–28. Paris: Seuil.

———. 1992. "Mass Higher Education and the Religious Imagination in Contemporary Arab Societies." *American Ethnologist,* 19, no. 4: 643–55.

Eickelman, Dale F., and Jon W. Anderson. 1997. "Print, Islam, and the Prospects for Civic Pluralism: New Religious Writings and Their Audiences." *Journal of Islamic Studies* 8, no. 1: 43–62.

Foreign Broadcast Information Service. 1992. "Structure, Aims of Muslim Brotherhood Detailed." *al-Musawwar,* April 3, 1992, p. 5 (NES-92-069, April 9, 1992, p. 9).

Gaffney, Patrick D. 1994. *The Prophet's Pulpit: Islamic Preaching in Contemporary Egypt.* Berkeley and Los Angeles: University of California Press.

Galal, Nadir. 1994. *al-Irhabi* (The Terrorist). Cairo: Mustafa Mitwalli. Distributed in the U.S. and Canada by Diana Nour International Films, Inc. Film #2018.

Gazeteciler ve Yazarlar Vakfı. 1994. "Gazeteciler ve Yazarlar Vakfı" (brochure describing the newspaper and broadcast holdings of this non-profit organization). Istanbul.

al-Ghitani, Gamal. 1988 (1971). *Zayni Barakat,* trans. Farouk Abdel Wahab. New York: Viking.

Gonzalez-Quijano, Yves. 1998. *Les Gens du Livre: Édition et champ intellectuel dans l'Égypte Republicaine* (The People of the Book: Intellectual Field and Publication in Republican Egypt). Paris: CNRS Éditions.

Guho, Budhdhodeb. 1985. *Pardeshia* (The Foreigner). Dhaka: Shameem Ahmed.

Hedges, Chris. 1995. "Jokes from Underground Keep Morocco Laughing." *New York Times*, February 21.

Kamalipour, Yahya R., and Hamid Mowlana, eds. 1994. *Mass Media in the Middle East: A Comprehensive Handbook*. Westport: Greenwood Press.

Lakhsassi, Abderahmane. 1998. "Scandale national et chansons populaires." In *Miroirs maghrébins: Itinéraires de soi et paysages de rencontre*, ed. Susan Ossman, pp. 99–109. Paris: CNRS Éditions.

Mitchell, Timothy. 1988. *Colonising Egypt*. Cambridge: Cambridge University Press.

Poindexter, Mark. 1991. "Subscription Television in the Third World: The Moroccan Experience." *Journal of Communications* 41, no. 3: 26–39.

Pollock, David, and Elaine el Assal, eds. 1995. *In the Eye of the Beholder: Muslim and Non-Muslim Views of Islam, Islamic Politics, and Each Other*. Washington: United States Information Agency, Office of Research and Media Reaction.

"Prophetic." 1993. *The Economist* (London), June 5, p. 102.

Robinson, Francis. 1993. "Technology and Religious Change: Islam and the Impact of Print." *Modern Asian Studies* 27, no. 1: 229-51.

Rocco, Fiammetta. 1993. "The Shame of Casablanca." *The Independent on Sunday* (London), May 9.

Scott, James C. 1990. *Domination and the Arts of Resistance: Hidden Transcripts*. New Haven: Yale University Press.

al-Sharif, Muhamad Shakir. 1992. *Haqiqat al-Dimuqratiya* (The Truth About Democracy). Riyadh: Dar al-watan li-l-nashr.

al-Sharq al-Awsat. 1994. "Shaykh Muhammad al-'Utayman in a Discussion of Incendiary Publications: Whomever Publishes These Leaflets and Pamphlets, Copies Them, or Distributes Them Commits a Major Sin and Bears Responsibility for His Own Crime and for the Crime of All Those Influenced by Them" (in Arabic). November 20.

Sreberny-Mohammadi, Annabelle, and Ali Mohammadi. 1994. *Small Media, Big Revolution: Communication, Culture, and the Iranian Revolution*. Minneapolis: University of Minnesota Press.

Starrett, Gregory. 1995. "The Political Economy of Religious Commodities in Cairo." *American Anthropologist* 97, no. 1: 51–68.

———. 1996. "The Margins of Print: Children's Religious Literature in Egypt." *Journal of the Royal Anthropological Institute* 2, no. 1 (March): 117–39.

al-Tahtawi, Ahmad. 1987. *Ahwal al-qubur wa-ma ba'd al-mawt* (The Terrors of the Grave and What Follows Death). Cairo: Dar al-Bashir.

"Up to 70 Suspects in Omani Islamist Ring to Go on Trial." 1994. *Mideast Mirror*, August 31, p. 27.

4 /

THE INTERNET AND ISLAM'S
NEW INTERPRETERS

Jon W. Anderson

Recent discussion of civil society in comparative and international contexts of the Muslim world has focused largely on a search for voluntary associations as intermediate social forms between those of family and polity (Norton 1995, 1996). The hope of finding counterparts to de Tocqueville's key to democracy in America cannot escape ethnocentrism for defining civil society so narrowly and misses more important developments in the realms where "civility" frames social space. Behind voluntary associations and other "intermediate" institutions lie understandings of individual responsibility in a public sphere (Seligman 1992) that may provide more productive ground for comparison. Every society includes conceptions of trust and responsibility, and of their scope. Prominent among these in Muslim societies is responsibility for interpretation of religion, of its requirements, of its expressions and, above all, for handling its texts. Today, more and more individuals are assuming such responsibilities, in public and through media that help to define or extend the public space of religious discourse. The Internet is one of these new media, by some measures a new public space, which enables a new class of interpreters, who are facilitated by this medium to address and thereby to reframe Islam's authority and expression for those like themselves and others who come there.

This is not—or not yet—the world of Islamic organizations and activist intellectuals, who attract attention and exegesis of their views (for example, Kepel 1985; Moussalli 1992; Roy 1994; Rahnema 1994; Appleby 1997).

Surrounding them is a larger, more inchoate context of seekers and various other Muslims similarly if less dramatically engaged in defining a Muslim life in a world in which Muslim and non-Muslim are increasingly intertwined. A common issue across the range of discussions, positions, and arguments associated with Islamic activism is taking responsibility for interpreting religion in a world of competing voices, multiple authorities, and problematic legitimacies. This wider context of interpretive practices and discursive authorities sets the narrower, more solemnized and abstracted forms of the activists in worlds beyond those they would essentialize.

This larger public sphere is marked by a coming into public view, and discussion, of interpretive practices between the high textualism of *'ulama*, marked by the super-literacy of an interpretive elite, and more mystical, participative expressions of the non-literate sometimes identified as "folk" Islam. Such orientations form more of a continuum than suggested by Hodgson's and similar distinctions between *shari'a*-minded and sufi-minded Islam (Hodgson 1974). Recent research shows fundamental similarities in modes of transmission, patron-client (master-pupil) relations, and cohort networks from those of *sufi* (Gilsenan 1973; Trix 1993) to *'ulama* (Fischer 1980; Eickelman 1985; Messick 1993) forms. Still, class and mass Islam have been treated as analytically separable domains, one subject to an updated version of textual analysis that probes for meaning (Moussalli 1992; Lawrence 1989) and the other subject to a more behaviorist analysis that probes for social forces (Sivan 1990; Goldberg 1991).[1] But contemporary Islamist discourse occupies, expands, and makes public a range of intermediate positions between these, combining features of traditional modes of representing the experience and interpretation of Islam with contemporary ones (for example, Gaffney 1994).

This linkage to social experience and contemporary cultural resources that expands the social space between elite and folk is crucially facilitated by media that feature the migration of discourse from narrower to broader, more "public" realms. Media make public what previously circulated in narrower, face-to-face interpersonal settings, such as coffee houses, *dowrehs*, the *majlis,* and informal discussion circles from university dormitories to parlors to dissident cells and other places where familiars meet, by giving messages additional circulation. The examples of cassette sermons against the former Shah of Iran (Sreberny-Mohammadi and Mohammadi 1994) and faxed *fatwas* of today's opponents of the Saudi regime (Sardar 1993) are joined by pamphlets and graffiti (Starrett 1995) that move messages from more restricted to less restricted spaces of circulation. In this move, relatively greater anonymity conveys an aura of more social—or at least more common—authority than that of face-to-face transmission between master and pupil, *pir* and *murid,* mullah and congregant. Media not only place messages into wider circulation, but also rebalance their authority from that of the sender to include the circulation itself. What is "new" here is the enhanced visibility that media afford.

Since the Salafiyya movement in the nineteenth century (Cole 1994), new interpreters of Islam have been tied to innovations in media. The founding figures of Islamic reform in this century such as Muhammed 'Abduh (1849–1905) and Mowlana Mawdudi (1903–1979) have been journalists whose work was enabled by the arrival of printing and of print news with new audiences for the written word. They filled and expanded the space between previously restricted circulations of text and talk. A century ago, printed books were the "new" media of Islamic reformist movements that spread from British India (Metcalf 1982). An important medium for the rising influence of the Iranian clergy in this century has been the circulation of religious interpretation and guidance in printed booklets of religious counsel, often in simple question-and-answer format, that preceded the tape cassette sermons of the exiled Ayatollah Khomeni and others. And today, television makes stars of conservative vernacular preachers. In their time, all new media have a certain "down-market" quality from high-textualist perspectives. They employ vernaculars and are often cheaply produced and ephemeral; but they expand the domain of Muslim discourse by engaging a wider public than previously had access to elite-controlled discourse and a more problematic public than other non-elite, "folk" forms reach.

THE INTERNET'S PUBLIC SPACE

Through the increasingly worldwide and nearly instantaneous Internet, Muslims adept at its use are increasingly able to reach out to each other and to publics beyond the Muslim world. They put into wider circulation views that previously circulated only in narrower circles and bring additional techniques for interpreting Islam, drawn first from those that facilitate access to the Internet itself. This extends the process that Eickelman (1992) has identified with the massification of education in the contemporary Muslim world, which has given wider access both to the texts of Islam and to a wider range of interpretation than developed in mosque-university (madrasa) and religious lodge (zawiya). Born in the world of higher education, the Internet facilitates and links specific new interpreters lodged within or enabled by it to form an extended discursive space, marked by new techniques not only for interpretation but also for creating a public that lies between, draws on, and links previously discrete discourses.

This is a process I have described as "creolization" (Anderson 1995) in the extended sense not just of mixing codes but also of forming what Drummond (1980) recast as special-purpose, intermediate communities of discourse that array in a continuum between otherwise (for example, socially) separate communities of communication. Islam is represented on-line in a mélange of wire-service news copy, transcribed sermons, scanned texts of the Qur'an and *hadith* collections, advice and self-help information ranging from where to find *halal* butchers and mosques to matrimonials and cheap travel to prayer-timers and Islamic educational materials. It is commonly driven by and often wrapped in intense discussion and debate about how to square Islamic requirements with modern life and how to lead a Muslim life in a non-Muslim society. Traditional apologia appear alongside attempts to think about Islam with techniques drawn from engineering and applied science. Islam on the Internet emerges as an intermediate realm of mixed content, mixed intellectual technique, and mixed persons who are not divided into the senders and receivers of mass (or of class) media but instead form a sort of community—commonly called "virtual." This is a social-communicative sphere more comparable to the "creoles" that Benedict Anderson (1991) identified with the civic publics that arose, without prior design, with the earlier spread of print capitalism and particularly with early modern newspapers. That is, the Internet and its surroundings that enthusiasts call "cyberspace" or envision as a new "information age" do not facilitate the spokesperson-activists of established institutions, but draw instead on a broader range of new interpreters or newly visible interpreters of Islam (Fig. 4.1).

Organization as a speech community, rather than of mass media, is built into the Internet. Representations of the Internet as a new paradigm of work, community, thought, and utopia (or dystopia) of unfettered communication tend to generalize from a narrow range of experience and often the worldview of programmers (for example, Lammers 1989; Gates 1995; Negroponte 1995) or enthusiastic annointers of the *avant garde* (for example, Rheingold 1993; Rifkin 1995; Levy 1984). The Internet originated as a collaborative tool, constructed by engineers and applied scientists in accord with their work habits and values (Hafner and Lyon 1996; Leiner et al. 1997). They built into it open access, flattened hierarchies, freedom of information, and, more subtly, notions of transient, purposive connections among people and between pieces of information. Their Internet is organized not so much around transmission as around sharing of information. Their scheme, in turn, diffused to and was taken up by the larger world of higher education and allied activities and, subsequently, in an increasingly commercial communication ecology of business and leisure. This, in the view of one of its creators, is composed of a changing community of users, technologies linking them, schemes for managing the system, and now commercialization of access and content (McLellan 1997).

The Internet's transformations to successively wider realms has been one of partial translations of engineer's tools to the larger worlds of research and higher education and then to realms engaged by their occupants. They develop as extensions of the physical network of computers, the pro-

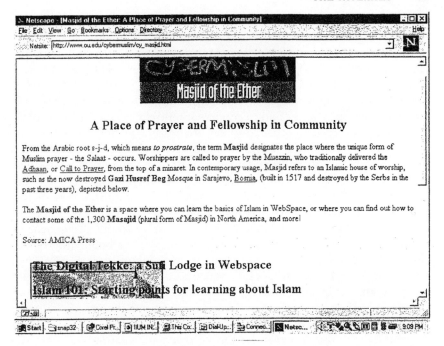

Figure 4.1. Early Islamic sites, like this Cybermuslim Webpage, displayed a clear "creole" character in their mix of forms (Western, Islamic, youth, university) and address to both believers and seekers. Sites like this one provided guides and links to similar efforts and material in cyberspace.

grams and protocols written by engineers to connect them, a social organization of work that engineers built into them, and a culture translating that organization into more general values. On the foundational technologies for remote access or connection to distant computers and for making files accessible, created in the 1960s, are built the functional technologies of electronic mail (1972), electronic mailing lists for groups of subscribers, newsgroups (1980) or electronic bulletin boards for discussion of special interests, and schemes for more ordered publication, which culminate today in the World Wide Web (1990).[2] With each, initial interest in professional communication has been quickly followed by avocational interests, first of engineers and then of others sharing those interests, including Muslims, first in the high-tech realms that invented and built the Internet and then in the wider world.

Setting aside the technologies primarily accessible to specialists and electronic mail, which is not a public medium, on-line communication for religious and other special interests breaks into roughly two kinds (Kinney 1995). One is found on Usenet newsgroups or electronic bulletin boards and e-mail lists. The dozen or so devoted to Islamic and Middle Eastern topics tend to be dominated by people with professional-technical qualifications who happen to be Muslims. Many, perhaps most, are students and expatriate professionals in the Middle East's "overseas." They belong to the world of or are enabled by higher education and range from ordinary Muslims to dedicated polemicists. Newsgroups and mailing lists are nominally articulated by open access and freedom of interpretation, into which practically intrude other values that routinely are negotiated, and often hotly debated. Tension commonly arises between access and desires, usually not fully articulated until challenged, to construct something like a home away from home around values and attitudes of hospitality. Interpretive freedom escalates into disagreements and sometimes into accusations less of bad manners or bad faith than of personal "ignorance" or willful "violation" of previously unstated or lately ignored rules—in other words, disagreements over interpretation, followed by attempts to redraw the boundaries of discussion. For all its artificiality and newness, there is a sense of transforming information into knowledge, at the same time that boundaries are fluid and change with participants, through the practices they bring on-line. On an electronic mailing list devoted to discussions among Palestinians, limits on access were waived to admit Israelis professing sympathies with the Palestinian cause; but their interventions to "provide information" were repeatedly censured as "Zionist" violations of a Palestinian space, that is, an on-line home for Palestinians ordered by guest-host relations in which they were charged with being bad guests.[3] Another list devoted to discussions of the history of Islam altered to a forum for participants and for seekers' questions about correct practice, and attendant disputes, that effectively excluded "objectivist" views offered by historians and drove them away.

By comparison, World Wide Web homepages, typically produced by individuals or groups to provide information, generally take the form of publications. Web technology facilitates linkage over discursiveness, and Web pages run the gamut from lists of links to other Web pages (and other on-line information) to extended presentations of original material. Here, interpretation is practically a matter of making and commenting on connections. The same material is often relinked over and over, with variations in organization, selection, and emphasis. In these respects, the Web is comparable in a contemporary context to early printing presses in the world of the scriptorium: it escapes the world of editors and arbiters of thought and interpretation by displaying the materials of interpretation and providing alternative organizations for them. And it brings together something of the moment. Into this world come people with views about Islam who are able thereby to extend those views into newly public forums—a "public" that is defined (like the readership of early newspapers) by those with access to its techniques (Fig. 4.2).

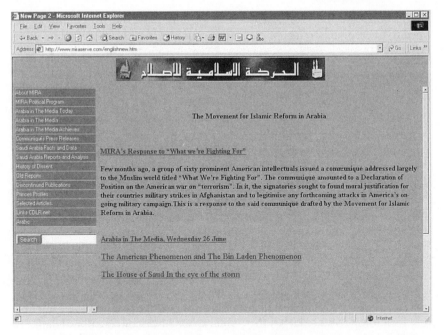

Figure 4.2. The movement for Islamic Reform in Arabia (*al-Harakat al-Islamiyya li-l-Islah*), established in London in 1966 as an offshoot of the Committee for Defense of Legitimate Rights in Saudi Arabia, takes advantage of Internet technology to add a "media watch," responses to international intellectuals, and links to other media to its own chronology of dissent in Saudi Arabia, critiques, and data on Saudi leaders. The site is now fully bilingual in Arabic and English. <www.miraserve.com/englishnew.htm>

INTERNET SOCIOLOGY AND COMMUNICATION ECOLOGY

Internet sociology follows this continuum of forms between conversation and publication. Muslims initially located in the high-tech precincts that created the Internet included students who found their way overseas for advanced training in engineering and applied sciences and expatriate professionals. Located in universities and polytechnic institutions of the West or in corporate and government research labs, they have brought other interests on-line, including interests in the religion, culture, and politics of their home countries, and brought these on-line with a sense of empowerment by the technology they commanded. In this respect, they are no different from non-Muslims, who also bring interests outside of their work and interests in making connections; indeed, technologies such as Usenet newsgroups and the World Wide Web were, in part, motivated and developed to overcome barriers of dispersion and to connect people of like interests.

Around these cores accumulate others who are similarly situated but in other fields, similarly seeking to make contact, to share views, and to recruit others. Through the Internet, these activities create worldwide networks that significantly extend conversations, expressions, and representations of and about Islam that were previously confined to coffee houses, university dormitories, cells, peer circles, and other off-hours sites of discussion and debate. The Internet unites such people, not just electronically but also through shared intellectual techniques derived from higher education, including techniques other than those classically associated with religious discussion and exegesis that are organized by and delivered in *madrasa* and other "traditional" forms. Balance of personnel affects the balance of communication. This is a realm in which engineers and applied scientists, followed by others with access to international-standard higher education, followed by others in their circles and increasingly by wider, more anonymous circles with similar access can try their hands at religious interpretation in a new medium of publication that extends the reach of their intellectual technology and enlarges the public space of discourse about Islam.

This enlargement echoes those new senses of agency that Eickelman (1992) has associated with the spread of mass education—especially secondary and higher education—throughout the Muslim world that de-monopolizes access to the texts of religion and opens their interpretation to new techniques. The process is reflected in the migration on-line first of translations and then of Arabic transcriptions of the Qur'an, collections of *hadith*, and other documents from history to apologia by those adept in the technology of the Internet. Use of the Internet as a channel is quickly overtaken by use of its techniques and the sense of confidence in their authority to carry messages of mutual recognition in a public of others like oneself. Texts are not only made available; what begins as a pious act of witness is followed by interpretations that apply intellectual techniques developed elsewhere than the texts themselves, along with the practical lessons of interpretive freedom, including responsibility for interpretation that goes beyond challenging received views to a broader pattern of expanding the public space.

The pattern goes back at least to Salafiyya and similar movements in South Asia in the nineteenth century, in which new interpreters of Islam have arisen in conjunction with new media to take responsibility for interpreting Islam. It has become a commonplace that "fundamentalists" embrace the techniques of "modernity" in order to challenge its goals (Lawrence 1989, Appleby 1997); but reformer-critics are not alone in creating a public space for Islam between the traditional style of the 'ulama and those merging Sufi with "folk" Islam. The bourgeois character of this space was revealed in Gilsenan's (1973) account of the recasting of Egypt's fastest grow-ing Sufi order in modern times to the practices and values of rising first-generation clerks, teachers, and new urbanites of Egypt's new middle class. In his account, the rule of this order—modeled on bureaucratic prac-tice and training office holders—is hardly to be described as "folk" as that term has been deployed by historians and indigenous observers to indicate something, especially something rural, beyond 'ulama control. It is the more professional middle-class end of this spectrum that is engaged on the Internet. The rising curve of expanded education to which Eickelman (1992) pointed as giving unprecedented access to the texts of Islam and opening interpreta-tion to techniques outside the traditional frameworks of *madrasa* training intersects the rising curve of the Internet's spread to more people and tasks and development as a public space. The Internet, which begins globally in high-tech precincts, arrives in Muslim spheres in hands committed to com-bining their values and expanding the public space for them through this means.

This more professional end of the middle classes attracts relatively less attention,[4] but it is the natural home also of representations and systemati-zations of Islam ranging from views that Islam is inseparable from all life (thus problematizing its integration in contemporary forms) to modernist views of Islam as a system in a world of systems (for example, Rahman 1982). Brought to the Internet, these make it an arena for alternative ex-pressions of Islam both to popular and to traditional elite views that are soon joined by oppositional and alternative groups speaking to Western and other non-Muslim media and opinion publics. They range from politi-cal activists to Sufi orders, from mobilization to witness. They both recruit and propagandize, bringing their issues into a wider, already public sphere in some cases but in others carving out a new one that encompasses or repackages existing ones, compelling dialogue by leveraging forms of com-munication that reshape the social field.

The complexities of this process sort into stages by which it proceeds. Islam on the Internet is first a story of new interpreters, newly emboldened by confidence in and command of the channel. The channel's foundational values, drawn from the work habits and values of engineers and applied scientists' need to collaborate and share in flattened hierarchies—in other words, specific senses of responsibility for statements—are extended into broader "cultural" values about open access, freedom of information, and taking responsibility for, rather than merely receiving, interpretations. Its context is an emerging bourgeois, essentially middle-class, and importantly a professional world, authorized by skills and increasingly transnational by virtue of the spread of professions through mass higher education and mod-ern means of communication among them.

Until recently, the story of Islam coming on-line would have been lim-ited to creole pioneers, located in the high-tech precincts that produced the

Internet and drawing on a transnational population of Muslims. They still bring religious interests on-line as after-hours interests, essentially as devotions and as witness in a public space that they define and in which they give a new dimension to their interests. Such Islam on the Internet is shaped much like anything else relocated there by techniques, including intellectual techniques, from the world of higher education and research. The early creoles link up with others like themselves and extend their links to realms surrounding and served by higher education and research, especially in communication agencies and businesses that increasingly convey the Internet to the wider world. After the pioneers also come activists, some to recruit within this world, others to address a wider audience through the channel widely believed to be a leading edge and symbol of a globalizing "age of information." Until recently, also, "official" Islamic voices—of the *madrasa*, *'ulama*, and authorized institutions such as the Organization of the Islamic Conference or the Muslim World League—have been largely absent from these arenas, except as others brought bits and pieces of their discourse and documents on-line. Conventional, established voices of Muslim authority as such are unrepresented here, in part because the effect of the channel was to foster intermediate sorts of discourse that could be dismissed as naïve, if pious in its own terms.

Increasingly, however, just as the creole pioneers were followed by activists, so both are now followed by officializing discourses that range from conventional *da'wa* organizations and, recently, Sufi orders to governments of Muslim countries. Forced to adopt the forms and formats already present, some organizations manage better than others a convergence on increasingly international, increasingly uniform formats. Al-Azhar, for instance, is not on-line. What are on-line are a School of Islamic and Social Sciences (SISS) in suburban Virginia that offers international-standard master's degrees in Islamic studies and pastoral training, an International Islamic University in Malaysia (IIUM), which presents a public face, a table of organization, and programs formally identical to those of Western universities. In the United Kingdom, a Muslim national council presents the face of a religious denomination with houses of worship and ancillary charitable, educational, and community activities. SISS grew out of a project supported by pious foundations to update Muslim apologetics; the IIUM is a joint project of the Malaysian government and the Organization of the Islamic Conference to create an international-standard Islamic university for training professionals (Fig. 4.3); and the national Muslim council evokes parallels with other national religious establishments.

These convergences and measures of uniformity characterize presentations that do not homogenize the faith brought on-line so much as affirm universal access and a sense of participation in a pubic sphere of listeners, watchers, or, in cyberspeak, "browsers." This affirms new senses of interpretive freedom to go beyond previous forms and responsibility to speak

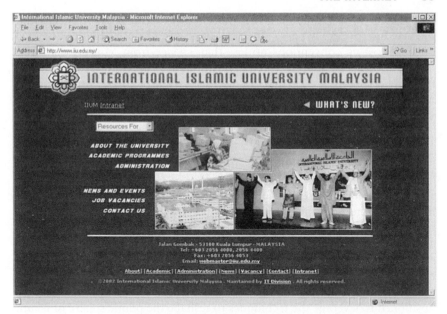

Figure 4.3. The homepage of the International Islamic University Malaysia is regularly updated with the latest Internet technology—here, a rotating picture gallery. IIUM was founded by the government of Malaysia and several member countries of the Organization of the Islamic Conference in 1983 as an English-medium institution for "integrating sources of revealed knowledge with an arts and sciences curriculum," which it proudly displays on its web site <www.iiu.edu.my/>.

for Islam in a "civic" public that goes beyond transferring discussions from more restricted to less restricted realms. Getting the word out supplants the earlier felt need to reach out to others like oneself; public space replaces virtual community. The move is not just from private to public, but a blurring of that distinction through communication and interpretation that bypasses the gatekeeping and sanctions embedded in older media. Just as print bypassed the scriptorium, so the Internet bypasses institutions of mass media and those attached to it and currently institutionalized through editors, publishers, acceptable genre, and marketing to specific "readerships."

While many of the views expressed in these media are intolerant in that context and are often driven into the underground or "minor" media, the larger contexts where they occur register a practical pluralism that problematizes responsibility and what Bourdieu (1991) called the social capital that enables interpretation. Among the first opposition met by these new interpreters are liberal humanists, whose social capital is tied to media that the new interpreters bypass.[5] They call to account responsibilities assumed outside existing conventions no less than silence from Muslim establishments. For a social analysis, such oppositions are part of the redefinition of the public sphere, a part that points to rarely articulated, often implicit notions of taking responsibility for interpretation otherwise met as rights to interpret.

CONCLUSION

The Internet is a significant new medium in expanding the public sphere, where Islamic discourse is altered by new positioning and new interpreters. Like other media, from cassettes to novels and tracts, it is fast and flexible, not least for providing opportunities for alternative expressions, networking, and interpretations that draw on and extend its techniques. Additionally, the Internet is worldwide in its reach and rooted in, as well as rooting, a professional class not yet so widely represented but uniquely positioned to leverage the techniques to reshape the public sphere of Islam. The process is an emerging one, and absolute numbers are small. It is their extent and the techniques they bring that is significant. Initially, they joined others' migrating discussions from more private to more public spaces that media make accessible and, ultimately, create. Increasingly, however, they reshape that space and what it means to be public.

What is happening with Islam on the Internet is a forging of at least three sets of related links. One set links individual Muslims via the medium of the Internet, individuals often in similar situations and often similar to each other, in social networks of communication. What begins as a home away from home extends to and then transforms the space in which "home" exists as this technology spreads, in part in these hands. Broadly speaking, these are the modern skill-based professions of expanding middle classes, whose mutual recognition and negotiation of rights to speak set the issues and character of on-line communities. The discourse itself reflects a creolization that does not so much mix religious with other talk as foster intermediate speech communities as contexts with rules that describe rights and responsibilities. They cast religious talk in idioms of speech and thought previously or otherwise allocated to separate speech communities, forming a continuum instead of a dichotomization between elite and mass, literate and folk. The significant feature of these links is the application to religious subjects and contents the techniques and models drawn from higher education generally and from science and engineering specifically. What emerges with the Internet is thus a sphere of intermediate people, new interpreters, drawn from these realms and linking them in a new social, public space of alternative voices and authorities.

Bringing these to the Internet also makes them more public. Internet discourse, in the first instance, migrated from less public to more public spheres by linking people, social networks, and modalities of thought in transnational networks of which they are in part the expression and in part its builders. Technology, not association, enables participation and is the means of participation in a space defined by taking it upon oneself to participate. In taking these as responsibilities to think about religion in the world, irrespective of the presence or absence of familiar institutions, a wider body of new interpreters of Islam beyond merely activists emerges, as does a context other than that of conventional and folk religiosities.

Islam on the Internet highlights not just new interpreters but also the presence of intermediate contexts that reflect a more nuanced diversity of views, settings, projects, and expressions of Islam today. This context is also occupied by Islamist critiques of both elite and folk traditions; but activists may not be its diagnostic creatures. Just as print—especially newspapers—opened a channel for what became recognized as Islamist critique and cassettes opened a channel for the circulation of sermons and other didactic material, so too the Internet opens arenas where responsibility is both problematic and engaged. These interpreters are part of a real diversity of opinion, interests, and variously formed programs, and part of a more general and diagnostic context shared with activists of sharper profile. The medium overlaps with others, as did those of previous interpreters. And the most striking features of the Internet are how it brings out the broadly intermediate character and location, the "in-between" and ordinary character, of the efforts that mark it, and its practical diversity. Finally, the recency of the introduction of its interpreters to a more public realm brings out the priority of responsibility and how taking responsibility, particularly for interpretation, in public (instead of forming associations) is the intermediating step for "civil" society.

NOTES

1. Gaffney (1994) has corrected this view by showing, on the one hand, how, at the level of expression and interpretation, activists are part of the same social field as *shaykh*s and *pir*s and, on the other, how they connect with their publics through emphasis on practical interpretation. A similar point is developed in more comparative terms by Eickelman and Piscatori's (1996) discussion of political Islam's many and local resonances.

2. The World Wide Web, which has become the Internet for most users outside the research world, superseded earlier technologies of WAIS (Wide Area Information Servers) and Gopher, which were created to index and systematize access to information on networked computers.

3. I am grateful to Rachel Rumberger for bringing this example, and this interpretation, to my attention.

4. But compare the singular study by Clement Henry Moore (1980) of Egyptian engineers, Göle (1993) on Turkish engineers, Palmer et al. (1988) on senior bureaucrats, and Vitalis (1995) on businessmen. Goldberg (1992) and Robinson (1991) focus on mobilization in this portion of the middle class.

5. This is equally true in realms closer to debate about the Internet itself, from the anti-Internet screed by the conservative literary theorist Gertrude Himmelfarb (1996) to reservations by journalists (Wald 1995) over the lack of "standards" and the rights of "experts" to judge what is acceptable.

WORKS CITED

Anderson, Benedict. 1991. *Imagined Communities: Reflections on the Origin and Spread of Nationalism*, 2nd ed. New York: Verso.

Anderson, Jon. 1995. "Cybarites, Knowledge Workers and New Creoles of the Information Superhighway." *Anthropology Today* 11, no. 4 (August): 13–15.

Appleby, Scott, ed. 1997. *Spokesmen for the Despised: Fundamentalist Leaders of the Middle East*. Chicago: University of Chicago Press.

Bourdieu, Pierre. 1991. *Language and Symbolic Power*, ed. John B. Thompson, trans. Gino Raymond and Matthew Adamson. Cambridge: Harvard University Press.

Cole, Juan R. I. 1994. "Printing and the Salafiyyah." Paper presented at the Annual Meeting of the Middle East Studies Association, Symposium on Print and Mass Communication in the Middle East, November.

Drummond, Lee. 1980. "The Cultural Continuum: A Theory of Intersystems." *Man* (N.S.) 15, no. 2 (June): 352–74.

Eickelman, Dale F. 1985. *Knowledge and Power in Morocco: The Education of a Twentieth-Century Notable*. Princeton: Princeton University Press.

———. 1992. "Mass Higher Education and the Religious Imagination in Contemporary Arab Societies." *American Ethnologist* 19, no. 4: (November): 643–55.

Eickelman, Dale F., and James Piscatori. 1996. *Muslim Politics*. Princeton: Princeton University Press.

Fischer, Michael M. J. 1980. *Iran: From Religious Dispute to Revolution*. Cambridge: Harvard University Press.

Gaffney, Patrick D. 1994. *The Prophet's Pulpit: Islamic Preaching in Contemporary Egypt*. Berkeley: University of California Press.

Gates, William. 1995. *The Road Ahead*. New York: Viking.

Gilsenan, Michael. 1973. *Saint and Sufi in Modern Egypt: An Essay in the Sociology of Religion*. Oxford: Clarendon Press.

Goldberg, Ellis. 1991. "Smashing Idols and the State: The Protestant Ethic and Egyptian Sunni Radicalism." *Comparative Studies in Society and History* 33, no. 1 (January): 3–35.

Göle, Nilüfer. 1993. "Engineers and the Emergence of a Technist Identity." In *Turkey and the West: Changing Political and Cultural Identities*, ed. Metin Heper, Ayse Öncü, and Heinz Kramer, pp. 199–218. London and New York: I. B. Tauris.

Hafner, Katie and Matthew Lyon. 1996. *Where Wizards Stay Up Late: The Origins of the Internet*. New York: Simon and Schuster.

Himmelfarb, Gertrude. 1996. "A Neo-Luddite Reflects on the Internet." *Chronicle of Higher Education,* 1 November, p. A56

Hodgson, Marshall S. 1974. *The Venture of Islam: Conscience and History in a*

World Civilization. Chicago: University of Chicago Press.

Kepel, Gilles. 1985. *The Prophet and Pharaoh: Muslim Extremism in Egypt.* London: Al-Saqi Books.

Kinney, Jay. 1995. "Net Worth? Religion, Cyberspace and the Future." *Futures* 27, no. 7 (September): 763–75.

Lammers, Susan M. 1989. *Programmers at Work: Interviews with 19 Programmers Who Shaped the Computer Industry.* Redmond, Wash.: Tempus Books of Microsoft Press.

Lawrence, Bruce B. 1989. *Defenders of God: The Fundamentalist Revolt Against the Modern Age.* San Francisco: Harper and Row.

Leiner, Barry M., Vinton G. Cerf, David D. Clark, Robert E. Kahn, Leonard Kleinrock, Daniel C. Lynch, Jon Postel, Larry G. Roberts, and Stephen Wolff. 1997. *A Brief History of the Internet.* The Internet Society. <http://www.isoc.org/internet-history/>

Levy, Steven. 1984. *Hackers: Heroes of the Computer Revolution.* New York: Dell.

McLellan, Hilary. 1997. "Diplomacy in Cyberspace: Report on the Virtual Diplomacy Conference, April 1-2, 1997." <http://www.tech-head.com/diplomacy.html>

Messick, Brinkley. 1993. *The Calligraphic State: Textual Domination and History in a Muslim Society.* Berkeley: University of California Press.

Metcalf, Barbara Daly. 1982. *Islamic Revival in British India: Deoband, 1860–1900.* Princeton: Princeton University Press.

Moore, Clement Henry. 1980. *Images of Development: Egyptian Engineers in Search of Identity.* Cambridge: MIT Press.

Moussalli, Ahmad S. 1992. *Radical Islamic Fundamentalism: The Ideological and Political Discourse of Sayyid Qutb.* Beirut: American University of Beirut.

Negroponte, Nicholas. 1995. *Being Digital.* New York: Knopf.

Norton, Augustus Richard, ed. 1995/1996. *Civil Society in the Middle East*, vols. I and II. New York: E. J. Brill.

Palmer, Monte, Ali Leila and El Sayed Yassin. 1988. *The Egyptian Bureaucracy.* Syracuse: Syracuse University Press.

Rahman, Fazlur. 1982. *Islam and Modernity: The Transformation of an Intellectual Tradition.* Chicago: University of Chicago Press.

Rahnema, Ali, ed. 1994. *Pioneers of Islamic Revival.* London: Zed Books.

Rheingold, Howard. 1993. *The Virtual Community: Homesteading on the Electronic Frontier.* New York: HarperCollins.

Rifkin, Jeremy. 1995 *The End of Work: The Decline of the Global Labor Force and the Dawn of the Post-Market Era.* New York: G. P. Putnam's Sons.

Robinson, Glenn E. 1993. "The Role of the Professional Middle Class in the Mobilization of Palestinian Society: The Medical and Agricultural Committees." *International Journal of Middle East Studies* 25, no. 2 (May): 301–26.

Roy, Olivier. 1994. *The Failure of Political Islam*, trans. Carol Volk. Cambridge: Harvard University Press.

Sardar, Ziauddin. 1993. "Paper, Printing, and Compact Disks: The Making and Unmaking of Islamic Culture." *Media, Culture, and Society* 15, no. 1 (January): 43–60.

Seligman, Adam B. 1992. *The Idea of Civil Society.* Princeton: Princeton University Press.

Sivan, Emmanuel. 1990. *Radical Islam: Medieval Theology and Modern Politics.* New Haven: Yale University Press.

Sreberny-Mohammadi, Annabelle and Ali Mohammadi. 1994. *Small Media, Big Revolution: Communication, Culture, and the Iranian Revolution.* Minneapolis: University of Minnesota Press.

Starrett, Gregory. 1995. "Signposts Along the Road: Monumental Public Writing in Egypt." *Anthropology Today* 11, no. 4 (August): 8–13.

Stoll, Clifford. 1995. *Silicon Snake Oil: Second Thoughts on the Information Highway*. New York: Doubleday.

Trix, Frances. 1993. *Spiritual Discourses: Learning with an Islamic Master*. Philadelphia: University of Pennsylvania Press.

Vitalis, Robert. 1995. *When Capitalists Collide: Business Conflict and the End of Empire in Egypt*. Berkeley and Los Angeles: University of California Press.

Wald, Matthew L. 1995. "A Disillusioned Devotee Says The Internet Is Wearing No Clothes." *New York Times*, 30 April, p. E7.

5 /

THE BIRTH OF A MEDIA ECOSYSTEM: LEBANON IN THE INTERNET AGE

Yves Gonzalez-Quijano

(translated by Dale F. Eickelman and William F. P. Raynolds)

Until a few years ago, a visitor to Beirut could escape the commotion of Hamra Street, West Beirut's main commercial road, by entering a large exhibition hall in the basement of a modern building on Sadat Street. It was the Permanent Book Exhibit (*maʿrad al-kitab al-daʾim*), where most of the Lebanese publishers—the most important ones in the Arab world—had exhibition space. Today, the exhibition hall is just as calm, but the bookshelves have given way to an orderly array of computers. Only a soft drink machine and a counter at which clients, most of them young, pay for Internet connection time, break the impeccable array of computers.

As in most large Arab cities where this new type of business has flourished—Cairo, Casablanca, and Amman, of course, but also Damascus, Nouakchott, and Sanaʿa—the large bookstores of an earlier era have given way to Internet cafés. Many Beirut intellectuals invoke this symbolic replacement with bitterness. For them, it underlines the dangers of a new "culture" in which books have given way to video screens. In practice, today's concerns merely prolong the laments that the local intelligentsia has expressed since the time that the new technologies began to appear at an ever accelerating pace several decades ago. These new "mid-range" media technologies (Alterman 2001) and their associated techniques do not always need large financial investments and complex skills. It has become increasingly clear that this complex package of instruments and tools has profoundly modified the shape of the intellectual field. By means of these new instruments and skills, unexpected and at times bizarre new voices have begun increasingly to mix with those of the earlier "legitimate interpreters"—that is, when these new voices fail completely to replace their predecessors. These new voices get the attention of a radically different public, one that belongs to their generation. It accepts the cultural and intellectual practices that modern technology facilitates (Eickelman and Anderson, this volume).

These new practices are fundamentally altering how information and ideas are shared, communicated, and produced. They are accompanied by, and partially explain, social and political change in contemporary Arab societies. Sometimes they take spectacular forms, especially in the case of technical changes with visible consequences, such as the proliferation of parabolic antennas for satellite television. However, the influence of these new techniques and technologies can also be less visible and more far-reaching. They can even radically transform established, "traditional" practices considered so old that they appear impermeable to change. Thus, the tremendous commercial success of the contemporary "Islamic book" (al-kitab al-islami) —which has totally reshaped the idea of religious books in conception, production, and marketing (Gonzalez-Quijano 1998)—offers a perfect illustration of the re-invention (Hobsbawm 1983) of "traditional" and "sacred" forms of knowledge in Muslim societies (see Eickelman, this volume, and Huq, this volume).

The re-invention of the modern Islamic book, made possible by the spread of desktop publishing techniques, could not have occurred without an associated decisive technological development, the creation of software applications to digitize Arabic. Word-processing programs for typesetting Arabic, such as al-nashr al-maktabi (literally, "desktop publisher"), were first developed in the mid-1980s.[1] These programs facilitated the creation of newspapers accessible to a worldwide Arabic readership. This first occurred in London in 1978 with the appearance of al-Sharq al-Awsat. Then in 1987, al-Hayat became the first Arabic daily with an entirely computerized editorial process. Since the early 1990s, these technological innovations spread with the first on-line editions of daily Arabic language newspapers, beginning with al-Sharq al-Awsat in 1995 in image (PDF) format, and direct on-line text in more recent years. Today hundreds of Arabic publications are available on the Internet,[2] to which one must add a larger number of Arabic-speaking and/or Arab-oriented sites that distribute information in one form or another.

As part of the linkages and mergers of traditional media actors (the press and broadcast media) with financial enterprises, information technology, and telecommunications companies, a stiff competition is taking place for global domination of the emerging Arab information market (Anderson and Eickelman 1999: 59). As of March 2001, there were more than 3.5 million Internet users in the Arab world, a number predicted to grow to 25 million by 2005.[3] This growth has facilitated a wide array of entrepreneurial initiatives. Some of these are based on passing fashions and will probably soon collapse and disappear. Others, like web portals, on-line newsletters, and webzines are better adapted to the still uncertain market for on-line information in Arabic and have already succeeded in finding a niche in the regional Arab media scene.

For at least half a century, scholars have recognized the importance of public opinion and the media to the growth of Arab societies and, in recent years, to such developments as the Internet and its uses as a new channel for information. In spite of this, few studies on the new media focus on this development. They focus instead on international[4] or "Western" (Bunt 2000) subjects, or privilege the transnational mass media and their effects from a global perspective (for example, Alterman 1998) at the expense of detailed case studies. Victims of a sort of fascination with technology-oriented ideologies (Wolton 2000: 13), most of those who produce such studies take for granted that the new media have completely surpassed and replaced prior systems for disseminating information and opinion. This chapter takes a different point of departure and is based on Lebanon, a case study with special regional significance. It requires us to note—in as detailed and specific a manner as possible—how an existing media system absorbs innovations, adapting new information techniques to its own needs.

LEBANON: THE CROSSROADS OF ARABIC-BASED INFORMATION

Lebanon stands out from all other arenas for technological transformation that influences the production of information in Arabic. Based on the changes that can be seen in editorial production techniques alone, Lebanon is at the core of a regional media network with global implications. The Lebanese played major roles in what can be called the incubation period of information technologies in the Arab world (1995–2000). Now that these innovators are crossing another development threshold, Beirut retains a number of features that allow it to remain an obligatory hub for the "Arab information highway." It will remain so even if a good part of regional information flows shift, in the not-so-distant future, to states such as the United Arab Emirates, which have made important investments (more than a billion and a half dollars, for example, with Dubai Media City, Dubai Internet Media, and Dubai Ideas Oasis, launched at the end of 2000).

In spite of numerous challenges, the importance of the Lebanese press, initially favored by the weakening in the early 1950s of its Egyptian rivals, was not entirely weakened by nearly two and a half decades of civil war. In the context of a regional crisis that remains unsolvable, the political formula devised during the 1989 Taif Accords is not yet fully realized. In spite of everything, however, it has permitted the implementation of certain important legal measures vital to Lebanon's future, including the fields of information and media technology. This new legislation, developed and applied with difficulty between 1992 and 1996, drastically reduced the number of media outlets. A decade earlier some three million Lebanese had access to some fifty television stations, and more than 150 radio stations, as well as a hard-to-calculate number of periodicals, not always legal, that occupied the many commercial niches of the local political market (Dajani 1992).

Clearly motivated by the political goals of maintaining a Lebanese national coalition and respecting the "privileged" relations with neighboring Syria, the Lebanese media reforms favored certain businesses able to use their "know-how" to help one of the political forces present on the local or regional scene. After this "cleanup" of the Lebanese media scene, a dozen important periodicals continued to appear and, of these, only a few—the most outstanding of which were the fairly liberal *al-Nahar* and the nationalist *al-Safir*—had a voice beyond Lebanon's borders. As for central Beirut, now reconstructed, it once again contains the reopened offices of the international wire services and, just recently, those of *al-Hayat,* whose main offices have returned from their London exile.

If print journalism taken as a whole has regained working conditions that permit it to recapture its traditional markets, the growth of Lebanese satellite television has been even more spectacular. Among the most popular regional satellite TV channels—including Middle East Broadcasting Centre (MBC) in London, Orbit in Rome, the Egyptian Satellite Channel, Emirates Dubai Television, and, of course, al-Jazeera from Qatar—are two Lebanese enterprises: the Lebanese Broadcasting Company International (LBCI) and Future TV, without forgetting al-Manar TV, a channel close to the Shi'i population which seems to gain more and more international influence. Even though the political ties of these corporations are mysteries to no one,[5] LBCI and Future TV are the only two private channels that broadcast from the Arab world, a situation made possible because Lebanon is the only Arab state to have legally relinquished its monopoly on televised information (al-Rammal 1999–2000: 62).

Finally, in spite of the inherent difficulties of rebuilding a technical infrastructure after the damages incurred during the civil war, it is remarkable that Lebanon became one of the first Arab countries to embrace the Internet. The information professionals of the Beirut daily newspapers were among the first in the region to make use of a technology that has been available since 1994. Competing against European-based rivals equipped with better financial support and technology, three Lebanese dailies (*al-Anwar, al-Nahar,* and *al-Safir*) placed themselves on-line by 1996. For the Arabic language press, *al-Anwar* launched a highly condensed version of its paper edition called *al-Anwar fax*. *Al-Nahar,* on the basis of a major investment in technology, launched the first real electronic edition on January 1, 1996. It was followed several months later by *al-Safir*. After this first wave and the en1try into play of foreign language journals (the *Daily Star* in October 1997, followed by *L'Orient-Le Jour*), *al-Liwa* followed (summer 1998), then *al-Mustaqbal* (August 1999), a mere two months after the launch of its print version. *Al-Kifah al-'arab* opened a site with a PDF version in 1999, and soon followed it with a full-text format.

These pioneering efforts served as a model for many others, both existing newspapers and those created to take advantage of the Internet. By the beginning of 2002, Lebanon had around 200 web sites (of a total, probably underestimated, of 5,000) providing information and news of one sort or another (Mokaddem 2001).

A Cartography of Shifting Borders

The Arab information market has paradoxically benefited from its delay in investing in infrastructure. For the most part, it has escaped the economic crisis permeating the dot-com economy as a whole, particularly initiatives in developing and selling on-line information (Gonzalez-Quijano 2002). Quite the opposite; due to an increase in the number of users and hardware purchases, the growth of on-line commerce and advertising, the creation of local branches of international corporations, and the launch of important public development programs, even in countries such as Yemen and Mauritania, the overall impression is that the new technologies have entered a new phase of growth. In Beirut, as in the other regional capitals, Internet usage was confined for a time to a narrow segment of the population drawn from the economic and cultural elite and largely imbued with a cosmopolitan spirit. This experimental period has been over for some time, because there is a much larger public now familiar with the "new" media technology. This implies, among other factors, the progressive Arabization of site content together with a lowering of communication costs, as Muhammad al-Shareh, the CEO of Sakhr Software, the principal IT firm in the region, explained to a gathering of political and economic advisors in Beirut in April 2001 ("Ajeeb.com" 2001).

Despite the many difficulties associated with two decades of a civil war that had barely ended just as the U.S. public discovered the Internet—the 1989 Taif Accords were signed just as html became the industry standard and the first browsers emerged—Lebanon was nonetheless one of the first countries in the region to rapidly develop a market interest in exploring the possibilities offered by this new and poorly understood media. Beginning in 1995, the first local Internet service providers (ISPs) offered people in Beirut a chance to connect to the global network. Today, many specialized firms (Gonzalez-Quijano and Taha 2001: 6) offer businesses and individuals connection rates that are mid-range for the region (about a $15 monthly connection fee).[6] This is even more advantageous because the standard of living in Lebanon is higher than in many neighboring countries. The number of Internet users in Lebanon was estimated at slightly more than 30,000 in July 1997, and is expected to pass 300,000, or roughly 8 percent of the population, by the beginning of 2002. Lebanese Internet usage is much higher than the average for the Arab world as a whole, which was only 1.29 percent as of March 2001. At this earlier date, the United Arab Emirates had the highest number of Internet users (around 25 percent), followed by Bahrain (17 percent), Qatar (10 percent), Kuwait (8 percent), and Lebanon (6.5 percent) (see note 3).

Different factors explain the relative success of the Internet in Lebanon in contrast to other countries in the region—its relative political liberalism, its higher level of socio-economic and educational development—Lebanese private and public universities offer some 22 academic degree programs in information technology—and a long and strong history of emigration, principally to industrialized nations. However, in spite of these characteristics, which make Lebanon seem like the most advanced Arab nation to put local information on-line, attempts remain largely embryonic. Nevertheless, limited as these early efforts may be, they offer a sense of the direction that later developments, vital for the region's future, will take.

Even for a country as small as Lebanon, creating a reliable overview of Internet information sites, let alone evaluating their content, is a major challenge. The capital needed to start a business is minimal, and businesses disappear as fast as they are created, a situation further complicated by a multitude of mergers and acquisitions. This development can be interpreted as confirming the maturity of the market. For example, after the Inconet and Datanet companies merged under the name Inconet Data Management in early 2002, it became the most important private ISP operating in the region, with 120,000 subscribers. Now only three providers—the other two are Cyberia and Terranet—control the entire market for private subscriptions, a market that was once much more open. Just before the Inconet and Datanet merger, the acquisition of the web-site portal Lebanon-online by Arabia.online based in Dubai and Amman—one of the biggest players in the local Net-economy—clearly suggests a regional trend of restructuring and consolidating the new information technology market.

Evaluating the implications of on-line information for Lebanon is equally difficult because of the gap that often exists between the services offered by different sites or even the same site during different stages of its existence. It is easy to note that many of the local companies, magazines for example, and also radio stations, limit their Internet presence to a simple publicity page, often devoid of other content. It is as though these companies are acceding to a passing trend and acquired an Internet address to give their enterprise a "modern" look.[7] Those responsible for these sites, many of which were created in 2000 or 2001 during a frenzied speculation over network potential, are content to maintain an Internet presence without exerting any effort on updating, simply to keep their options open should a change in circumstances justify increased investment.

Because the number of Internet users remains relatively small, the authorities in Lebanon have not yet found it necessary to set up a separate administrative and legal framework specifically for those new fields of information and communication. Out of roughly 200 on-line information sites operating from Lebanon, fewer than half have addresses that end with Lebanon's characteristic "lb." One reason might be that it is much cheaper and easier for a Lebanese webmaster to get a foreign URL address—often from the USA rather than from Lebanon (Tabbarah 2000). There are positive benefits to this governmental neglect, such as the absence of censorship,[8] but in the eyes of some there is also the negative consequence of a lack of any form of effective local regulation.

Any account of information-producing web sites must take into consideration the transnational nature of Internet activities, which makes it difficult to determine the identity of even the most important sites. For example, the daily *al-Hayat* has two addresses, one of which hosts two other publications of the same publishing group. Historically it has been Lebanese, including its editorial staff, but it has been subject to English law since it opened offices in London. Owned by Saudis, the newspaper has done well in the past few years since its return to Beirut, but its Internet site is still managed in London. Adding further to this "global" touch, the web site's technical base is the program Sakhr Press Solution, developed by a firm based in Cairo's duty-free zone operated by a Kuwaiti businessman. In contrast, *al-watan al-'arabi,* a weekly political magazine based in Paris since 1977 in order to escape political pressure, chose (perhaps because of costs) to repatriate only its Internet site to Beirut, while maintaining its offices abroad. In addition, www.naharnet.com, one of the most important web portals in the region, is registered in Cyprus.

In general, the Lebanese case, characterized by a strong émigré influence, confirms that the new media technologies transcend and in some cases efface state boundaries. Thus, many emigrants contribute to the creation of a new professional space in which American corporations such as the *Beirut Times,* printed in California, or an "ethnic portal" such as <www.lebanon.com>, created in 1995, can become players in the information market of their country of origin because of the lack of firm national boundaries on the Internet.

Of course, the idea of what is "information" on the Internet has been totally overtaken by the rapid technical, legal, and economic changes introduced by the use of new media. To assess the current situation, one must look beyond the conventional print media and focus instead on the new information forms made possible by the technologies. Some of these are readily identifiable—like web portals and on-line newsletters—because they share many points of resemblance with the earlier conventions of information professionals, especially of journalists. Other features are more difficult to discern because the new forms of publishing and disseminating digital data involve a change not only in the hardware associated with producing information, but in the idea of information itself. To sense this change, one need only visit the web site of a public figure such as Shaykh Husayn Fadlallah, the religious authority of Hizbullah, whose sermons and *fatwa*s are available on the Internet (www.bayynet.org.lb). One can also visit the web site of a local militant based in south Lebanon (www.geocities.com/ sajedz), who reports on Shi'i resistance activities. Either web site can be legitimately considered—as do certain search engines such as <www.thedaleel. com>—as information/media sites; all the more so as they sometimes reach a large public.

Besides these examples, where ideology is the sole motive, many web sites have an economic dimension in one form or another. One advantage of the Internet, particularly in societies where information is limited by political control or merely through a lack of a structured marketplace, is the possibility for communicating with a wide public at a cost considerably lower than that of other media, including recent ones such as fax. The spread of new media technologies in Lebanon has contributed to changing radically the economic value placed on obtaining certain types of information. For example, Lebanese authorities have placed some administrative information on-line. The result has been to break up the networks of petty corruption because certain essential administrative forms that some officials previously made available only at a high price are now available at the government web site. The same logic prevails among a larger number of actors who utilize the seemingly inexhaustible Web-based information resources, including political, economic, and technical bulletins, as well as chat rooms, practical advice sites, and even want ads. Observing the Internet scene in Lebanon demonstrates that the majority of these numerous initiatives flounder quickly. The few that survive today, and those that are bound to follow when conditions are better, lead not only to an increase in the supply of information, but also to a radical transformation in the idea of information.

THE IMPACT OF THE ONLINE LEBANESE PRESS

Is it possible to conclude that the first years of Lebanese sites on the Internet have begun to have specific consequences on the supply of information in Lebanon? It is difficult even to provide an exact number of sites. Some information providers share the same Internet address; others have multiple web-site addresses, and their visibility, according to the number of links that lead to them, can vary greatly.[9] On a strictly qualitative basis, of 160 Lebanese sites mentioned on the Web, 100 offer regularly updated information, another 40 appear dormant (without any regularly renewed content), and more than 20 have disappeared (their URL addresses no longer function). On the whole, the number of information web sites does not appear to be a major challenge to the traditional information sector, where there were officially more than 400 periodicals published in 1994 (Kalamipour and Mowlana 1994: 163). Moreover, among the Internet information sites created on the Internet, roughly two out of every three belong to a business already involved with the media. Nevertheless, this figure suggests that the growth of new media technologies has permitted the appearance, in a media form that is still poorly developed, of a significant number of new actors who are entering and modifying the local media landscape.

To elaborate on one such modification, there have been notable changes in language use on these sites. While the "traditional" actors have typically addressed their audience on the Internet in English as well as French and Arabic, the new actors favor English at the expense of the other two languages. The technical constraints, which are now completely identical for all actors, do not explain everything. In fact, a more precise observation of language choice, often linked to graphics, results in two general orientations that correspond to two different communication strategies. On the one hand, today the majority of the "cosmopolitan" sites directly introduce to the local region different models that were developed in other parts of the world that are more advanced in terms of new media technologies. On the other hand, a smaller group of sites where Arabic plays a much greater role (and is often the only language used) shows specific efforts to adapt the Internet to local conditions, especially in terms of graphics.

While the "cosmopolitan" sites remain dominant, it is increasingly clear that the predominantly Arabic sites are attracting an increasing number of users. In fact, large international sites like MSN (since November of 2001) and CNN (since January 2002) now offer their content in Arabic to facilitate reaching the local market.[10] In Lebanon as elsewhere, it is difficult to obtain reliable information about the number and frequency of web-site hits. In an emerging market that is still poorly regulated, one must view available figures with caution because the number of visitors at any given site may have been exaggerated as advertising budgets are determined by the number of people likely to be reached. Nevertheless, when the claims of the public and private Internet actors agree with the information available among specialists or with information suppliers, some general trends can be discerned. The number of advertising banners (which cost up to US$2,000 monthly for the best placements), the frequency of site update, and the status of advertisers (local businesses close to the company that opened the site

Figure 5.1. The multilingual web site of Hizbullah's spiritual guide, Shaykh Fadlallah, has been redesigned more than three times since its opening in 1997. The earlier "oriental" touch has been replaced with this new welcome page, which integrates the graphic conventions of the Web with proper Arabic. <http://www.bayynat.org/www/arabic/>

or prestigious international organizations) are among the best indicators, as Lebanon is particularly active in the advertising industry. The main Arab advertising agencies and the regional representatives for the large international agencies are in Lebanon, which is also where *Arabad*, the main advertising periodical, is published. Seen in this light it is clear that the sites that advertisers prefer are those of the principal local web-site portals, Cyberia, Naharnet, and Yalla! as well as the sites of the major Beirut dailies.

The importance of the local dailies is confirmed by the fact that after several years of activity on the Internet, Beirut's foreign-language press (the *Daily Star* and *L'Orient-Le Jour*) already attract a number of readers equivalent to their hard-copy circulation (8,000 to 10,000 visitors daily for the *Daily Star*, for example, with more than 1,000 people registered to use its on-line forum).[11] Admittedly, these publications are marked by their small

Figure 5.2. Yalla! (Let's go!), a principal Lebanese portal directed especially to youth, illustrates the "cosmopolitan style": Arabic text is only provided through links and some ads, and the global emphasis of the home page is superficially adapted to local users, thanks to an agreement with al-Manar TV, whose importance on the local media scene is thus confirmed.
<http://www.yalla.com.lb/NASApp/portal/YallaHome>

local readership; their profitability is assured because these individuals are of high social standing, and the use of European languages makes them readily accessible to Internet users around the world. For the most part this has not been the case for the Arabic dailies, whose on-line readership increasingly resembles that of their print version. However, if the *al-Nahar* newspaper develops ambitious Internet projects, notably with the launch of its trilingual port, <www.naharnet.com>, it is because its business managers know that the two or three thousand paying subscribers in the late 1990s are currently many thousands more and the number is rapidly increasing (Nagi Tuéni, interview with Gonzalez-Quijano, September 2000).

In the aftermath of important political events such as local elections and bombings, web-site visits peak. In Lebanon, the May 2000 Israeli army withdrawal from south Lebanon created an increase of 60 percent over normal usage in attempts to connect to certain sites, forcing some servers, such as the one used by Hizbullah, to shut down to avoid attacks from hackers).[12] Nevertheless, it is still the case that the number of on-line readers of the Arabic press remains small, especially if one takes into account the world daily information flow on the Internet. Even so, with the public informed by the local media and the small number of Arabic language Internet users, it can be noted that the usage rate of the on-line press, particularly among the elite, has become significant.

A "SMALL" INFORMATION REVOLUTION

Now that the Arab world—or, more specifically, certain Arab states or certain sectors of the Arab population—seems to be entering the Information Age more than before, the case of Lebanon, whose regional importance has already been noted, suggests that the new technologies have accelerated the modernization of the local media that had already been underway for some time. Although the first Arab satellite television dates only from the early 1990s—the Middle East Broadcasting Company (MBC) began in London in September 1991—this development was preceded, as noted earlier, by the use of digital data transmission techniques by the Arabic-language press in the mid-1980s. The local media's current Internet use highlights a certain number of current developments.

The case of Beirut does not significantly differ from what is happening elsewhere in the Arab world. The inevitable shift to new technologies has everywhere accelerated generational change. In every niche of the information industry, but especially in the daily press, the introduction of new technologies has been accompanied by a significant turnover of personnel. Journalists have been the first to be affected because the work styles accompanying the new technologies differ significantly from the earlier locally prevailing mode in which editorial commentary overshadowed new reporting. The current style increasingly approximates international standards for the on-line press, in which news content has become more important.

In a milieu in which social and professional mobility is rather limited, the new technologies have significantly accelerated the circulation of elites. The old guard of well-known writers have not adapted well to the specific format of electronic writing. A new generation of "inheritors" has been able to accede more rapidly to important posts on the basis of a technical competence largely acquired from abroad. Considering only the Beirut dailies, names such as Ahmad Salman (*al-Safir*), Nagi and Wadih Tuéni (*al-Nahar*), Saïd Freiha (*al-Anwar*), and Majed Mneimeh (*al-Liwa*) come immediately to mind. They all belong to publishing families who have placed them in charge of projects for digitizing texts.

The winds of change are present in conventional enterprises, but they naturally blow much stronger in companies created thanks to the development of new technologies. These companies are often founded by émigré Lebanese professionals who have frequently trained abroad—like Ahmad Omari, the young founder of Cyberia, an Internet Service Provider that currently dominates the Lebanese market and is also active in the regional market through contracts with Jordan, Saudi Arabia, and projects in North Africa. In their offices, which fully resemble those that can be found in the most modern Western metropolis, teams of young bilingual editors, in addition to technicians, webmasters, and businessmen, share the experience of returning to their country of origin in following the technological flow. Convinced that they are the pioneers of a future Arab Silicon Valley, the names that they have chosen for their sites—Yallah! (Let's go!) or even ThisisCyberia—directly reflect their inspiration.

Under their influence, on-line publication has significantly contributed to spreading a new journalistic style that places more value on the sheer amount of information at the expense of contextualization and analysis. Linked to feedback from the public, which is more apparent thanks to increased interactivity—forums, e-mail, guest books, and surveys—the home pages of sites indicate a new information hierarchy of which one sees categories highly valued earlier for ideological reasons—foreign affairs, for example—lose their prestige in favor of more everyday concerns such as local, practical, or financial information.

The younger actors who are taking charge of publishing enterprises facilitate the implementation of strategies better adapted to the needs of a global digital information market. Throughout the Arab Middle East, the openness to new styles of information management is often associated with the rise in influence on the political scene of a new generation—for example, in Qatar, Bahrain, Jordan, and Morocco, and soon perhaps in Syria and Libya. Following this trend, the Lebanese press thus chose to go on-line in order to strengthen its ties with its foreign-based readership and, thus, at the same time minimize the costs of overseas distribution. This decision also corresponds to their aspiration to play a major role in a new regional and even global space, as well as to become the local relay for the global media giants. As a function of their own market position and their available political and economic resources, the various Lebanese media have opted for a style of modernization that permits them to retain and, if possible, to reinforce their market share at a time when the new media technologies facilitate a means of exchange that is specifically Arab in terms of language and interests. At a time of information globalization, this option remains open for a market that can develop only due to production costs that remain low—in a region whose strategic importance makes it a continuing political hot spot ("al-iʿlam al-ʿarabi" 2002).

The convergence among digital media has opened the way to strategies of syndication already evident in several sites. When *al-Safir* made an agreement in 2001 with the Arabic service of the BBC, *al-Nahar* responded with an agreement with the Arabic service of Radio Monte Carlo, a particularly popular regional service, and by developing a radio version of its print newspaper. Television stations have adopted the same strategy and have begun to use pictures and texts from their broadcasts on the Internet. In terms of the success achieved by the al-Jazeera Satellite Television web site launched in early 2001—unquestionably the first Arabic web site, with around 12 million hits daily, capable of competing with the major international sites[13]—the major private Lebanese broadcasters lag somewhat behind. However, they have a different market strategy and the Arab public values them less for their information than for their entertainment value. The "Arab street" recognizes these essential features through a word play based on the acronym of one of them, the Lebanese Broadcasting Corporation (LBC)—in Arabic, *albisi* ("Get undressed!"), alluding to the dress code of some of the female announcers!

An unexpected rival of al-Jazeera may be another Lebanese station situated in a south Beirut suburb, al-Manar TV, in spite of the fact that it plays on a register diametrically opposed to al-Jazeera—or perhaps because of it. Started in 1991 as an offshoot of a radio station close to the Shiʻi resistance and becoming since then a formally established television station in 1996, al-Manar opened an Internet site in the same year. Having made its local reputation by televising videos taken by Hizbullah combatants fighting the Israeli army in south Lebanon, al-Manar sought to acquire a regional reputation, especially after it received authorization to broadcast via satellite. These transmissions began on May 24, 2000, the day that the Israeli army withdrew completely from south Lebanon. Perhaps to capture market share, the station sometimes sets aside journalistic scruples. In October 2001, for example, it televised video footage that it falsely claimed was taken in Afghanistan (*Libération,* October 13, 2001). These methods notwithstanding, al-Manar appears to have gained an increasingly important audience, especially in the Arab Gulf, where it directly competes with major Arab stations such as Dubai television (for example, al-Sammak 2002). The Shiʻi or, more specifically, Iranian flavor of these programs only partially explains the audience gains that observers attribute to its editorial slant, notably concerning the Palestinian conflict, as well as the quality of its generally open debates involving different opinions in the Arab world, including non-religious ones. The success of its Internet site is evident in the fact that its owners had to add a new web-site address in late 2000 to accommodate the large number of users. However, this site, along with similar ones, frequently finds itself at the front line of an information battle between pro- and anti-Israeli web-site hackers. Al-Manar is also deprived—because of the close ties that it maintains with Hizbullah (as a local ISP called "Destination")—of advertising revenues from American companies such as Microsoft and Amazon ("The Odd Tale" 2001).

In sum, the rise of a media player such as al-Manar TV, which focuses on issues specific to the region, is even more significant than the presence of the Arab media giants so well represented in Lebanon. No doubt these "giants" are aware of the important changes, but they have not significantly altered their relationship with the political authorities. Although modernized and consolidated through regional and international alliances, the local media remain indentured to local financial circles and to technical networks over which the state authorities retain significant control. Even if a broadcaster such as al-Manar TV knows how to take advantage of Lebanon's local political context to develop (like LBCI and Future TV), its placement on the media scene situates it amid new categories of actors who have appeared with the spread of new technologies. Their goal, that of reaching wide audiences and, if possible, to spread their worldview, may no longer be merely a utopian dream.

NEW USES FOR MEDIA

Jon Anderson (1997) stresses not only the technological but also the social stakes of the Arab information revolution. One conclusion to draw from an analysis of new media in Lebanon is the emergence, albeit still modest, of new media uses. Some signs of this are already apparent among the professionals who supply a good part of on-line information, but it is at the other end of the communications spectrum, that of the public, where one must look for more telling examples.

In a country like Lebanon, where political and even moral censorship is lighter than elsewhere—without being totally absent—the Internet contributes significantly to the trend underway since the introduction of new media technologies of diminishing the control that state authorities can exercise over the circulation of information. These openings are realized by various sites such as the Campaign for Good Governance (www.cggl.org) and by El-Sohof (www.elsohof.com), a site maintained by young, local journalists who critically monitor the media. In a less formal manner, they express dissident opinions while creating new forms of political and social mobilization. Even on the web sites of the conventional press, sensitive stories are sometimes available, even if only in the form of links to other web sites. Gradually, under the influence of technical developments that range beyond the transfer to screen of reproductions (usually in PDF format) of print editions, the content of on-line editions is becoming independent. Following the trend of the foreign language press, often more liberal in tone than its Arabic equivalents—the case of the *Al-Ahram Weekly* is a prime example—the on-line press benefits from a greater degree of freedom, largely due to the nature of its readers. They feel freer to express themselves in the on-line forums associated with the majority of sites.

The anonymity offered by the various forms of digital communication is one of its strong attractions. Sheltered from the negative consequences associated with free expression in other contexts, Arab internauts do not shut themselves off in a virtual universe. Instead, they take advantage of the new spaces for exchanging ideas to contribute to public discussion. Polls that directly tackle taboo subjects, chat rooms focusing on political and religious issues as well as relations between women and men, and e-mail messaging services offered by different sites,[14] suggest the need felt for more open discussion on many issues. Because these web sites offer the opportunity to compare different sources of information, intensify the (virtual) coming and going between different local and international places, and transcend physical and intellectual barriers between political worlds previously sealed from one another—for example, exchanges, including hostile ones, between Arab and Israeli Internet users—the new techniques have been taken up by sectors of the population, such as women, who were earlier barred from public expression.

In grafting a horizontal communication network onto the traditionally vertical one of the traditional media, the Internet no doubt contributes to bypassing the older elite hierarchies to widen communications with a public that is only beginning to be envisaged. Because of the new media technologies, new understandings of the world are becoming increasingly accessible, including in a material sense. Digitalization expands, with the addition of sound and images, the limits of textual readings which gaps in the educational system make difficult for many people. In contrast to the *nahda* ("renaissance") and the earlier print revolution in the Arab world during the second half of the nineteenth century, partially held in check because of difficulties in integrating the Muslim cultural and religious heritage (Graham 1987: 165), the experience of a country such as Lebanon offers hope that the entire region is on the verge of taking part in the new age of communication and information in a positive way.

NOTES

The research for this chapter was conducted during four periods of field study in Beirut between January 2000 and June 2001. The data, brought up to date wherever possible, is presented in more detail in Gonzalez-Quijano (in press).

1. The program developed by the firm Diwan (London) in late 1985 for Apple Macintosh. In its more advanced form, it remains the standard program for Arabic (see <www.diwan.com>). However, this situation may change due to the technical constraints of Internet browsers, mainly Microsoft's Internet Explorer.

2. The site <www.mafhoum.com>, which is not limited to Arabic-language publication sites based in the Arab world, contains more than 600 addresses.

3. "Over 3.5 millions Arabs accessing the Net, according to Ajeeb.com survey," a study published March 25, 2001, on the portal <www.ajeeb.com>. This portal was started at the end of 2000 by the company Sakhr (founded in 1982), a pioneer in Arabizing information technologies (www.sakhr.com).

4. As suggested in work published by the American University in Cairo's *Transnational Broadcasting Studies* (www.tbsjournal.com).

5. LBCI, founded by the Lebanese Forces (a Christian militia) in 1985, is now controlled by politicians known for their good relations with Syria. Future TV, as well as the daily *Al-Mustaqbal* and Radio-Orient (based in Paris but relayed in Lebanon) were created by the Lebanese prime minister, Rafic Hariri, who remains one of their principal shareholders. Al-Manar TV, founded in 1991 during Lebanon's war against the Israeli occupation in south Lebanon, was legalized under the pressure of the Hizbullah Party.

6. At one point in 2001, monthly rates were down to US$10 due to a price war between providers, but prices later increased. However, in the absence of strict regulation, there are many local arrangements, especially the use of illegal but tolerated cable links (see "Kayfa nasilu" 2002).

7. For example, see <www.snobmagazine.com>.

8. The only recent example of censorship occurred in April 2000, with the trial of Kamal El Batal, the head of a human rights organization, and Muhamad Mugraby, the owner of the ISP "Destination" (which has Hizbullah among its clients). The proceedings, formally undertaken for reasons of public morals (the offense was that "Destination" intended to host the site <www.gaylebanon.com>), ended with a lenient judgment. Nevertheless, the political interference with the press was clearly evident. See "Documents" on the web site for Campaign for Good Governance in Lebanon (www.cggl.org).

9. *Al-Hayat* can be found at <www.alhayat.com> and <www.daralhayat.com>; *Al-Nahar* can be found at <www.annaharonline.com> and <www.annahar.com.lb>, not to mention the portal opened by the press group <www.naharnet.com>. The web site for the town of Tripoli, in the north of the country, <www.tripoli-city.org/news/index.html>, gives excerpts from three local publications.

10. This decision, taken in the context of the post–September 11 world and the war in Afghanistan, coincides with the launch of American media endeavors designed for the Arab public, such as the youth-oriented FM radio station "Sawa" (Together) on the Arabian Peninsula.

11. Information given by various sources and confirmed by Ali Mneimeh, the webmaster for the *Daily Star* (personal correspondence, June 2000).

12. At the time, the local press (see *al-Safir,* June 6, 2000) believed there had been 500,000 visits to Hizbullah's web site. On information warfare in the region, see "Hasilat 'amm" (2000).

13. Al-Jazeera's webmaster claims 41 million daily hits following September 11, 2001 (al-Makki 2002).

14. The significance of e-mail messaging services was indicated when the web portal <www.maktoob.com> reported in June 2001 that its messaging service had more than a million members, or one-third of all Arabic-language Internet users.

WORKS CITED

"Ajeeb.com's CEO Urges Regional Dot-coms to Rethink Their Business Model." 2001. April 16 (www.ajeeb.com).

Alterman, Jon B. 1998. *New Media, New Politics? From Satellite Television to the Internet in the Arab World.* Washington, D.C.: Washington Institute for Near East Policy.

———. 2001. "Mid-Tech Revolution." *Middle East Insight* 16, no. 3 (June–July) (http://www.mideastinsight.org/5_01/midtech.html). Accessed October 2002.

Anderson, Jon W. 1995. "Cyberites, Knowledge Workers and New Creoles on the Information Superhighway." *Anthropology Today* 11, no. 4: 13–15.

————. 1997. "The Internet and the Middle East: Commerce Brings Region On-Line." *Middle East Executive Reports* 20, no. 12: 8, 11–16 (www.georgetown.edu/research/arabtech/meer97.htm). Accessed October 2002.

Anderson, Jon W., and Dale F. Eickelman. 1999. "Media Convergence and Its Consequences." *Middle East Insight* 14, no. 2: 59–61.

Bunt, Gary. 2000. *Virtually Islamic: Computer-Mediated Communication and Cyber Islamic Environments*. Cardiff: University of Wales Press.

Chartier, Roger. 1987. *Les usages de l'imprimé*. Paris: Fayard.

Dajani, Nabil. 1992. *Disoriented Media in a Fragmented Society*. Beirut: The American University of Beirut.

Gonzalez-Quijano, Yves. 1998. *Les gens du livre: Édition et champ intellectuel dans l'Égypte républicaine*. Paris: CNRS Éditions.

————. 2002. "La révolution de l'information arabe aura-t-elle lieu?" *Politique étrangère* 67, no. 1: 135–48.

————. In press. *Le Liban et les nouveaux médias arabe*. Paris: CNRS Éditions.

Gonzalez-Quijano, Yves, and Mohamad Taha. 2001. "Internet et l'offre d'information au Liban." *Document du Cermoc* (Beirut), no. 11 (www. pisweb.net/mmm). Accessed June 2002.

Graham, William A. 1987. *Beyond the Written Word: Oral Aspects of Scripture in the History of Religion*. Cambridge: Cambridge University Press.

"Hasilat ʿamm 2000: hal shahadat al-ʿamm 2000 awwal harb ʿarabiyya-israʾiliyya raqmiyya?" (The year 2000 in review: Did the year 2000 witness the first Arab-Israeli digital war?). 2000. *al-Hayat*, Dec. 18.

Hobsbawm, Eric. 1983. "Introduction: Inventing Traditions." In *The Invention of Tradition*, ed. Eric Hobsbawm and Terence Ranger, pp. 1–14. Cambridge: Cambridge University Press.

"al-iʿlam al-ʿarabi amama al-tahaddi: al-munafasa wa-l-taknulujiya wa-l-mawduʿiyya" (Arab information confronts a challenge: Competition, technology, and objectivity). 2002. *al-Wasat* (Beirut), April 1.

Kalamipour, Yahya R., and Hamid Mowlana, eds. 1994. *Mass Media in the Middle East: A Comprehensive Handbook*. London: Greenwood Press.

"Kayfa nasilu ila shabakat al-intarnit fi lubnan" (How to connect to the Internet in Lebanon). 2000. *al-Nahar*, January 30.

Lerner, Daniel. 1958. *The Passing of Traditional Society: Modernizing the Middle East*. New York: Free Press.

al-Makki, A. M. 2002. "12 milyun itlala yawmiyan. Al-Jazira nit: nahwa mawqiʿ bi-l-lugha al-inkliziyya yukhatibu al-ʿalam wa-yunafisu al-mawaqiʿ al-duwaliyya" (12 million daily hits: al-Jazeera for an English-language site speaking to the world and competing with the international sites), *al-Hayat*, February 2.

Mokaddem, Misbah. 2001. "Le numérique en ébullition." *Le Commerce du Levant* (February): 78–80.

"The Odd Tale of al-Manar's US Advisers. Warren Singh-Bartlett Finds that American Companies Are Applying Double Standards in Their Definition of Terrorism." *The Daily Star* (Beirut), January 30, 2001 (www.dailystar.com.lb/30_01/art3.htm). Accessed June 2002.

al-Rammal, Ali. 1999–2000. "Tatawwur mulkiyyat wasaʾil al-iʿlam al-marʾi wal-masmuʿ" (Development of the ownership of audio and video media). *Bahithat* (Beirut) 6: 37–63.

al-Sammak, Rida. 2002. "al-jazira wa-l-manar: ma la-huwa wa ma ʿalayhima" (Al-Jazeera and Al-Manar: In and against their favor) (www.elsohof.com).

Tabbarah, Riad. 2000. *Information and Communication in Lebanon*. Beirut: Middle East Research and Studies.

Wolton, Dominique. 2000. *Internet et après? Une théorie critique des nouveaux médias*. Paris: Flammarion.

PRINCIPAL WEB SITES CITED

Web sites were accessed June 2002.

www.ajeeb.com
www.alanwar.com
www.alhayat.com / www.daralhayat.com
www.aljazeera.net
www.alliwaa.com
www.almustaqbal.com
www.alwatanalarabi.com
www.annahar.com.lb
www.arabia.com
www.arabiamsn.com
www.arabic.cnn.com
www.assafir.com
www.bayynat.org.lb
www.beiruttimes.com
www.cggl.org
www.cyberia.net.lb
www.dailystar.com.lb
www.diwan.co
www.elsohof.com
www.geocities.com/sajedz
www.lbci.com.lb
www.lebanon.com
www.lebanon-online.com.lb
www.lissan-ul-hal.com
www.lorient-lejour.com.lb
www.mafhoum.com
www.naharnet.com
www.terranet.net.lb
www.thedaleel.com
www.thisiscyberia.com
www.yalla.com.lb
www.zen-tv.com

6 /

MUSLIM IDENTITIES AND
THE GREAT CHAIN OF BUYING

Gregory Starrett

It is obvious how economic goods satisfy physical needs such as those for food and shelter; less evident, but of overwhelming significance in understanding modern society, is how merchandise can fill needs of the imagination. (Williams 1982: 65)

The protean capacities of new communications technologies are quickly making their way into the popular imagination through political speeches, phone company advertisements, and the anxious experiences of information workers threatened with obsolescence. Among Muslim groups, such technological and market-driven changes in information distribution have very diverse effects. It has been argued (Eickelman 1985, 1992; Roy 1994; Sardar 1993; Starrett 1998) that such obsolescence has to some extent already begun to overtake traditionally trained indigenous religious intellectuals in urban areas of the Middle East as growing literacy rates, publishing, and changing discursive practices bring growing numbers of literate citizens into public debates on religious, social, and political questions. But for African-American Muslims, who have not experienced Islam in the context of comprehensive institutional orthodoxies, issues of counter-hegemony currently so important in the Arab world (Eickelman and Piscatori 1996; see also Dannin 1996), are often less significant than creating a Muslim identity in the first place through forming a community with its own body of knowledge and interpretive traditions.

The process through which new technologies and channels of information distribution come into play is one of creating a space for the production, appropriation, and consumption of intellectual commodities. Since the mode of consumption of such products is not a simple function of their availability, we need to study the way specific communities acquire and use information media and to understand this "consumption . . . [as] a key instrument in . . . the creation of . . . particular social relations and group identity" (Miller 1987: 204). Group identities and the public spheres in which they are negotiated are increasingly mediated by such consumption practices. A suggestive example of the way information and material goods help construct new publics has been provided by historian Colin Jones (1996), who writes of the change over the course of the eighteenth century in French notions of social order, especially the shift from a view of social institutions as hierarchically arranged in a vertical chain whose topmost link was in the hand of the king to a view "horizontally disposed: grounded in human sociability and exchange, . . . posit[ing] an open and relatively egalitarian social organization [which] undergirds a commercial society" (Jones 1996: 14). Imagining these horizontal linkages as a "Great Chain of Buying,"[1] he discusses a new kind of product in the latter half of the eighteenth century: weekly provincial advertising newspapers that addressed different classes, occupations, and localities as one consuming public. The commodification of culture and its circulation through these newspapers established "new links that transcended geographical localism, social particularism . . . and occupational restrictiveness . . . [through] the social and cultural capillarity" of advertisement (Jones 1996: 26). Jones's image also suggests senses in which contemporary Muslim communities are formed through the cultural appropriation and consumption of intellectual goods. Following a brief overview of the nature of these products obtained through the market, this chapter examines an inventory of intellectual goods and how they are coded and used in an African-American Muslim community in the Southeastern United States.

Globally, the sheer scale of information on Muslim topics is enormous, taking advantage—to point in only one direction—of Anglophone publishers and research and educational foundations in Britain, Nigeria, Malaysia, Pakistan, and North America. A broad indicator of the availability of intellectual goods in this marketplace is the most recent catalog of the Iqra᾿ Islamic Foundation in Chicago, which lists 250 titles in English and Arabic. One can also order an entire pre-packaged K-6 curriculum, including books, charts, and curriculum guides for setting up an Islamic school. Islamic Publications International, based in Teaneck, New Jersey, lists nearly 1,500 book titles and offers 250 videotapes, as well as Qur᾿anic CDs, perfumed oils, inspirational plaques and bumper stickers, T-shirts, calligraphic watches, three-dimensional models, posters and jigsaw puzzles depicting the mosques in Mecca and Medina, greeting cards, board games, and computer software, including Qur᾿an and *hadith* databases, and computerized aids to Arabic learning. Other companies, like Chicago's SoundVision (the media arm of the Islamic Circle of North America), produce and distribute specialty videotapes for children, as well as computer software like *SalatBase* (prayer base), and a new serial publication, *Young Muslim*. Arabic-language

Islamic software, including games, databases, and interactive guided tours of the Pilgrimage sites, are available from Egypt through distributors in the Middle East, Malaysia, Indonesia, Britain, and North America.[2]

Given the linguistic, socioeconomic, and cultural diversity of the Muslim world, the flow and spread of these products into different communities is necessarily uneven. Geographical and ethnic origins, wealth, taste, tradition, education, association membership, community structure, and other factors influence the availability and use of Muslim intellectual commodities. For African-American Muslims, links to this market are forged primarily at the household level, as religious media—primarily books and videotapes—are purchased with personal funds and shared with other community members in the mosque, which serves as a public forum where the use and interpretation of these commodities are negotiated. At the same time, the gradual construction of an inventory of communally held intellectual commodities and practices is shaped by multiple links to a wide range of non-Islamic media.

COMMUNITIES OF KNOWLEDGE

In the United States, a number of African-American Muslim movements have developed during the twentieth century (see Haddad 1991; Haddad and Smith 1993, 1994; Waugh et al. 1983), each of which has constructed a unique relationship to the texts and traditions of the wider Muslim world, often in competition with one another. In 1975 Wallace D. Muhammad, the son of the Honorable Elijah Muhammad, succeeded his father as leader of the 44-year-old Nation of Islam (NOI). Diverging sharply from his father's precedent, Wallace Muhammad embarked on an Islamization program that repudiated the racial separatism of the NOI and sought to bring the movement into line with international Islamic practices. In 1976 he renamed the organization the "World Community of al-Islam in the West" (WCI), isolating and demoting some of his father's associates, including Louis Farrakhan, who revived the Nation of Islam in 1977 under his own leadership and promised to remain true to the legacy of Elijah Muhammad. In the ensuing years, Wallace Muhammad's WCI was renamed, first as the "American Muslim Mission" and then as the "Ministry of W. D. Muhammad, Muslim-American Spokesman for Human Salvation." W. D. Muhammad's movement began to benefit from close relationships with international Muslim and ecumenical organizations, the leaders of some of the Gulf states, and even the U.S. government, which had so assiduously spied on and persecuted its predecessor, the NOI, throughout the 1940s, 1950s, and 1960s as a perceived threat to national security. In part because of the movement's historical origin and in part because of ethnic, class, and political differences, many immigrant Muslim groups are suspicious of

W. D. Muhammad's Ministry, stereotyping it as a prison ministry and not to be mistaken for "real" Islam. W. D. Muhammad's followers, on the other hand, consider themselves victims both of Farrakhan's ethnic separatism and of the general misunderstanding and suspicion of Islam in the West.

According to W. D. Muhammad's followers, the extent and development of the NOI has been retarded because little of its theology and practice is shared by the world Muslim community. NOI members, they say, are not taught proper Muslim prayers, fasting during Ramadan, or Arabic. There is a rumor, though, that a cadre of leaders close to Farrakhan has this knowledge but does not share it, either with the mass of the believers or with visitors. One former member recalled that NOI centers ran public religious services in ground-floor meeting halls and afterward held different private services in the basement for members only. Such secrecy confirmed for him that the NOI, unlike the Ministry of W. D. Muhammad, has something to hide from the rest of the world. The right to speak authoritatively about Islam is tied to the issue of free access to knowledge, both on the part of local community members and on the part of the world community.

The Masjid al-Nur of al-Islam is a local affiliate of the Ministry of W. D. Muhammad, occupying a rented clapboard building on a corner of a main thoroughfare through the African-American section of a mid-sized city in the Carolinas. The street has been the site of thefts and narcotics sales, and since only a handful of the 100 or so families who belong to the *masjid* actually live in the surrounding neighborhood, the directors plan a move to a recently acquired three-acre lot in a better location. Members feel that their young community is still growing from the kernel planted in 1975. The head of the Education Committee, Brother Shaheed Bilal, told one of his classes that

> We're still pioneering [here]. We're not established. You're established when everybody knows when the 'Id is, when they put it on the calendar like Christmas is or like Rosh Ha Shana or Hannukah is. They had an 'Id at the White House last year, and you'd think if Bill and Hillary are getting in on the act, someone would be smart enough to put the 'Id on the calendar. But because we're just establishing Islam here, we really ought to give more [in *sadaqa* and *zakat*, to build up the community]. (September 15, 1996)

The *masjid* hosts activities every day. On Tuesdays there are adult Arabic classes, taught until recently by a Mauritanian graduate student from the Sorbonne who had married a local woman. Thursday is for committee meetings, Friday for collective prayer, and Saturday has social activities and seminars, including a Sisters class. On Sunday, there are three levels of regular classes for children and adults. From 10:00 A.M. to noon, a preschool and an elementary Islamic school operate simultaneously in the mosque's main room. The younger children draw, write, and listen to stories read by Sister

Kenyatta, a young graduate of one of the state's historically black land-grant colleges who is taking graduate courses in education at the local urban university to complete her teacher certification. The Islamic Sunday School, for older children, is taught by Brother Bilal, a public middle-school teacher who recently relocated from Georgia. From noon to one o'clock, there is an Orientation to Islam class for new believers (many of them former NOI members, some new Muslims, others curious members of the local black community). Finally, from one o'clock until the mid-day prayer, Brother Ansari holds a *hadith* class where new and more advanced students study the sciences of evaluating and interpreting the traditions of the Prophet, using chapters photocopied at his own expense and books purchased from a home-based book distribution business operated by one of the Sisters.

In contrast to those of the other two Islamic centers in town, the library at the Masjid al-Nur is tiny. It holds a dozen copies of the Saudi reprint of Pakistani A. Yusuf 'Ali's translation and annotation of the Qur'an, a two-volume *hadith* collection, and four or five Arabic reference works on morals and theology. Also on the shelves are a set of Funk and Wagnall's Encyclopedia, an English dictionary, and a student writing manual. The collection in the adjoining Sister Clara Muhammad School office is far more extensive.[3] Aside from a single copy of the Qur'an and a few Arabic workbooks and dictionaries, the collection consists mostly of general-interest books and old college texts from the 1970s. There are do-it-yourself legal manuals, IBM CAD and OS/2 manuals, tax and test preparation guides, several books on basketball and baseball, a dozen or so children's picture and story books, four identical fuel-injection manuals, a text on film criticism, four volumes on "Insect Life" first published in 1890 and harvested recently from a used book store, and a row of thirty trade paperbacks ranging from Nietzsche's *Genealogy of Morals* to *The Book of Lists*. The collection was mostly donated by Brother Bilal.

The bookshelves also hold stacks of twenty different photocopied documents. Two are school planning and fund-raising documents outlining plans for the establishment of a full-time Islamic school; the other eighteen are 11" x 17" copies of material from children's books meant to be folded in half and used as worksheets: Islamic crossword puzzles, charts outlining activities that Islam discourages, color-in Arabic calligraphy and transliterated Islamic phrases, 'Id songs. There were excerpts from more advanced books on the Caliphs 'Umar and 'Uthman, tips for "Raising Your Child with Faith," and a dot-matrix printed sheet of advice on "The Selling of Our Children—Coping with Commercials." These materials were compiled for an intensive two-week Islamic day camp held in mid-summer and are not currently used in Sunday School classes.

On shelves to the right of the book collection are the school's videos. Three two-volume sets of "Religion and Politics in Contemporary Society" show Imam Muhammad's guest lecture at The Citadel earlier this year. A video featuring an African-American woman storyteller stands next to two nature videos, one taped from broadcast and the other the introductory piece to a Time-Life subscription series, two videos about the history of baseball, episodes from the civil rights series *Eyes on the Prize*, a video biography of 1920s dance sensation Josephine Baker, two copies (either taped from broadcast or copied) of "The Book of Signs" about scientific knowledge in the Qur'an, and a copy of "The Furthest Mosque," about the history of Jerusalem and al-Aqsa mosque. There are two purchased Islamic videos: "Salam's Journey," an animated cartoon about the evil king Abraha, who tried to destroy the Ka'ba in the sixth century, and "Fatih," a two-hour animated epic produced in Turkey and dubbed in English, chronicling the collapse of Byzantium at the hands of the rising Ottoman Empire.

More tapes are expected soon. The school has more than one hundred dollars' worth of the *Adam's World* series on order from SoundVision. Bilal was impressed when he saw some of the series on cable television during a visit to Washington. The *AW* series features a bright green, red-headed Muslim muppet and his multi-ethnic friends learning about Islam while traveling about the Muslim world courtesy of Adam's high-tech Trans-Visualizer, all while producing a basement talk show with famous and not-so-famous Muslim guests. Alphabet songs, segments about the wonders of nature, plays illustrating Islamic values like honesty and courage, and Adam's fantasies about what he'll be when he grows up (Adam the Wonder Journalist), alternate with Adam reading Islamic children's stories and folksy songs about prayer and pilgrimage.

Videos, though, are special and infrequently used. In weekly classroom use, the more usual instructional aids are books, which come and go as personal copies in the briefcases of the teachers. The range of texts in use both privately and in class enforces a continual interpretive project in public discussions. Bilal, Ansari, and other visiting teachers bring books from their home collections—from the Anglo-African Islamic Foundation's *Islam for Children*, *Short Suras*, and *The Promise*, to hefty tomes of scholarship for adults—and read excerpts or use them as references for the class. Adult students in the Orientation to Islam class, too, often bring books they have come across in stores or ordered through the mail. Bilal warns them constantly that they have to take secondary works and translations with a grain of salt and that even the best English translations of the Qur'an are flawed. "You've got to learn the Arabic," he tells them, even if only well enough to look up a word here or there in Hans Wehr's *Dictionary of Modern Written Arabic*. One day an adult student was comparing two paperbacks before class, one of which Bilal had recommended some weeks before, the other of which he had brought with him from his former home in Philadelphia. The two books presented such different English texts of the *tashahhud*, the ritual statement of intention to pray, that he brought them first to me and then to Brother Bilal, who initially attributed the difference to translation. But closer inspection revealed that the Arabic texts were not the same either. Checking the publicity statements on the back covers, we discovered that the student's older book was a reprint of a work originally published by the Ahmadiyya, an Indian Muslim movement that had done significant missionary work among African-Americans in the 1920s. Bilal shook his head. "There shouldn't be any sects or schools in Islam. That's why we left the Nation. Sometimes there are just different versions of what you say. Basically, I suppose either one's fine. The important thing is their statement of intention."

Working with texts from multiple sources creates other uncertainties as well. The use of English as a lingua franca of the world Muslim community (see Metcalf 1996) disperses texts far beyond their original target markets, sometimes rendering incomprehensible ideas and ritual requirements that have been translated into local terms. During one discussion of *zakat* during the Orientation class, Brother Bilal produced from his briefcase the paperback *Elementary Teachings of Islam*, an unusual Indian volume written by Maulana Abdul-Aleem Siddiqui in catechistic, question-and-answer format. "Now," he said, "about specific items you have to pay *zakat* on, the book says, 'You should pay on gold in the amount over—' . . . hmm, the note gives the equivalent of 'Pakistani *tola*s,' but I have no idea what a Pakistani *tola* is. This doesn't do *me* any good." He sighed, looking up at the audience.

> You see, that's why we need to have something for *America*. . . . We've got a lot to do, and we've got a road to pave that nobody's ever paved before. In every area there's plenty of work for us to do. When a Muslim intends to do something, he seeks to perfect it, that's what the Prophet said. Do it so nobody could come behind you and do it any better. . . . We need to do one of these *zakat* tables for the United States. Hardly anybody owns goats anymore! We need to put together a *zakat* information package so that when new believers come and convert over from Christianity, they know. Right now they think it's the same; you just give over ten percent of your check.

He called on Brother Karim, an accountant and construction contractor who serves as the mosque's treasurer, to form a committee to put together an easy-to-use *zakat* table and contribution form so that members could understand how their financial obligations to the community are part of their ritual obligations as practicing Muslims.

MEDIATIONS OF KNOWLEDGE

Creating a community of correct practice is one way in which the mosque works to distinguish itself from the Nation of Islam and to integrate itself with the world Muslim community. In support of correct practice, a community of reliable knowledge has to be forged and expanded,[4] and as part of this project, the mosque's educational programs deal both with the specifics of Islamic tradition and with the character of knowledge itself. The Sunday *hadith* class, for example, offers a substantive review of Prophetic traditions and a course in epistemology. For several weeks the teacher, Imam Ansari, distributed photocopies and read to his students from the book *Hadith Methodology and Criticism*, both about the process of *hadith* verification and about the way the Prophet distributed knowledge to the Believers during his lifetime. First, the Prophet did so orally, repeating important parts three times so that his companions might remember. Second, he did so through writing, including letters and treaties dictated to the forty-five scribes who recorded his words. And finally, he did so by means of practical demonstration. "Islam is *easy*," Ansari assured the class,

> because it's natural. It agrees with your nature. The Qur'an is the manual for all human beings. Allah sent the manual, but also sent a demonstrator, Muhammad. He *was* a Qur'an. A living, walking, talking Qur'an. You should emulate the Prophet in your actions, in your speech. You should always carry the Prophet inside of you. We need to have a course on the Companions—and that way we'll learn that we are the Sahaba— we're his companions, in their place, and we have to do what they did. (September 15, 1996)

The Prophet was both an embodiment of Qur'anic knowledge and, through his behavior, a commentary on the Qur'an. In studying this behavior and thus *being* the companions of the Prophet (Metcalf 1993), members of the community are bound in turn to share their knowledge with others, particularly those who are less involved with activities in the *masjid*. "There are a lot of Muslims walking around out there who don't come to these classes," Bilal told the Orientation students, "who don't hear what we're saying, who don't know this. People need to know this stuff, and it's up to you to tell them" (28 September 1996). "Islam is the way to go for human beings," he had said two weeks before. "Allah's trying to show you; he shows you the signs. Some information can renovate your personal life and then the whole community. *Use* the information we give; we'll run off some copies, but don't hog it—spread it around." In the children's Sunday School class, a visiting teacher, Sister Khadija, repeated the theme. "Knowledge increases your faith," she explained.

> "As we walk through our lives, this is what Allah has given us. We have to think about garments not just as shirts and shoes, but as knowledge. Knowledge gives you a protection and a covering. Faith gives us the *shahada*, and prayer, *sawm*, *zakat*, *hajj*. The things Allah gives us should be as close to us as a garment, to protect and cover us. You have to

guard your own soul first, and then you are responsible for guarding the souls of families and others around you. What are you supposed to do with knowledge?"

"Practice it," suggested one student.

"Recite it," offered a second.

"Study it," answered a third.

"And aren't you supposed to teach it, to give it to someone else? That's the worldview. You're not supposed to just keep it, to see how big it makes you, but to share it with others." (October 27, 1996)

In both children's and adults' classes, these oral and personal channels for transmitting knowledge of the sacred tradition are supplemented by, and refer to, media outside the domain of Islamic intellectual production, including general newspapers, movies, television, public school textbooks, mass-market paperbacks, and the signs of nature. Experiences at meetings and conventions, local and national news stories, television series, and films stimulate discussion of the global values shared with other Muslim nations, as well as considerations of the difference between American and foreign Muslim contexts.[5] Both teachers and students use such examples, which rely for their force on the assumption of common knowledge of extra-scriptural media.[6] Illustrating the necessity for self-control during Ramadan, Bilal told adult students that they needed to control their environments so as not to fall into tempting thoughts during the fast. If you fall asleep watching a football game and wake up with the lithe dancing bodies on "Soul Train" staring you in the face, he said, you've got to get up and turn it off. You can't predict when Satan will slip through the cable on the back of your television set, he argued, but you can control whether or not you listen to his whispering. This is a media culture, and the market is evoked as one context of Islamic messages.

Teaching the children about etiquette on another occasion, Bilal told a story from David Carradine's 1970s television show *Kung Fu*. The children knew the series well enough to remind him of the name of the Chinese temple—Shaolin—where the action took place. The week before, a discussion of proper dress had included a *hadith* condemning cross-dressing, which ignited an unprompted and enthusiastic student recital of examples from the media, from basketball star Dennis Rodman to transvestite pop-culture figure RuPaul. As an extreme example of the moral degradation manifest in the practice of men wearing women's covering, one student eagerly recited details from the 1991 Jodie Foster/Anthony Hopkins movie, *Silence of the Lambs*, in which the male villain constructed a body suit from the skin of his female victims.

Even though the mass media and its referents provide useful fodder for religious critique (Moore 1994), the media should also confirm and amplify positive understandings gained through public discussion. When an adult student asked whether there was going to be an advanced class after the Orientation to Islam was completed, Ansari replied, "Listen to the Imam [W. D. Muhammad]. He will take you where you want to go. His teaching is precise, clear, simple. Imam Muhammad *is* an advanced Islamic class: listen to him on the radio on Sunday. Attend his class on WBAV 1600, every week" (September 8, 1996). If Imam Muhammad is a person, a class, and a radio broadcast all at once, this is in part because the lines between the media of knowledge are permeable. They include not only intellectual commodities like books and the technologies of broadcast, but also, according to mosque members, the signs of the human body and the observable structure of God's creation.

LORD OF ALL THE SYSTEMS OF KNOWLEDGE

Media used in the classroom are broadly merged under a common purpose and a conception of their source in God. On a flyer tacked to the bulletin board of the mosque's anteroom, one of the state functionaries of the Ministry's Office of Public Relations makes this point theologically in stressing the importance of the Sister Clara Muhammad School as a basis for community building:

> Prophet Muhammad said it best: "Knowledge is the lost property of the believer." Imam W. D. Muhammad has recently given a new and clearer translation for the Qur'anic verse, *"al-hamdu li-llahi rabb al-'alamin."*[7] Imam Mohammed translates this, "Praise be to Allah, Lord of all the Systems of Knowledge."

This new label for God is starting to circulate beyond the Ministry's flyers and is gaining currency in public discussions. Anything with instructive value is fair game, whether it is specifically "Islamic" or not, and consequently, instructional themes range widely. The Islamic Sunday School begins each week with twenty to forty-five minutes of Arabic, using elementary workbooks for learning the alphabet and vocabulary. It ends with a story read from a Muslim children's story collection or from Aesop's fables, or told by the teacher. These are usually focused on the theme of leadership. Otherwise, science, Islamic history, and etiquette are treated as interchangeable subjects, all unified ultimately through their relationship to God, as the Lord of all the systems of knowledge, and the needs of the community He established.

This theme is also developed by appropriating additional material for the classroom. For the first few weeks of the fall semester, Brother Bilal assigned homework not only from the Arabic workbook but also from the *Jurassic Park Puzzle Book*, a short volume of logic, mathematical, and word puzzles (anagrams, word searches, crosswords) based on the 1993 Steven Spielberg blockbuster movie, which he had purchased in bulk from a local discount store. He discussed scientific method with the students and told them to use their own minds to find out about the world, including topics like the life of the Prophet. "You have to check it for yourself to see if what people tell you is true. Don't just believe me when I tell you something. Think about how you would check on it, verify it, research it" (September 15, 1996). On other days he brought in large-format (18" x 24") photo books he used for his sixth-grade public school class on topics like *The Rain Forest* or *Recycling*. "What's science?" he asked the children. After they mentioned technology and finding out about nature, Bilal confided to them,

> Now, I can't say this in the public school, but I can tell this to you all: science is the study of Allah's creation. *Science is the study of Allah's creation.* Any word you see with an "-ology" at the end is part of science. Like biology, the study of life. Ecology, the study of how living things relate to each other. And that includes people as living things.

He showed them the photo book on recycling, counseling them to get their parents to use the bright plastic recycling bins the city provides for cans, bottles, and paper. "Allah designed the world," he said, "in a way that everything gets recycled back to where it came from. Allah has put a recycling system in nature. A lot of recycling systems. One of them is called the Water Cycle. . . ." "I teach the children about science," he told me later, not only to provide extra attention to children the public schools define as at-risk, but "because I want to show them the unity of creation and how they can understand it. I want to show them that God *is* mathematics."

The unity of God, the unity of creation, and the consequent importance of science and knowledge are themes that consistently run through public discourse at the mosque, drawing on and tying together various media and sources. "We need to have a workshop on diet and nutrition for Muslims," Bilal told the adult students:

> There's a book out called *Medicine of the Prophet*; you should *have* that. Any food mentioned in the Qur'an is good for you. Lentils, cucumber, olive oil. In fact, everything that's in the earth is in your body: gold, silver, phosphorus, magnesium—and you need all of that to be a healthy adult. (September 28, 1996)

He had drawn this latter image from one of his favorite videos, "The Book of Signs," a lavish 1986 production of the Regional Daʿwa Council of Southeast Asia and the Pacific. Narrated by Briton Robert Powell, the video was approved by the Malaysian Prime Minister's Office, a Saudi *daʿwa* council, and al-Azhar University in Egypt. It is based on a book by Frenchman Maurice Bucaille, which details the parallels between the Qur'anic worldview and that of modern science, asserting that the Qur'an anticipates modern knowledge of everything from embryology to meteorology. Islam, one with human nature, reveals its plan through the signs of the observable world. "When Jibril told Muhammad, 'Read!'," Bilal told his adult class,

> He didn't have a book to read, so what did he read? What was the angel telling him to read? Read Allah's creation! Read the sunrise, read the world! Jibril is not talking about a physical book; he's talking about the creation. When we start kids in school, they don't know how to read, so we start them off with picture books. There were slaves that couldn't read, but they could read the north star, to keep the star in front of them as they walked to freedom! (September 28, 1996)

Being encouraged to read the natural world as they might read a book bestows a measure of interpretive authority on each member of the community and not only frees them to deepen their own understanding but makes them responsible to enter into discussion with other community members in the context of the mosque as a public forum. A young substitute *hadith* teacher, weaving together a complex set of images comparing the sun and its planets to the Ka'ba and its pilgrims, explained that "God's creation shows the virtue of taking one's place and allowing others to have their place. You have to know who you are, have your culture and let others have theirs. The sun is symbolic of God's light and also of our work enlightening others through spirituality." And not only the natural world, but the body especially, is a sign of God. When a local Muslim politician substituted in the Orientation class one day, he elaborated on the meaning borne by the body:

> God doesn't pay attention to the intellect, he pays attention to the heart, to the human *sensitivity*. You see, your body is a *sign*. But the *sign* won't be held accountable on the Day of Judgment. The *body* is Muslim; in fact, on the Day of Judgment the *body* will testify against the soul; the *body* is made to *follow* the soul. So when you see, move toward the light. Don't go back! (October 27, 1996)

Being Muslim, the body will follow Islam naturally. The soul, on the other hand, is subject to temptation, to error, to falling away from the truth. "The Qur'an says your body parts will testify against you on the Day of Judgment," the substitute *hadith* teacher agreed. "You need to think about the symbolism here. The hand, for example, is symbolic of your actions; your arm is symbolic of your power. Take the literal meaning, but don't be limited by that literal meaning" (December 8, 1996). Others contrasted this ongoing interpretive project, the continuous intellectual challenge of Islam, to the emotionally expressive tradition of black Christian churches. "Part of the reason I became a Muslim," Bilal told the adult students, "is because it gave me academics, and it gave me knowledge, and it gave me facts. It's not about emotion. Lots of things can make you feel good. If I just wanted to feel good I could go to a nightclub!" (November 7, 1996). Another *hadith* student agreed:

> When Allah says, "submit," you've got to submit *everything*. You have to become a *scientist* when you become a Muslim. You have to have a *whole curriculum*. Give up your Afrocentric way of thinking, give up your whole way of life, and *submit*. Everything is a schoolhouse for Muslims. You have to become a storehouse, submit not only to the rituals, but you have to study, establish a community, be the pioneer, the forerunner, rewrite *everything*. (December 29, 1996)

OFFSHORE INVESTMENTS

Not everything can be easily rewritten by the growing Muslim community. There are communities and cultural networks already in place whose boundaries and intersections—whether local or international, ethnic or confessional—require effort to cross, adjust, exploit, or transcend. One of the links strengthened through participation in a globalized market for Islamic intellectual commodities is an investment of identity in the larger Muslim world. In making this investment, the followers of W. D. Muhammad are forced into a complex series of negotiations with the local African-American community, with the imagined community of Africa, and with the larger Muslim community, both regionally and internationally. "I don't even like to say 'American Muslim,'" Bilal explained to the adult students,

> because I don't like divisiveness. Or "Black Muslim," like the Nation of Islam. One of our brothers went to Pakistan, and while he was there, they were always talking about a Muslim writer named Maududi. It was Maududi this, and Maududi that. Maududi represents a leader for them, like the Grand Mufti of Russia who was here visiting the States a while back. These people represent different communities. Now, I have to accept other ways of doing things, [but] I don't have to be an Arab to be Muslim or eat camel meat to be Muslim. African-Americans have a unique problem. There *is* an Islamic culture. We don't eat pork. But in the plantation culture we were taught to eat everything off the pig—the feet, the intestines; and it's a real adjustment. (December 8, 1996)

National, regional, and local identifiers, whether writers, leaders, clothing, or culinary traditions, set communities apart from each other, despite belief in a transcendent Islamic culture. Different expressive and consumption habits provide students with points of articulation to different communities. The boys come to class in winter coats emblazoned with NFL logos, while Amina, the one girl in the Sunday School, covers her hair with a plain white scarf like one of her Arab sisters might. When a class on appropriate dress turned into a discussion of cultural differences in bodily decoration, some of the boys described the scarification rituals undergone by immigrant acquaintances from Nigeria, and Amina gasped, "I sure am glad I'm not from Africa!" (December 8, 1996). Similar sentiments expressed publicly have recently caused controversy in local African-American communities (Young 1997). But particularly where multiple orders of identity are in play, the sense in which any of them are local or transnational, authentic or authoritative, becomes problematic (Eickelman and Piscatori 1996: 149–55). In a June 7, 1996, sermon in Philadelphia, Imam Muhammad Abdul-Aleem proclaimed,

> My dear Brother and Sister Muslims, let us stop feeling that we have to abandon what is the best of our cultural tradition to be Muslim. When we come to the table, our other brother may bring chicken curried. However, I may like chicken smothered in gravy, like Grandma used to cook. So I am going to bring that to the table. My chicken smothered in gravy has to have the same respect as the brother who brings the chicken with curry. . . . If we come to the table looking identical, then you won't recognize me, because I don't know myself. I must get to know myself and feel comfortable coming to the table as who I am.
>
> We have to stop being carbon copies. . . . Let me just give you one example. . . . You would think that African-Americans would at least look at Africa for Islamic models. Yet too many of us look past Africa, like it has never been Muslim and try to be something from the Middle East. That's not us, Brother and Sister Muslims. Let's be comfortable. Our last contact with Islam was on the African continent. We should reconnect ourselves with that life and stop trying to graft a life that is not for us. The Islam we are used to is colorful and has vibrant life to it, it isn't dark or drab. No, Sister, that isn't you. . . . You are the best educated Muslim women in the world. So use your knowledge. Use your insight. Use your flair for style to create a beautiful Islamic expression that is native to here, and stop trying to import and graft yourself onto a life that isn't you. You won't last. After a while, you will get tired of that same old shabby dress, as Otis Redding once said. You have to come alive. Be more creative in the way you dress, the scarves and everything. Don't just have an old drab look, because you know it won't hold up. (Abdul-Aleem 1996: 12)

The authentic African/American/Islamic modes of expression should be native to "here," the United States, a space defined in part by the shared vocabulary of popular culture. Bilal and others feel that in some ways it's easier for African-Americans to be Muslims in the U.S. because they already have a place in the culture; unlike immigrant Muslims, they already know how to deal with the potentials and problems of living in the majority white Christian culture, with all its temptations and distractions.

These different points of articulation were mediated in one of the two instances I've seen so far of a commercial video being used in class.[8] One cold day in fall Bilal had the older students watch a portion of *Fatih*, the 1995 video about the Ottoman Empire produced in Istanbul and marketed in the United States by SoundVision. Detailing the life and times of Sultan Muhammad II, founder of the Ottoman empire "through his struggles dealing with the plotting and aggression of the Byzantine Emperor Constantine XI, . . . it shows his creative planning for defense against an inevitable clash with the Crusaders" (cover blurb). The protagonist—who looks remarkably like Sean Connery on the video case—is portrayed as a precocious leader who refuses the pomp and luxury accorded to his Byzantine rival. When it comes time to build a strategic fortress, for example, Sultan Muhammad rolls up his sleeves and acts as the construction foreman, to the bemusement of visiting Byzantine messengers.

The four older students were shivering in the cold building and distracted by the noise of the younger children playing nearby. On top of that, they were slightly unsure of the conventions of the Epic Civilizational Clash movie genre (they had no idea, for example, what the video and their teacher meant when they said the Ottomans "laid siege on Constantinople"). After half an hour or so, Bilal stopped the video and began asking questions, always referring to the Ottomans as "we."

> "Who," he asked, "were the Byzantines?" Silence. "The Byzantines," he answered his own question, "were the enemies, in the ancient times, of the Muslims. Who was Constantine?"
>
> "Emperor."
>
> "Emperor of who?" Silence. "I see we're gonna need to watch the whole thing again two or three times." He shifted his line of attack. "Remember when the Byzantine messenger came and knelt down? Why did the Sultan [Muhammad] tell him to get up?"
>
> "You don't worship no one."
>
> Bilal nodded, "You don't bow down to any man. In Islam we don't do that. . . . What else did you notice about the Sultan?"
>
> "The first one or the second one?"
>
> "They were both pretty much the same," Bilal explained. "The second was fulfilling his father's dream, building that fortress." He paused. "If I told you to write an essay contrasting the Sultan with Constantine, what would you say?"
>
> "What's 'contrast'?"
>
> "Show the differences between two things."
>
> "Constantine had servants cleaning his feet and stuff."
>
> The teacher nodded. "What are some other ways the Sultan and Constantine are different?" Long silence. "Have you studied the Ottoman Empire?"
>
> "The what?"
>
> "The Ottoman Empire. I *know* that in your [public school] social studies books, in the world history part, that they say something about

the Ottoman Empire, because when I teach Social Studies [in the public school], I talk about it. You never heard of the Ottoman Empire?" One of the boys shook his head. "All we study," he said, "is about Africa."

The sensitivities of the American majority culture that prompt it to provide limited resources for the creation of a non-Eurocentric identity for young African-Americans are sometimes wide of the mark. The majority culture's limited and homogeneous perception of African-Americans derives from an understanding of origin and identity as constituted by a system of naturally discontinuous spaces rather than by the intersection and convergence of cultural, political, and economic processes (Gupta and Ferguson 1992). The case illustrates, among other things, that the "we" of the African/American/Muslim (or Muslim-American, as in the label W. D. Muhammad has chosen for himself) community is labile and does not necessarily presume or privilege Islamic Africa as an intermediary. For Muslim Americans like the followers of W. D. Muhammad, the investment in broader identities pays a higher dividend, insofar as it can move beyond a specific Africanness and connect with wider global currents (Dannin 1996: 142) and Islamic histories alternative to both America-centered and Afrocentric identities.

At the same time, the linkage with multiple offshore identities coincides with the creation of a comfortable space of consumption and entrepreneurship on a local and national level. While some scholars have pointed to an "anticommercial" bias in the bourgeois black community, which associates commerce with hustling (Austin 1994: 240–41), the Muslim community tends to treat the market with cautious respect, interpreting its potential as enormous and its lapses as the result of moral rather than economic forces. For example, Brother Bilal once quizzed his young students on the life of Muhammad.

> "Now Muhammad was married to Khadija, and he was known as a trustworthy man in his business transactions. People admired him, people respected him. While he was working for Khadija, did he make her a profit?"
>
> The children misunderstood. "Was she a Prophet too?"
>
> Bilal puzzled for a moment, then smiled. "No, no. P-R-O-F-I-T. You're thinking P-R-O-P-H-E-T. He *was* a Prophet, and he *made her* a profit; he made money for her business."

Islamic history provides plentiful support for the dignity of the merchant life, and one of the items advertised on the back page of the *Muslim Journal* is a book by W. D. Muhammad, *Islam's Climate for Business Success*. During the class section on recycling, Bilal had emphasized that the recycling industry not only was morally important but was the site of enormous economic potential and that some of them might one day be in the recycling business. The unspoken implication was that, given God's interest in creating a world where recycling of material is a natural process, the creation of profit from the enterprise not only fulfilled the economic needs of the family and the community but could be interpreted as a pious act in itself.

THE GREAT CHAIN OF BUYING

Given this predominantly positive view of commerce, communities like this, which construct their identities in part through the market, experience the market as liberating, empowering, and creative. Jones (1996) demonstrates that, for France, the provincial advertising newsletters that proliferated in the latter half of the eighteenth century helped shape their readers—from domestic servants and women to artisans, physicians, lawyers, merchants, and the minor nobility—into a consuming public. In this world of the market, wealth and taste rather than the social rank of birth or nobility defined an audience linked together in a "communication and commerce of minds," "'a reciprocal commerce in enlightenment' . . . tied closely with their belief in the enlightening and civilizing powers of trade" (Jones 1996: 24–25). As the century wore on to its revolutionary climax, these newsletters came to carry more and more literary and political material, although they still relied on their subscribers and on each other for most of their copy, providing a mechanism through which "the parish pump spoke to the world, and the world to the parish pump," effectively preparing the ground for a bourgeois public sphere "that transcended geographical localism, social particularism, gender exclusivity, and occupational restrictiveness" (Jones 1996: 26). Likewise this Muslim community is oriented and situated through the commodities linking it with others.

Intellectual commodities play a key role in the contemporary Muslim world, as they did in creating France. But instead of focusing only on the market *for* printed materials like books or periodicals (Anderson 1983), we can look also at the ways that printed materials act as a window *to* a market, the sense in which printed materials like newspapers are self-sustaining links to other products, other services, other communications, and in general are links to the imagined community of world commerce. Large parts of Muslim periodicals, like other periodicals, are given to these sorts of links through advertising.[9] A comparison of three popular journals suggests the extent to which they provide these extra linkages.

The type of advertising in the sample periodicals differs somewhat. While the Nation of Islam and the Ministry of W. D. Muhammad devote most advertising to products, the Islamic Society of North America—largely comprising educated and relatively prosperous immigrant Muslims and WASMs (White Anglo-Saxon Muslim converts)—devotes its largest single block of ads to services, largely financial planning services that proportionally fewer African-American Muslims have the means to benefit from. But these ser-

Figure 6.1.
A Content Comparison of Three American Muslim Periodicals

JOURNAL TITLE

What Is Advertised	Muslim Journal (WDM)		Final Call (NOI)		Islamic Horizons (ISNA)	
	% of Total Space	% of Advert Space	% of Total Space	% of Advert Space	% of Total Space	% of Advert Space
Conventions	17.0	32.0	3.0	10.0	9.0	19.0
Speeches, Broadcasts, Services	0.4	0.8	3.0	7.0	17.0	35.0
Products (Total)	27.0	51.0	22.0	72.0	11.0	23.0
Print	9.0	17.0	5.0	16.0	6.0	12.0
Audio/ Videotapes	3.0	5.0	14.0	46.0	3.0	6.0
Charities	4.0	8.0	1.0	4.0	4.0	8.0
Help Wanted	7.0	15.0	0.0	9.0	7.0	15.0
Total Proportion of Space Devoted to Advertising		52.0		31.0		49.0

vices, international in scope and serving to construct the financial underpinnings of other sets of connections, can diffuse through multiple links (for example, entities like the Iqra' Foundation or the Islamic Circle of North America's SoundVision corporation, which advertise in the *Muslim Journal*),[10] to benefit communities like the Masjid al-Nur, whose new lot was donated by a consortium of thirty or so "Arab Brothers."

Like any periodicals, Muslim tabloids and magazines depend on market linkages to subsidize their cover or subscription price. But it would be a mistake to assume that advertisements are unwelcome distractions breaking up blocks of "real" content. Given the high percentage of space devoted to them (a percentage that is much higher in some other mass periodicals), it is likely that both editors and readers experience advertising as part of the informational content of periodicals (Miller 1987: 171–72). The advertisements, which define and grant access to constellations of goods that demarcate particular communities and lifestyles, are part of the reason magazines and newspapers are purchased.

Habermas (1989: 16) reminds us that the original newspapers were really newsletters distributed by the guild-like organizations of sixteenth-century merchants seeking to construct their own larger-scale imagined community, a point repeated by Anderson (1983: 62) and Jones (1996) with respect to later developments in North America and France. They were engaged in constructing an imagined universalism of distribution and consumption, a universalism of the same type we see being built by the world Muslim community through its entry into intellectual commodity production and distribution on an international scale. As we have seen, the availability of particular products on the market has not led to their universal adoption[11] but to a selective and strategic use of materials to create both a local community and investment in broader identities. These two elements are clearly reciprocal, for it is only by establishing a strong and responsible local Muslim community that individuals can feel a part of the world community of Muslims. Hence the emphasis on knowledge, which is held to be the core of Muslim identity, and the effort to identify, acquire, and consume intellectual commodities from a variety of sources, marking a cosmopolitan participation in a global market of ideas rather than a particularist one consuming mostly proprietary goods, like the Nation of Islam.

CONCLUSIONS

The diversity of sources that shape given interpretive worlds and the diversity of those worlds themselves are facts of the first order. The sense of investing in the historical and geographical community defined by Mecca as the Center-Out-There is shared by the African/American/Muslim as well as by the Islamist radical in Egypt (Goldberg 1991). Both strive to create an encompassing local community in which personal and public virtue can be achieved. For both, the creation of this community is perceived as liberation stemming from a return to the sources. The difference between them lies in the different structures of power and networks of position and identity to which and through which new markets in intellectual sources are responding. Returning to the sources amidst the enervating abundance of Islamic literature in Egypt (Starrett 1998) means locating a culturally specific purity of knowledge and practice that transcends the globally corrupting influences of power, careless imitation, and worldly desire. Activists strive to "make the discursively mediated public sphere govern the public environment influenced by commodification, . . . reimposing a politics of high meaningfulness on what appears to them the exteriority of consumption" (Salvatore 1997: 15–16). The paucity of similar literature in the American context stimulates, conversely, an omnivorous appetite for a corpus of knowledge that transcends cultural specificity, either that of domestic black nationalism or that of Middle Eastern tradition. The local Muslim community looks outward toward the global *umma* as a storehouse of materials for building a sense of identity *in situ*. Returning to the sources means focusing on the universality and naturalness of Muslim identity, those aspects of Islam that are independent of culture and of place.

Only by looking precisely at what are the sources for specific communities can we identify real interpretive worlds, worlds not deducible either from individual media or from the constellations of intellectual commodities assembled in advertisements, bookstore shelves, or market stalls. In the process of returning to the sources, members of the Masjid al-Nur combine two strategies: pooling individually held commodities (books, videos, software) and forging linkages between religiously inflected materials that are consciously sought through the market and those that represent the common knowledge of the community (the unavoidable mass media, the historical experience of African-Americans, the signs of the human body or of the physical world). These strategies underline the sense in which the religious imagination in both its public and its private forms is stimulated and circumscribed by the vehicles at its disposal. The multiple links forged through the market elaborate, unavoidably, multiple communities of Muslim knowledge and practice.

NOTES

The research for this chapter is part of a larger project, "Disks, Games, and Videotape: The Impact of Technological and Market Forces on Islamic Education," conducted with Kathryn Johnson and funded by the University of North Carolina at Charlotte. My thanks go to the panelists, discussants, and audience of the original panel, "Civic Pluralism and Mass Communication: New Media in the Muslim World," for their constructive suggestions. The editors, in particular, have provided vital direction and criticism. The paper has also received many useful comments from Allen Roberts and from members of the Department of Anthropology at the University of Chicago.

1. Jones derived the phrase as a pun on Arthur Lovejoy's classic examination of ancient and medieval understandings of the ascending linkages between living things, *The Great Chain of Being.*

2. Another important set of questions about these developments—unfortunately, far beyond the scope of the present chapter—has to do with the formal transformation of fourteen centuries of textual and embodied knowledge into new representa-

tional conventions, distributed through new mechanisms and intended for new audiences (Eickelman 1985; Messick 1993; Starrett 1996, 1998; Anderson, this volume).

3. Sister Clara Muhammad was the wife of Elijah Muhammad. Her interest in education led to the naming of NOI and WCI schools after her.

4. During a heated discussion of the mosque's financial troubles, several people pointed out that during Friday prayers the parking lot has more than one Mercedes Benz in it but that the wealthier members of the community did not seem to be contributing their share. One of the regular participants in the *hadith* class attributed this to the casual but well-to-do believer's lack of "scientific Islamic information." He insisted, and several others agreed, that the basis of the community is knowledge and education, on which everything else depends.

5. At one point there was a lively discussion of the fact that young Arab and Pakistani children visiting *masjid*s in the U.S. can sometimes recite the whole Qur'an from memory. When it was pointed out by Brother Bilal's wife, Angela, that they didn't understand much of what they were reciting, admiration for the feat of memory turned into disappointment in the flaws of such an approach to schooling.

6. Bowen has noted the same process in Indonesia, where the Gayo "would at times elucidate an Arabic text (or its translation) with a Gayo proverb or compare the power exercised by Moses with that wielded by a local ancestor spirit" (Bowen 1992: 496).

7. This is usually translated "Praise be to God, Lord of the Worlds." The verb *'alam* is derived from a verbal root denoting knowledge; the noun *'alam* means "that which is known."

8. The other case was on a day when Sister Kenyatta didn't make it to school; Bilal hooked up the TV and used the storytelling video and "Salam's Journey" as babysitters for the younger children.

9. The *Muslim Journal* is published weekly by the Ministry of Wallace Muhammad; *The Final Call* is published weekly by the Nation of Islam. *Islamic Horizons* is published bimonthly by the Islamic Society of North America. This is a rapid comparison of single issues of these periodicals and is thus suggestive of questions rather than representative.

10. Each devotes between 43 (MJ) and 83 (FC) percent of its product advertisements to intellectual commodities—books, other periodicals, informational video- and audiotapes. In general, products advertised in *The Final Call* are proprietary—for example, videos of speeches by Minister Farrakhan and other NOI officials.

11. At the Masjid al-Nur, only the Imam, who works full-time as a county prison chaplain, has access to a computerized Islamic database—at work—and the school's one ancient IBM PC currently gathers dust in the office, too slow and small to run Islamic computer games or databases, even if the school could afford them.

WORKS CITED

Abdul-Aleem, Muhammad. 1996. "Freedom of Religion: An Islamic Perspective." *Muslim Journal* 21, no. 46 (August 30), pp. 12, 20.

Anderson, Benedict. 1983. *Imagined Communities: Reflections on the Origin and Spread of Nationalism.* London: Verso.

Austin, Regina. 1994. "'A Nation of Thieves': Consumption, Commerce, and the Black Public Sphere." *Public Culture* 7, no. 1 (Fall): 225–48.

Bowen, John. 1992. "Elaborating Scriptures: Cain and Abel in Gayo Society." *Man* 27, no. 3 (September): 495–516.

Dannin, Robert. 1996. "Island in a Sea of Ignorance: Dimensions of the Prison Mosque." *Making Muslim Space in North America and Europe*, ed. Barbara D. Metcalf, pp. 131–46. Berkeley: University of California Press.

Eickelman, Dale F. 1985. *Knowledge and Power in Morocco*. Princeton: Princeton University Press.

———. 1992. "Mass Higher Education and the Religious Imagination in Contemporary Arab Societies." *American Ethnologist* 19, no. 4 (November): 643–54.

Eickelman, Dale F., and James Piscatori. 1996. *Muslim Politics*. Princeton: Princeton University Press.

Goldberg, Ellis. 1991. "Smashing Idols and the State: The Protestant Ethic and Egyptian Sunni Radicalism." *Comparative Studies in Society and History* 33, no. 1 (January): 3–35.

Gupta, Akhil, and James Ferguson. 1992. "Beyond 'Culture': Space, Identity, and the Politics of Difference." *Cultural Anthropology* 7, no. 1 (February): 6–23.

Habermas, Jürgen. 1989 (1962). *The Structural Transformation of the Public Sphere*, trans. Thomas Burger and Frederick Lawrence. Cambridge: MIT Press.

Haddad, Yvonne, ed. 1991. *The Muslims of America*. New York: Oxford University Press.

Haddad, Yvonne, and Jane I. Smith. 1993. *Mission to America: Five Islamic Sectarian Communities in North America*. Gainesville: University Press of Florida.

Haddad, Yvonne, and Jane I. Smith, eds. 1994. *Muslim Communities in North America*. Albany: State University of New York Press.

Jones, Colin. 1996. "The Great Chain of Buying: Medical Advertisement, the Bourgeois Public Sphere, and the Origins of the French Revolution." *American Historical Review* 101, no. 1 (February): 13–40.

Messick, Brinkley D. 1993. *The Calligraphic State: Textual Domination and History in a Muslim Society*. Berkeley and Los Angeles: University of California Press.

Metcalf, Barbara D. 1993. "Living *Hadith* in the Tablighi Jama'at." *Journal of Asian Studies* 52, no. 3 (August): 584–608.

———. 1996. "Introduction: Sacred Words, Sanctioned Practice, New Communities." In *Making Muslim Space in North America and Europe*, ed. Barbara D. Metcalf, pp. 1–27. Berkeley: University of California Press.

Miller, Daniel. 1987. *Material Culture and Mass Consumption*. Oxford: Basil Blackwell.

Moore, R. Laurence. 1994. *Selling God: American Religion in the Marketplace of Culture*. New York: Oxford University Press.

Roy, Olivier. 1994. *The Failure of Political Islam*. Cambridge: Harvard University Press.

Salvatore, Armando. 1997. *Islam and the Political Discourse of Modernity*. Reading, UK: Ithaca.

Sardar, Ziauddin. 1993. "Paper, Printing, and Compact Disks: The Making and Unmaking of Islamic Culture." *Media Culture and Society* 15, no. 1 (January): 43–60.

Starrett, Gregory. 1996. "The Margins of Print: Children's Religious Literature in Egypt." *Journal of the Royal Anthropological Institute* (N.S.) 2, no. 1 (March): 117–39.

———. 1998. *Putting Islam to Work: Education, Politics, and Religious Transformation in Egypt*. Berkeley: University of California Press.

Waugh, Earle H., Baha Abu-Laban, and Regula B. Qureshi, eds. 1983. *The Muslim Community in North America*. Edmonton: University of Alberta Press.

Williams, Rosalind. 1982. *Dream Worlds: Mass Consumption in Late Nineteenth-Century France*. Berkeley: University of California Press.

Young, Jeri. 1997. "Out of Africa." Review of *Out of America*, by Keith Richburg. *Charlotte Post*, February 13, p. 10A.

7 /

BOURGEOIS LEISURE AND
EGYPTIAN MEDIA FANTASIES

Walter Armbrust

Egypt has rich and diverse mass media that have grown up and expanded with the country's modernization. Modernization, in turn, has been one of the Egyptian media's major topics. In exploring the meaning of modernization, mass media are part of the public space that is explored in them, and they help to define it. They not only describe, they also simulate, in the words of John Hall, the spaces "in which people could try out, at first or second hand, different social roles" in "a lively sphere marked by the spread of new codes of manners" (Hall 1995: 7). Such a "lively sphere" in Egypt has been all but invisible to analyses that focus on associational life and its structures as measures of freedom of expression. But media do more than record or promote. They are especially significant sites of social experimentation because they are at once removed and engaged, observers of the public space that their activities also define.

Tester (1992: 11) has suggested that social experimentation is especially significant for its ability to enable the transcending of social bonds previously thought to be immutable (or as likely, previously not thought about). Leisure is such an experimental site for modernizing societies; in the perspective that goes back to ideas about mass culture and mass media developed by the Frankfurt school sociologists, particularly Adorno and Horkheimer (1944), leisure channels disruptive emotions into a controlled release that is part of modernity (Rojek 1995: 51–52). While reducing mass culture and mass media to a "safety valve," such functional views still allow a place for

disorder, ambiguities, and, most important, the exploration of change. Leisure—particularly as constructed and disseminated in the mass media—consists of ideologically informed texts, but it is also experienced by consumers. It is "mediated," presented as well as represented in the media, in the
company of incentives to consume products and practices associated with
it. But leisure consumption is also inseparable from an imperative to imagine a world in which the givens of the social order no longer remain un-
examined, and so also falls within a sober discourse on civic pluralism and
the shape of public space.

To tease out these connections, I focus here on representations of a
particular instance of leisure and consumption: the practice of going to the
beach, particularly the practice of men and women going to beaches where
mixed bathing occurs. This practice pointedly depicts women in public space.
These are, furthermore, not just representations of women in public space
but, in varying degrees, attempts to sanction behavior that clashes with
traditional social practices relevant to gender roles. They bear a superficial
resemblance to orientalism's use of women to imagine an unbridled space
(Graham-Brown 1988, Alloula 1986) and to the more recent neo-orientalist
strategy of juxtaposing images of "Westernized" Middle Eastern women
with images of tradition to suggest a sense of inevitable modernization
(Graham-Brown 1988: 241). Indigenous representations of women in public space are also modernizing, but in a different way. Here nationalist imagery often dominates (Graham-Brown 1988: 244), including representations of idealized motherhood and iconographies of emancipated social
progress, which, Graham-Brown contends, are not necessarily matched by
substantive changes in the status of women. Graham-Brown also notes that
representations of women have been used in locally produced Middle Eastern media to eroticize Western-style consumption (1988: 247).

Representations of going to the beach similarly contain a great deal of
such visual juxtaposition that has, like beach-going itself, been dismissed as
Western-influenced and passed over as unworthy of further analysis. But
media commentary on the beach, with its controversial mixing of partially
dressed men and women in public, indicates that "the beach" as a destination of leisure and a topic of representation implicates the reality of Western involvement in popularizing this form of leisure. Still, it is not reducible
to Western hegemony. Neither does it represent a purely indigenous, traditional "response." Instead, it presents a zone of danger that media representing it share, symbolized by their treatment of women as the most contentious issue in East/West polemics. Beach representations always pointedly
include women. If they did not, there would be nothing to say or represent,
nothing to register the zone of social experimentation that they mark out
and share.

These representations have been formally continuous over time and
across different media, suggesting that while the issue is not new, it does

find new homes or vehicles of expression. Beach representations, like political cartoons, are topical; they are a fluid representational genre that maintains an internal consistency, while at the same time responding to the political and social contingencies of particular periods. What the different media
used to convey these representations have in common is that they are also
the vehicles of modernity's public spaces and its modes of representing social experimentation. Here, I examine the iconography of such representations at different moments in time and in different media that, having no
prior counterparts, are intrinsically definitive of the new public space they
examine.

Beach representations operate in the space between "the super-literacy
of traditional religious specialists and mass sub-literacy or illiteracy" (Anderson and Eickelman, this volume; Anderson 1995). Such a space can be
thought of as "interstitial," for it does indeed stand between all sorts of
differences conceptualized as tradition and modernity, male and female, elite
and common, or literate and illiterate. However, interstitiality suggests a
misleading image of an emergent bourgeoisie wedged uncomfortably between well-defined hegemonic cultural formations. In fact the imagery described below has been ubiquitous in Cairo for decades, and present to
varying degrees in the rest of Egypt and the Arabic-speaking world. It has
become naturalized; its hybrid character is more apparent from an outside
perspective than from that of someone who grows up with it. New media in
Muslim societies are new to the extent that they are inseparable from the
content they convey. An analysis of the content properly begins with an
understanding of how these media carry forth, and sometimes transform,
processes with established trajectories.

BEACH DISCOURSE: 1992

"Aristocratic Girl for a Pack of Cigarettes" was the title of a
cover story of a 1992 issue of *Ruz al-Yusuf* (no. 3348, August 8), one of
Egypt's largest and oldest mass-circulation weeklies. The picture on the cover
is a lurid drawing of a woman reclining on a beach towel. She has exaggerated bare thighs, big hair, and sunglasses, and she stares boldly at the viewer.
In front of her are a bottle of suntan lotion, a pack of Marlboros, and a
cigarette lighter. The picture is repeated inside the magazine (Fig. 7.1), along
with a text by 'Adil Hamuda, a well-known columnist.

> Eyes born of the temptations of the night. . . . The hunger of the sun for
> the water of the sea. Passion. Caprice. Quenching the thirst. Satisfac-
> tion. Sunset. Pain. Boredom. Departure. Waiting for the winter to wash
> away the sins of summer. This is the story of every summer in al-Agami.
> Firdus: beach of hot bikinis, excessive liberty, the madness of pleasure
> reaching into the brain. This is the private beach, only for the rich.
> (Hamuda 1992: 38)

Figure 7.1. "Aristocratic Girl for a Pack of Cigarettes." *Ruz al-Yusuf* 3348 (August 19, 1992): 38–41.

Hamuda explains that Firdus, this private beach in an area west of Alexandria known as Agami, was, until a short time ago, undeveloped and owned by bedouin. He scathingly characterizes the bedouin as ignorant, boorish overnight millionaires, enriched by easy profits from beachfront development projects. Now rich foreigners in scandalous "French-cut" bikinis expose most of their backsides (but not, he notes sourly, their midriffs) alongside similarly attired corrupt Egyptian elites. An Egyptian woman (Hamuda claims she is a real person but mentions no names) spends her summers on this beach by herself because her parents have divorced and moved to Spain and Australia. With no family to protect her, the woman lives the life of a prostitute, so desperate for sex that she will sell herself for a pack of cigarettes—hence the article's title.

At a glance this article seems to be anti-leisure—to have everything to do with creeping fundamentalism and class resentment and nothing to do with tolerance or Hall's "lively sphere marked off by the spread of the new." The article points to massive social contradictions that could threaten the painful rebirth of civil society that some observers (for example, Ibrahim 1995) see as having come about in the 1980s, after decades of state domination. Indeed, at one point the article strongly implies that "liberty [and] the madness of pleasure reaching into the brain" is a recent corruption of more innocent pleasures experienced by ordinary Egyptians. The decadent Firdus beach, Hamuda tells his readers pointedly, is a *private* beach—a product of the *infitah*, Egypt's post-1973 "open door" economic policy. The *infitah* was an early instance of what is now termed (in Egypt and elsewhere) "structural adjustment" of state-dominated Third World economies: forced capitalism under threat of withdrawal of support from the IMF and World Bank. Beside the decadent *infitahi* beach are more wholesome outlets for the summertime leisure urge.

> There are public beaches on either side. The distance from those beaches to the public beaches takes you from one world to another; from an exciting beach—naked, wealthy—to a modest, crowded beach from which women enter the water wearing *galabiyyas*. The line between the two beaches appears to be imaginary, but it really isn't. It divides between whiskey and *mi'assil* [a honey-steeped tobacco associated with a more modest lifestyle]; between arrogance and humility; between debauchery and sedateness; between the motor boat and the raft. But in the end all of them are swimming in the same sea. (Hamuda 1992: 39)

This image of women entering the water fully dressed has a power to fascinate imagemakers, although the way they employ these presumably contradictory juxtapositions of extreme modesty and extreme bodily exposure varies. Yusuf Shahin's semi-documentary film, *Cairo Enlightened by Its People* (Shahin 1991),[1] used juxtaposition of flesh and modesty to show a city groaning under the weight of its contradictions and ripe for trouble. Unemployment, sexual frustration, dirt, dilapidated public housing projects, seedy foreigners on sex vacations, and the ever-present lurking menace of fundamentalism run together throughout the film. At one point we see people praying in the shadow of a giant movie billboard showing a big-breasted film starlet. The juxtaposition of fundamentalist and sexual imagery, together with the film's relentless pessimism on the likely fate of freedom of expression if the situation is not bettered, suggest a city on the point of explosion. Shahin's film debuted at the Cannes Film Festival just as American and IMF officials were deliberating on whether Egypt would be rewarded by debt relief.

Neither the state nor the public was pleased with *Cairo Enlightened by Its People*. Shahin had not shown the finished version of the film to the censorship authorities before releasing it at Cannes. Journalists attacked him mercilessly, calling him "*khawaga* Yusuf" (more or less, "Gringo Joe"). Although nobody in Cairo had yet seen the film, the general feeling was that it "slandered Egypt's reputation" abroad. The key to this feeling is that it was first shown abroad; nothing in the film was markedly different from the contents of many commercial Egyptian films, which are, however, not shown widely outside the Arabic-speaking world.

Another recent film shown in the West, *Marriage Egyptian Style* (Head 1991), touches on the assumed contradiction between bodily exposure and modesty less explicitly than in *Cairo*, but with a beach scene.[2] *Marriage Egyptian Style* is an ethnographic film that focuses on the life of an old woman who works as a domestic. The film explores the woman's hopes for remarriage (she is divorced) and for her children's marriages. In the course of the film, she, her son, and the family of a prospective bride take a trip to the beach. The purpose of the trip is for the two families to get to know each other better prior to the marriage. On the beach the two families mix freely with other bathers. Some of the women in these scenes wear bathing suits, and some appear in more modest dress. Most of the men wear swimming trunks.

Such trips are in fact common. I have been told that, aside from providing a means for families to get to know one another in a leisurely setting, a groom's family can observe how the prospective bride behaves in a potentially licentious public setting. Given that such beach outings do occur and would strike few Egyptians as controversial when the young couple is accompanied by their families, the reaction of the Egyptian media to *Marriage Egyptian Style* was surprising. The film, it was said, was a complete scandal. In the opinion of Egyptian journalists, this was not how *real* Egyptians lived. Because a foreigner had been involved in making the film and because it was intended for foreign consumption, the film was instantly labeled a national shame. As one writer put it, "An Egyptian researcher helped to produce the film *Marriage Egyptian Style*—the director was a British woman. She chose everything that was wretched, disgusting, and ugly, and photographed it" (al-Gamal 1993: 97). As in the case of *Cairo Enlightened by Its People*, the objection was not to the content of the film, which was commonplace, but to the involvement of foreigners and the fact that foreigners were the intended audience. But even the foreign involvement might have been forgiven if the film had not focused on lower-class subjects. In Egyptian media discourse, leisure is an aspect of a "clean" middle-class lifestyle.

The problem is that what constitutes "middle class" in Egypt is difficult to pin down. It does not correlate with a material standard of living. There are, however, certain attitudes and expectations commonly associated with a middle-class ideal. Egyptians who have at least a high school education, and therefore basic literacy and familiarity with how modern institutions work, generally consider themselves middle class. Egyptians who think of themselves as middle class expect a lifestyle free from manual labor. In the media, the ideal of middle class is often associated with modernity, bureaucracy, and office work, and it is portrayed as having a degree of familiarity with an ideology of national identity that seeks to balance local Egyptian and classical Islamic cultural referents.[3] Certainly middle-class Egyptians, as previously mentioned, consume objects and images that they do not themselves produce "in the first instance" (Miller 1995: 1).

The juxtaposition of flesh and modesty in *Marriage Egyptian Style*, "Aristocratic Girl for a Pack of Cigarettes," and *Cairo Enlightened by Its People* allude to a class dimension in the way leisure is represented. "Aristocratic Girl" and the furor whipped up in the media over *Marriage Egyptian Style* mark the socioeconomic limits of leisure in Egypt. Leisure is not for the poor, and it is not healthy when the extremely wealthy indulge in it. The presumed decadence of both the poor and the rich brackets middle-class identity. The poor are suspect because of their "failure" to adjust their lives to modern institutions, the wealthy for a rootless cosmopolitanism at the opposite end of the socioeconomic spectrum. Thus failure to "get with the program" is marked by presumed backwardness in the case of the poor, and for the rich, by an inauthenticity tainted with foreignness. To be middle class is to refuse both extremes.

Cairo Enlightened by Its People suggests that social conservatism, alongside licentious imagery, presages an imminent explosion. The film depicts such juxtapositions as new, as the harbingers of change. It encourages viewers to assume that the society depicted in the film has been entirely covered and that leisure as represented in the lurid billboard's backdrop to prayers threatens the social equilibrium of traditional society. This implication of novelty marks the film for foreign consumption. The other two instances of covered/uncovered imagery—"Girl for a Pack of Cigarettes" and *Marriage Egyptian Style*—are more closely connected to a local discourse over the meaning of exposure in the pursuit of leisure.[4] It would be misleading to suggest that the local reading of these violent juxtapositions is only a constructed vision of an imposed modernization theory or of nationalism. Although both *Marriage Egyptian Style* and *Cairo Enlightened by Its People* were intended in part for foreign audiences, audiences that read novelty into juxtapositions of exposure and modesty, it is not necessarily the case that the sense of outrage conveyed by "Aristocratic Girl" arises from the same impulse. The article was published in the mass-circulation weekly *Ruz al-Yusuf*, intended primarily for an Egyptian readership. "Aristocratic Girl" was accompanied by a cartoon that emphasizes the starkness of visual juxtaposition by showing a man and a woman walking together on the beach, other bathers in the background. The man is grotesquely fat and hairy; the woman wears a bikini with a *niqab*—a Saudi-style face veil that covers her entire head, leaving only a slit for the eyes (Fig. 7.2). Such dress is considered a statement of radical fundamentalism in the Egyptian media and a sign of backwardness by many Egyptians. Of course it is normally worn with a long shapeless gown and gloves. As the pair walks, the man says to the woman, "Don't look back—there are informers." One might be tempted to interpret the cartoon, along with the article, as an instance of the lurid Western iconography that careens from the harem to the brothel. But in Egypt, these images are part of a long-standing discourse within the Egyptian media; there is in fact nothing new here. *Ruz al-Yusuf*'s "Aristocratic Girl for a Pack of Cigarettes" portrays a thoroughly modern sense of leisure fully entrenched in Egyptian society that has been represented uninterruptedly in Egypt for decades.

Figure 7.2. "Don't look back—there are informers." *Ruz al-Yusuf* 3348 (August 19, 1992): 40.

THE BEACH IN 1969

In 1969 the Egyptian public sector was near the pinnacle of its power and influence. Saad Eddin Ibrahim describes the 1960s, when Gamal Abdel Nasser led a wave of populist postcolonial regimes in nationalizing social institutions that had previously been in private hands, as the low tide of civil society (1995: 36–37). Starting in 1963, the Egyptian cinema was extensively nationalized. The state acquired almost all the means of production, distribution, and exhibition. Many Egyptian intellectuals remember the period as the golden age of Egyptian cinema, when state sponsorship of the industry gave filmmakers a freedom from constraints imposed by the marketplace. However, since 1967, when Egypt was crushed militarily by Israel, the public sector has declined. Public-sector film production was one of the first casualties. By 1971 the cinema had been "reprivatized," to the extent that direct state funding of films was ended, although the state has not yet relinquished control of the decaying studios.

Papa's up a Tree (Kamal 1969b), released in 1969, was one of the first significant films *not* made in the public sector since 1964. Intellectuals feel ambivalent about the film. *Papa's up a Tree*, unlike the expensive prestige projects of the public-sector period, could not be shown in European film festivals; it was geared to a popular Arabic-speaking market. The masses, however, were not ambivalent about the film and allegedly made it the most profitable film in the history of Egyptian cinema up to that time. *Papa's up a Tree* was a musical, starring 'Abd al-Halim Hafiz, the most popular singer of the Nasser period and the singer most closely linked to the fortunes of the state. 'Abd al-Halim was the heir apparent of another giant of Arabic music, Muhammad 'Abd al-Wahhab, and the only active performer who rivaled him in popularity was the female vocalist Umm Kulthum.

The director, Husayn Kamal, trained in France, was artistically ambitious and was given his first chance to direct by the public sector. His first film, *The Impossible* (1965), was a morality play.[5] A man and a woman, both married but not to each other, live lives of quiet desperation until they develop a powerful urge to have a torrid affair. Before the affair can really get off the ground, they decide not to go through with it for the sake of their children. *The Impossible* was not very successful at the box office. Kamal's second and third films, *The Postman* (1968) and *A Bit of Fear* (1969a), were adaptations of literature, and both films had limited appeal. *Papa's up a Tree*, written by novelist Ihsan 'Abd al-Qudus, was Kamal's first private-sector production and his first popular film.[6]

Papa's up a Tree is a beach film, and it gives a much more detailed exhibition of the discourse invoked in 1992 by "Aristocratic Girl." In particular, it elaborates a representation of what happens, in media fantasy, on the "other beaches" located on either side of the decadent locale described in the article. In a nutshell, the film is about the middle class only briefly alluded to in "Aristocratic Girl;"[7] its focus is ultimately a vision of what the beach should be with respect to middle-class ideals. 'Abd al-Halim plays a college student who goes to spend his summer at the beach with friends from school, one of whom is his girlfriend. He craves intimacy with her, but she is shy and insists that they stay safely with the group. He runs off with a prostitute and spends his summer trying to accept the fact that she has other lovers.

In the first fifteen minutes of the film (including a song), the film develops several themes, including (1) generational conflict, (2) romantic love between individuals before marriage, and (3) leisure as an escape from the ordered world of work. It begins with 'Adil (the character played by 'Abd al-Halim) preparing to travel from Cairo to Alexandria for his summer vacation. His teenage sister packs his bags for him. This is quintessentially conservative, as brothers and sisters in many Arab societies are held to have a special bond, a semi-romantic relationship in which a brother and sister's "masculinity and femininity were defined and practiced in a connective relationship that was often sexually charged" (Joseph 1994: 66). There could scarcely be a more efficient way to evoke a patriarchal social structure; the first five minutes of the film further evokes what Gellner (1995: 33) characterized as the "tyranny of cousins"—a more extended version of patriarchy that he argues is anathema to civil society. But mixed in with what are unquestionably tradition-bound family relations are copious references to order and modernity.

As 'Adil's sister packs his suitcase, she discovers that he has already written and addressed his postcards for the summer. He explains this as an attempt to better organize his time—he does not want to waste his summer having to worry about the "work" of corresponding with friends and family back in Cairo. As his sister finishes the packing, she complains that she does not get to go to the beach, even though she too has passed her exam. 'Adil tells her she is too young, and she retorts that girls grow faster than boys; her sixteen years make her the equivalent of twenty-six in relation to him, therefore she is "older" and should be allowed to go. This light-hearted joking in the first scene essentially states the film's theme in miniature: the younger generation yearns to be free of rules imposed by tradition. And of course a temporary relaxation of rules is inherent in leisure generally (Rojek 1995: 80). The rest of the film constantly reiterates a dialectic between order and disorder.

As the sister packs 'Adil's bags, their mother enters the room with a cake "for Khalid." The reason for the gift is that Khalid—'Adil's schoolmate and a native of Alexandria—will watch over him during the summer, just as they watch over Khalid during the school year. Khalid's parents will be there too. The film never explicitly describes Khalid's relationship to 'Adil, but the close connection between the two families suggests that he is kin, perhaps even a cousin. Furthermore, Khalid's sister Amal is 'Adil's girlfriend. Patrilineal parallel cousin marriage (between the children of male siblings) is so prominent in the anthropological literature on the Middle East as to be almost a cliché, and the issue of cousin marriage has, in fact, been present in the Egyptian cinema since its beginnings in the late 1920s. Some films portray cousin marriage as coercive and undesirable, and others as the perfect match. But in all films, the prospect of cousin marriage is an icon of tradition.

Papa's up a Tree, although it leaves ambiguous the issue of whether 'Adil and Amal are biological cousins, portrays their relationship as the traditional ideal, but also as problematic. It is ideal in that the eventual marriage of the two is condoned, or even arranged, by their parents, and problematic in that 'Adil chafes under the dead hand of tradition. He wants more than a conventional marriage to a family his parents know and respect (and may be related to). Not to put too fine a point on it, he wants a romantic relationship with an individual woman, a relationship not constrained by the overbearing presence of a group, whether the group is their friends from school or their parents.

The film's alternation between work, authority, and order on the one hand, and rumblings of rebellion on the other continues when 'Adil and Khalid arrive at an isolated bungalow on the beach. The bungalow is a mess, and 'Adil immediately starts cleaning. Khalid comments that he wishes his colleagues from college could see him so that they know what his real future will be: "engineer and janitor." 'Adil replies that their *shilla* (group of friends from college) has never seen him at the beach in anything but a bathing suit, and in a bathing suit everyone looks the same. One who sweeps the floors looks just like the boss of a company; someone who lives in a hut looks exactly the same as a person who lives in a palace. Khalid then excuses himself, saying he has to join the *shilla* because they are preparing a *mahkama*, a "court." 'Adil has an errand to run before his date in beach "court." The audience sees a dreamy juxtaposition of Amal, a woman who has light auburn tresses flowing in the breeze and wears a form-fitting pink blouse with tight pants, and 'Adil. Both are running, and eventually they meet and embrace. He tries to follow up the embrace with a kiss, but Amal pulls away. "Mother and father say hello. They've missed you too." And she walks away from the frustrated 'Adil.

Next the "court": It begins with young men in bathing suits blowing seashell "trumpets." Swimmers and boaters standing on kayaks come ashore like South Sea islanders. The orchestral music swells. A group of students run out from beneath a row of colorful umbrellas. A ring of them bend toward each other in a close-up shot, hands clasped, and as they rise, the sun blazes out from among them. The singing begins: *Bismi-l-hawa wi-sh-shams wi-l-viligat; bismi-sh-shabab wi-l-hubb wi-l-agazat* (in the name of the air, the sun, and "villages" [of beach bungalows]; in the name of youth, love, and vacations). The dancers form lines of women in tight shirts and pants, alternating with lines of boys in bathing suits. The overall effect up to this point is rather pagan—pointedly so, as their "in the name of . . ." invokes the sun and wind rather than the God of a traditional Islamic benediction. As they sing, they set up a podium, and the "judge" arrives with two officials of the "court." The officials, both men, wear tiny bikini bathing suits; the judge (played by 'Adil's friend, possibly relative, Khalid) wears a brown robe, a turban improvised from a towel, and a beard made of seaweed. The parody here is not of South Sea natives in canoes, but of an Islamic court. The joyful song about love, sun, and carefree vacations is interrupted by one of the judge's cronies yelling *Mahkama!* (Order in the court!).

The judge calls for 'Adil, son of Kamal, "a student on summer vacation." He approaches the podium guarded by soldiers carrying kayak paddles instead of swords. 'Adil sings his case: "Judge of the beach, O judge, I've been absent since last summer, and now I've come back to my dear friends" (he casts a glance at Amal, who stands in the line of students leading to the podium). "I've found my place still open, what are we waiting for, O judge?"

The judge points at him accusingly: "You're asking to spend the summer, boy?"

"I want to have my vacation both summer and winter."

"Raise your hand and take the oath," says the judge. "State your defense."

The music grows more lively, the stiffness of the "court" dissolves momentarily, and 'Adil dances back into the crowd of students, singing, "By God, I've studied all year; it gave me headaches and colds; but I've passed my exams, and that's why I want a vacation—I and my friends and festivity; it's all up to you, O judge, my love to you, O judge."

"*Al-niyaba*" (the prosecution), calls the judge.[8] One of the two men on the podium with the judge sings censoriously, "He's forbidden to spend his summer here: no beach, no love, not even an air-conditioner; and he has to take the first train back to Cairo." The guards hustle 'Adil off to a prison constructed of kayak paddles.

'Adil sings, "What is my crime? What have I done?" A female chorus repeats his plaintive appeal.

The prosecutor responds, "Why have you come here in a bathing suit without permission?" The women all rush to the kayak-paddle prison, exclaiming "*Ya Latif*" (O God—but perhaps also "How nice," a double entendre, as the women are looking over 'Abd al-Halim as they say the line). The prosecutor continues, "And why has he come here without bringing cookies or a cake?" ('Adil's mother had given him one to bring to Alexandria, but he ate it on the train). "*Ya Hafiz*" (O God), sings the female chorus in make-believe shock.

The judge then asks the opinion of his "jury," which consists of the various male "guards" holding kayak paddles. Some say, "Let him stay"; others say no. Finally, 'Adil breaks out of his "jail" and approaches the judge directly: "You mean I've left mother and father, fled from domestic lockup,[9] and now I can't enjoy my vacation? By the Prophet, you students, we're being oppressed!"

Order breaks down once again. The students, 'Adil, and even the judge and the prosecutor begin dancing and singing about the joys of vacation after a hard year's work. Then the court crier once again yells *Mahkama*! bringing the court to order once again. All three—the judge, prosecutor, and crier—sing portentously: "The legal interpretation of the beach court . . . is to give him the title *musayyif daraga 'ula* [summer vacationer first class]." The students erupt in cheers. They gleefully wash 'Adil in sea water and put him in the judge's place, dressing him in the robe, the towel-turban, and the seaweed beard. "Long live the judge," they sing. The scene is ritualistic in a fairly classical sense: the initiate ('Adil) is set apart and put in a liminal state and then reintegrated into society transformed to a new social state.

Now 'Adil gets to judge other students. A pretty young woman approaches the court, singing that she's finished prep school, high school, and most of college. "So how old would you say I am?" she asks.

"How should I know?" replies ʿAdil.

"What kind of judge are you?" she asks indignantly. ʿAdil replies that he knows all about legal interpretation, even statistics and agriculture, but nothing about women. She replies, "What would you say if I told you I'm seven years old?"

"Seven!" he exclaims.

She explains: "Mama and Papa think I'm not more than eight; they treat me like I'm still in kindergarten wearing ribbons in my hair; my whole life is 'Shame,' 'Don't talk back,' 'You can't have that.' When do I get to be myself? I want to live. Mama and Papa have become ancient."

The court descends once again into a chaos of joyous singing and dancing until the crier again yells *Mahkama*!

ʿAdil pronounces: "After legal deliberation of the beach court, family disputes branch, and after reviewing all the documents, we have decided the following: we will change her status, for those responsible for her, from the age of seven to the age of five."

The court tries several more cases, always reiterating the same pattern: order alternating with a sense of disorder that is barely contained. Eventually the lighthearted joking of students in this early beach song gives way to real rebellion, as ʿAdil temporarily abandons his conservative girlfriend and has an extended fling with a prostitute (the film's version of "Aristocratic Girl"). Patriarchal authority tries to intervene when ʿAdil's father comes looking for him, but the father too falls victim to the charms of the prostitutes. Eventually they meet in a seedy bar, both having been shamed by their wallowing in lewdness. They forgive each other; the conservative Amal forgives ʿAdil because she truly loves him; everybody goes back to their ordered lives (except the prostitute, who it seems, truly loved ʿAdil and is heartbroken).

BACK TO THE FUTURE: 1934–1969

Papa's up a Tree suggests that the novelty factor in the material from the 1990s (described above) is purely a function of our own stereotypes. The ability of racy Western style juxtaposed with what we assume to be icons of tradition to induce a sense of shock or urgency—to suggest barely contained social strife as in Yusuf Shahin's *Cairo*—depends in some cases on a certain separation from local traditions of representation. "The beach" is one of these and as a destination for leisure was certainly in full bloom in Egypt by 1969.

One might question whether *Papa's* was a novelty of an earlier time, an artifact of Nasserism—a kind of forced secularization with shallow social roots. The director, Husayn Kamal, was at that time in good graces with the regime, and his first three films were made in the public-sector cinema. Indeed, he was one of the few directors of any distinction to have made his first film while the cinema was nationalized. By the same token, ʿAbd al-Halim Hafiz, the singer who played ʿAdil, is also frequently associated with the Nasser regime. It might, in other words, be possible to look at *Papa's up a Tree* as a cultural artifact from a period in which, as Ibrahim has described it, "an explicit or implicit 'social contract' was forged by which the state was to effect development, ensure social justice, satisfy basic needs of its citizens, consolidate political independence, and achieve other national aspirations" (Ibrahim 1995: 37). The feisty near-nudity (by Egyptian standards) of young people cavorting in the sand could perhaps be seen as attractive window dressing for the film's rather obvious affinity with patriarchal attitudes. Even the carnivalistic beach court might be viewed as an indulgence by a regime determined to deflect attention from the far more serious political repression everybody knew was being carried out in the mid-to-late 1960s, not to mention the catastrophic collapse of the Egyptian army in the war against Israel only two summers earlier.

But to look at the film as only or even primarily an artifact of Nasserism would be overinterpretation, for the image of beach leisure noted in *Papa's up a Tree* was scarcely more original in 1969 than it was in 1992. Beach leisure has been the subject of a consistent discourse going back at least to the 1930s.[10] By the end of World War II, for example, many Egyptians resented the rise of allegedly boorish *nouveaux riches* who had profited from serving the British war effort and from hoarding scarce commodities to sell to their less fortunate neighbors. The campaign against these "war profiteers" (*aghniyaʾ al-harb*) was carried out in a long-running campaign in the magazine *al-Ithnayn*. The new class was mercilessly mocked in cartoons for their presumed ignorance and lack of taste. The cover of *al-Ithnayn*, no. 567 (not pictured), shows the stereotypical war profiteer as a grotesquely overweight man in slightly old-fashioned European clothes—the sort of outfit that might be worn by someone accustomed neither to finery nor to dressing like a European. The bottom of the page says, "In this issue—war profiteer contest." The contest is to invent a caption for the picture. A few issues later the winner was announced: "War profiteer [holding telephone]: I wonder what the number of the black market is?"

In summer issues the beach was a favorite site for these cartoons. Fig. 7.3 shows a pair of "war profiteer" cartoons from 1945. The story on the page matches the cartoon. A war profiteer and his wife plainly don't know what a beach is (Egyptians often use the French word *plage*—*bilaj* in Arabic—meaning, this ignorant, non-French-speaking clod doesn't know what *bilaj* means). They ask a lifeguard, and he tells them they're on it. "But I want to meet him *personally*" says the profiteer, who is accustomed to being able to buy an audience with anyone he pleases. They refuse to take off their clothes because it appears low-class to them. By the end of the story they enter the water fully clothed and are on the point of drowning (lower right-hand corner). These cartoons bear a striking resemblance to the way the *infitahi* class of 1990s Egypt is sometimes depicted (compare Fig. 7.3 with Fig. 7.2). The rhetoric of resentment, in other words, is hardly a new feature of the representational repertory of Egyptian public culture.

In popular imagery, the objectionable nature of war profiteers was often signaled by an obvious lack of taste and refinement, making them out of place on beaches, which were sold to the public as a place for cutting-edge modern habits. This is still true, as the media campaign against *Marriage Egyptian Style*, with its lower-class beach outing, suggests. This does not mean that the tables aren't occasionally turned. Some cartoons made fun of what must have been for many a strange new habit. Figure 7.4 shows a cartoon in which two peasants (by the look of their clothing) go to a beach. In the first frame (top) they see a sign that says "LE 50 reward for saving a person who is drowning." One man says to the other, "I'll throw myself in and you save me." In the second frame the man is in the sea drowning, while his friend, who was supposed to save him, lounges in a chair. In the third frame the nearly drowned man says, "Didn't we agree that you were going to save me?" In the fourth and final frame the lounging man says to his angry companion, "But I hadn't yet seen that other sign." The sign says, "LE 100 reward to anyone who pulls a corpse out of the sea."

Figure 7.3. War profiteers. Top cartoon (man and woman walking with servant carrying umbrella): "What fools. Why would anyone put an umbrella in the ground and sit under it?" Bottom cartoon (man soaking his wrist in a bucket of water). Wife of the war profiteer (in incorrect Arabic, suggesting that she either is a foreigner or has spent so much time abroad she no longer speaks Arabic well): "Look, sister [she is talking to a man], ever since he bought a 'waterproof' watch he hasn't taken his hand out of the water." *Al-Ithnayn* 577 (July 9, 1945): 5.

Figure 7.4. "Is This For Real?" First frame: sign says, "LE 50 reward for saving anyone drowning." One man says to his companion, "I'll throw myself in and you save me." Second frame: "Too bad, someone's drowning. Isn't anyone with him?" Third frame: "Didn't we agree that you'd save me?" Fourth frame: "But I hadn't yet read that sign." The sign says, "LE 100 reward for pulling corpses from the water." *Al-Ithnayn* 577 (July 9, 1945): 15.

In addition to its social commentary, representations of beach leisure have also been part of a broad network of consumerism.[11] Advertisements for leisure products run from the 1930s (and very likely from even earlier) to the present, including advertisements selling accessories for the beach. For example, Fig. 7.5 shows a man and woman with a beach ball in an advertisement for the store of Muhammad Hindi al-Khimi, which sells umbrellas and beach chairs.

Another subgenre of representations of beach leisure is advertisements for train rides to the beach. In one advertisement from *al-Ithnayn* (July 9, 1934, p. 47), the reduced price for tickets is 325 millimes (the ad doesn't give the regular price), which was not necessarily accessible to everyone (the magazine itself cost only 10 millimes), but it does suggest a broadening of interest in this particular kind of leisure. An article and accompanying drawing in another issue of the same magazine (July 2, 1934, pp. 32–33) shows hordes of people descending on the beaches of Alexandria.[12] The title is "Train of the Sea, or Train of the Resurrection" (*qitar al-bahr aw qitar al-hashr*—it rhymes in Arabic).[13] The article describes a man buying a newly discounted summer train ticket to the beach 24 hours in advance and going to the station half an hour early to buy more tickets for friends, only to find the place packed with people. The author finds all the cars full and finally jumps onto the last one in the train, where he finds Muhammad al-Qasabgi, a famous composer, who announces he will make the trip pleasant for everyone by playing his lute. The man leaves al-Qasabgi "drowning in his tunes" and finds himself in a crowd of bureaucrats from various government ministries, with the exception of the Ministry of Religious Endowments. "Are they [the Ministry of Religious Endowments] waiting for yet another reduction in price from the railroad company? Or has the price reduction been hurtful to them, and made them abstain from traveling and participating in this 'democracy'?" Suddenly he's joined by Zaki 'Ukasha (presumably the Minister of Religious Endowments), who tells the author to follow him, and they go to a car where four men give up their seats. The author discovers that his ticket cost 32.5 piasters, but the Minister of Religious Endowments paid 34.5. He wonders why 'Ukasha was charged 2 piasters more—initially he suspects this unworldly man of religion has been taken advantage of—but he learns that the four men who gave up their seats were the minister's employees, whom he'd sent to hold his place. The rugs the minister is carrying are not for prayer, as the author had assumed, but to furnish the villa he's rented at the shore, which is supposed to be finer than those leased by the really big ministers. The Minister of Religious Endowments, it seems, is no pious prude but something of a high roller.

The mocking of religious authority evident in the story is quite common, as is illustrated by a "beach laws" feature (Fig. 7.6) remarkably analogous to the "beach court" song in *Papa's up a Tree*. The accompanying picture includes a "*shaykh*" in robe, turban, beard (Fig. 7.7). There are also

Figure 7.5. Muhammad Hindi al-Khimi's store. "Rare opportunity" to buy umbrellas and beach chairs. *Al-Ithnayn* 577 (July 9, 1945): 30.

strong overtones of generational conflict, as is evident in the text. But this was in 1934, thirty-five years before *Papa's up a Tree*. The drawing of a bearded Azharite *shaykh* in robe and turban, strolling on the beach among reclining beauties conversing with boys in swimming trunks, accompanies the "Bathing Law" (Fig. 7.6). The caption by the *shaykh* says, "What is this 'unveiling' the women want? Isn't it supposed mean that they're taking off their long dresses?!" He says this as if the woman lying on the sand next to him with the shoulder strap on her bathing suit slipping off—an affront to standards of public decency—was somehow overdressed.

CONCLUSION:
CONSUMPTION, MODERNITY, AND MEDIA

Consumption is important in the analysis of media effects, but content also matters. The machinery of new media—and perhaps even of less novel media such as large-scale publishing and television—is controlled by metropolitan producers. Obviously consumption is far less controlled. A

Figure 7.6
Laws for Bathing

Article 1:   –Everyone must obey the law.
Article 2:   –Male and female bathers must be good.
Article 3:   –"Good" means that boys must be handsome and girls pretty.
Article 4:   –Those who are not "good" can swim under the following conditions:
a. they are rich
b. they are cultured
c. they are lighthearted
Article 5:   –Those who do not meet the conditions of article 4 will be expelled from the beach at the first sign of disagreeableness.

Old People (*shuyukh wa-'aga'iz*)

Article 6:   –God created them to cause fear.
Article 7:   –They can come to the beach under the following conditions:
a. they leave their "irritated faces" at home
b. they wear one of the protective masks used in the military club [presumably a fencing mask]
c. they can prove that they were once handsome
Article 8:   –An old woman can come to the beach only on the condition that she drown herself in the water (*tighraq*).
Article 9:   –If she cannot meet the conditions of article 8 she must stand far away so as not to bother the girls and the children.
Article 10:   –We assume no responsibility for lost items such as false teeth, glass eyes, wigs or the lives of any other old women (*al-baqi min 'umraha*).
Article 11:   –Before swimming with wives and children, men must know that morals are old-fashioned.
Article 12:   –Pray for the deceased spirit (*al-fatiha 'ala ruh . . .*) of modesty and jealousy.

This law has been issued for the shore, and is in effect 15 minutes after coming onto the beach.

Signed: Minister of Waves (*wazir al-amwag*);
Sultan of the Jinn (*sultan al-ginn*).
(*al-Ithnayn* 8 [August 6, 1934]: 26)

consumption-oriented research agenda draws us away from concern with the technological and commercial dominance of metropolitan societies, but should not cause us to lose sight of the production of media content.

The content in question here is a discourse about a particular kind of leisure—beach leisure. In Egypt there is a vocabulary for talking about lei-

Figure 7.7. "The Shaykh: What is this 'exposure' that the women want? Isn't 'exposure' taking off long clothes?!" (as if the women all around him aren't already exposed enough). *Al-Ithnayn* 8 (August 6 1934): 26.

sure, and for talking about the beach, and it has developed over a long period. None of the elements utilized in beach discourse of the periods discussed here—1934, 1945, 1969, and 1992—was original. To characterize the consumption patterns evident in "Aristocratic Girl" or *Papa's up a Tree* strictly in terms of such contemporary academic concerns as the expansion of transnational capital and culture or reaction to Islamist politics would be ahistorical. It would similarly be mistaken to think of this kind of consumption as a product of digital-age technology developed substantially over the past two decades, or even technology of the post–World War II era. The fat man walking with the woman in bikini and *niqab* on the "Aristocratic Girl" beach of 1992 is recognizably a variation on the corpulent war profiteer of 1945, and even in 1945 this was no longer a novel image. Simmering resentment of the overprivileged and excessively Westernized in the 1990s bears an eerie resemblance to resentment of the rootless cosmopolitanism of the 1930s and 1940s. Carnivalesque digs at religious and patriarchal authority in *Papa's up a Tree* reiterate the imagery of juxtaposed law and youthful rebellion in the "Bathing Law" of 1934, right down to the ridiculously robed and turbaned *shaykh* striding on the beach amid throngs of teenagers in revealing swimsuits. The recognition of such continuities protects analyses of new media from anachronism.

It is important to acknowledge the continuity and depth of this discourse. There is a tendency in discussions of the Middle East, and increasingly of Egypt in particular, to search for signs of imminent change, to point to social contradictions and say, "It's about to blow—the entire edifice of modern Egypt is about to come tumbling down," or conversely to point to Egypt's increasing integration into world systems and say, "They're over the hump—civil society must be just around the corner." Both the panicky rhetoric of those obsessed with "fundamentalism" and the cheery and self-serving association of globalism with democracy (and the presumption of open markets for metropolitan-based companies) associate new forms of media with sweeping change. And of course many things have changed in Egypt, including certain conventions in popular culture.[14] But there are also elements of popular culture that show strong continuities. And furthermore, some of the changes we associate with new media are arguably extensions of processes initiated through "old media."

Egyptian beach discourse fits readily within current emphases on creolized or hybrid cultural forms. But at what point does the emergence of such discursive practices as hybrid cultural form cease to be its most salient feature? All cultural forms are hybrid at some level, but hybrid for whom? Under what historical circumstances? And for how long is hybridity the most compelling aspect of the phenomenon? The representations described here appeared in media that are no longer strikingly new. Truly mass-circulation weeklies have been produced in Cairo for most of the century if not slightly longer, and films since the 1930s. The machinery of new media produce an appearance of continually shifting boundaries. And yet the machinery itself is locatable. Metropolitan societies produce it, and these same societies control the wealth generated by it, and this tends to force analytical attention up the scale and away from the continuities of popular forms. Reproduced on the English-language-dominated Internet, beach discourse would look as new as Yusuf Shahin's *Cairo Enlightened by Its People*. But in both cases the effect of novelty would be largely a product of our metropolitan location.

Beach leisure, and leisure in general, are not novelties, but they are modern. Change comes about partially through the tensions generated by the rigidity inherent in the more orthodox conception of modernity that rarely reflects the actual experiences of human beings. Conventional notions of modernity have channeled disorder into the field of leisure: leisure was for the betterment of individuals, a healthy release that enables one to function more efficiently in the rational world. Rojek (1995) suggests that confining disorder to the margins of society did not eliminate the unsavory aspects of life as much as it created a liminal zone in which new forms of social experience could take place. The liminal zone constructed in leisure activity is one area in which the social space necessary for the formation of civil society could take place. Rojek claims that this liminal zone could be exploited by leisure producers eager to create new commodities and by individuals whose leisure habits could never be completely controlled, and who might well experience leisure in deviant ways.

Whether beach leisure ultimately buttresses the hegemony of the bourgeoisie or creates a space in which people can experiment with freedom from it is ambiguous. For some, mass-mediated images of rebellion or freedom from the strictures of conventional social order can be nothing more than "insipid, enervated, co-optable forms of carnival" (Stam 1989: 92). Certainly, the portrayal of beach leisure in Egypt has always been tied to the construction of class through a pictorial grammar of consumption, and the excesses of unchecked commodity fetishism can be alarming.[15] But there are good reasons for paying attention to such representations. For one thing, the construction of class, particularly the bourgeoisie, is essential to discussions of civil society and the public space it occupies. Yet analyses of the manifestations of bourgeois culture in the Middle East are conspicuously lacking—as if civil society, artistic culture, or the intellectuals (both Western and Egyptian) who write about them are all ideally free from any taint of it. The promotion of consumption in general, so evident in the material described here, looks like the vanguard of dependent capitalism. Although one might readily concede that all these representations are shot through with Western influence, even Western hegemony, this does not diminish the importance of such material as a forum for a discourse that can only be understood through a historicized understanding of the local culture. Unless we reevaluate the importance of the mass media as a vital creator of modernity, we will restrict ourselves to talking about the failure or success of modernity experienced or not experienced by the Egyptian bourgeoisie without ever delving into how the bourgeoisie was created and how it experiences itself.

The idiom of leisure—in this case the imagery of trips to the beach—is a productive point of entry into this space, but of course by no means the only one. Such material is salient in magazines read by mass audiences, and it is often presented in ways that intersect with wider social concerns. Beach imagery is part of the growth of consumerism in Egypt, as it was in the West; but it is also a blank canvas upon which the concerns of the day could be painted. In Egyptian beach imagery specific issues, such as the economic *infitah*, war profiteering, and the phenomenon of neo-Islamic conservative dress appear beside the advertisements for summer villas, bathing suits, and beach blankets. The beach also comes to its audiences intertwined with more general issues of obvious relevance to discussions of the public spaces like courts, the rule of law, the regulation of commerce, the toleration of new practices, and, perhaps most important, the division of life into realms of ordered work, play, and family life, social obligations and individual fulfillment. Every drawing, photograph, and film discussed here can be dismissed as vulgar, but to do so is to use the word "vulgar" in a thoroughly modern way: as a morally charged aspect of lowbrow/highbrow distinctions used to create canons of taste (see Twitchell 1992). Beach imagery is one of many vocabularies used to construct such canons in ways that are both modern and distinctly Egyptian.

In the end, while the issues in going to the beach (or in imagining that one does so) are not identical to those in forming an opposition party, neither are they entirely separate from conventional politics. Associational life and the habit of leisure are each an aspect of modernity with political ramifications. Both are potentially important aspects of social change, and we should not automatically assume that the social consequences of leisure are always of a lower level of importance than the consequences of explicit politics. Politics may be easier for the state to identify and control. Hardly a day goes by that our own media fail to mention the authoritarian nature of Middle Eastern regimes, and more serious analyses than those typically found in the media must also take this troubling aspect of the region into account. By comparison, leisure, although ambiguous in its effect, is part of this discourse locally. Throughout the entire period, media—one after the other—have constructed beach leisure in persistent terms; habits and expectations were routinized; comparisons to other social institutions were made; and a new concept of work and non-work was instilled. These were not processes that were always imbued with explicit politics, but by facilitating both a sense of order and an expectation of change, they may in fact enable new kinds of politics.

A simple comparison makes the point. Women did not disappear from the public sphere once a majority of them started wearing the *hijab*, even though some of its proponents advocate restricting women to the domestic sphere. As Macleod (1991) notes, the *hijab* is an ambiguous symbol, a form of "accommodating protest," that for some legitimizes non-traditional activities of women even as it signals loyalty to a concept of tradition. And the neo-Islamic *hijab*—ascetic, class leveling, and radically pious in its original conception (el-Guindy 1981)—quickly became enmeshed in elaborate webs of commercialism. Styles proliferate, stores specialize in "modest women's clothing" that in fact is quite varied, advertisements appear in the middle of videotaped films that militant Islamists denounce as sinful. One now often sees the *hijab* worn with bright accessories and blue jeans rather than as the austere shapeless gowns associated with "fundamentalism." In other words, it "migrates" much as beach-leisure imagery moved among media as the local accent of what was "new" shifted. Moreover, it is a fashion statement that occupies the same commercial galaxy as the bathing suit. And like all fashion statements, the *hijab* and the bikini leave open the possibility—indeed, the expectation—that tomorrow's fashion will be different. This, of course, is the message in all modern media, which exemplify this restlessness in the very ways they examine such practices as the making of fashion statements.

NOTES

An earlier version of this chapter was written during the author's fellowship at the Institute for the Transregional Study of the Middle East, North Africa, and Central Asia, Princeton University, 1996–1997, and presented at the annual meeting of the American Anthropological Association, November 21, 1996. I also wish to thank Jon Anderson and Dale F. Eickelman for later comments on the paper.

1. *Cairo Enlightened by Its People* mixed genres indiscriminately. The film depicted numerous street scenes in Cairo but combined the anonymous masses with more intimate situations staged with actors. Which parts of the film were staged and which were not was not always immediately obvious to an audience unfamiliar with commercial Egyptian cinema.

2. Head worked with Egyptian anthropologist Reem Saad, whose role in the film was bitterly criticized in the media (see Saad 1998).

3. Elsewhere (Armbrust 1995, 1996) I have described the way "authenticity," including classicism and "folkloric" imagery, is constructed in the mediated popular culture of various periods. Lockman (1994: 167) describes Egyptian class consciousness in its formative stages (late nineteenth to early twentieth century) as a discursive process in which "the poor" is the most vaguely defined category. The middle class, by contrast, "comprises those who 'work for the benefit of the nation in such occupations as commerce and agriculture and industry,' as well as scholarship, writing, and government service" (Lockman 1994: 164). In contemporary Egypt, "middle-class" occupations such as these are often impoverished, and the social prestige associated with them is, at best, ambiguous.

4. *Marriage Egyptian Style* is the most complex of all these examples. A BBC production, the film was made to be shown in the West, but at the same time it conjures distinctly Egyptian assumptions about national identity. The differences in how the film is viewed in the West and in Egypt attest to the film's ability to speak a double language. To a Western audience, *Marriage* is a colorful glimpse into a social world that most Westerners do not associate with the Middle East—a world of a strong woman unafraid to speak her mind and very much in control of her life. The film will be shown almost entirely in educational settings, where the desired effect is to break up the prevalent image of a monolithic Middle East. To an Egyptian audience, *Marriage* challenges assumptions of class propriety, most generally by giving an unvarnished and unsentimental look at the lives of the poor and through showing lower-class people doing stereotypically middle-class things. But it is also true that the challenge to middle-class propriety comes from showing the film outside Egypt. In terms of domestic audiences, the film has practically no point. Without the crucial element of national identity brought to the film through its foreign audiences, it is little more than a collection of commonplace images and conversations.

5. *The Impossible* was written by Mustafa Mahmud, a medical doctor and former atheist who returned to Islam in the 1960s and began transforming himself into a government-sponsored religious commentator—essentially the government's fundamentalist. He has his own television show called *al-'Ilm wa al-Din* (Science and Religion), dedicated to promoting the idea that there is no inherent contradic-

tion between science and spirituality. He also writes a weekly column in the public-sector paper *al-Ahram*, as well as numerous short stories, novels, and essays.

6. ʿAbd al-Qudus is a novelist with numerous screenplays to his credit. He is also the son of Fatma Yusuf, the founder of *Ruz al-Yusuf*, the weekly that published "Aristocratic Girl."

7. Armbrust (1998) discusses the attitudes of spectators to *Papa's up a Tree*. Many Egyptians joke about the alleged sexiness of the film. It is also a film with a considerable cult following, and many young people today treat it almost as camp.

8. In the Egyptian court system, the *niyaba* has powers of both prosecution and investigation—rather like the chief of police and the district attorney combined.

9. *Harabt min il-bayt abu bawwaba*, "I've fled from the house of locked gates."

10. This is not to say that the depiction of youth culture and leisure were entirely devoid of a period style. *Marriage the Modern Way* (Karim 1967) and other films treat the beach theme; *Midterm Vacation* (Rida 1962) and *Love in Karnak* (Rida 1967) are about leisure. But the concerns of these films were not new in the 1960s. For example, "beach issue" magazine covers have been regular features of mass-circulation magazines since at least the 1930s, if not before (for example, *al-Ithnayn* 851 [October 2, 1950]; 786 [July 4, 1949]; 731 [June 14, 1948]; 572 [May 28, 1945]; 7 [July 30, 1934]). The models on these magazine covers tend to be almost exclusively European-looking. On the whole, the imagery is more *Papa's Up a Tree* than "Aristocratic Girl." But sometimes more resentful, critical, or even playful attitudes were on display inside the magazines.

11. By contrast, the commercialization of leisure in England began as early as 1690 and was well marked by the mid-eighteenth century (Plumb 1973).

12. The phenomenon of special rail transportation to oceanside leisure sites echoes a similar development in mid-to-late Victorian England. Railroads transformed visits to the sea, formerly a variation on "taking the waters" in a health spa, to a mass phenomenon involving, by the 1850s, the transport of hundreds of thousands of lower-to-middle-class visitors (Walvin 1978: 69–82). In England, as in Egypt, the advent of mass leisure caused some anxiety over the mixing of disparate social groups and quickly resulted in the socioeconomic stratification of beach recreation sites (Walvin 1978: 70).

13. "Train of the resurrection" is perhaps a play on *yawm al-hashr*, the "day of congregation" or day of resurrection (of the dead). In other words, the train is so crowded it looks as though it is taking all the desperate souls off to their salvation (or perhaps damnation) on the beach. The drawing gives an impression of complete chaos. *Hashar* means "to stuff," so the title might be a double entendre—the train is obviously stuffed, but the religious sense of *yawm al-hashr* also fits with the theme of the article (one of the passengers mentioned is a *shaykh*).

14. In earlier works (Armbrust 1995, 1996) I have argued that there was a broad sea change in the character of Egyptian popular culture, particularly with regard to the way images of the middle class are constructed. Before the 1970s, the cinema and, to some extent, the other arts were a synthesis of vernacular and classicist elements. After the 1970s, the tendency of popular culture was to refuse any kind of viable social synthesis of cultural elements.

15. For example, Sonallah Ibrahim's latest novel, *Sharaf* (1997), takes commodity fetishism to its extreme. The protagonist spends the novel in prison for a crime he did not commit, but his real prison is the iron grip of his desire for consumer goods. Ibrahim punctuates his prison narrative with commercialist reveries—essentially lists of products and brand names. The protagonist's memory of his outside life gradually fades as his stay in prison lengthens, but the grip of commodity fetishism remains forever fresh and inescapable.

WORKS CITED

Adorno, T. W., and Max Horkheimer. 1944. *Dialectic of Enlightenment*. London: Verso.

Alloula, Malek. 1986. *The Colonial Harem*, trans. Myrna Godzich and Wald Godzich. Minneapolis: University of Minnesota Press.

Anderson, Benedict. 1983. *Imagined Communities: Reflections on the Origin and Spread of Nationalism*. London: Verso.

Anderson, Jon. 1995. "Cybarites, Knowledge Workers and New Creoles on the Information Superhighway." *Anthropology Today* 11, no. 4 (August): 13–15.

Armbrust, Walter. 1995. "New Cinema, Commercial Cinema, and the Modernist Tradition in Egypt." *Alif: Journal of Comparative Poetics* 15: 81–129.

———. 1996. *Mass Culture and Modernism in Egypt*. Cambridge: Cambridge University Press.

———. 1998. "When the Lights Go Down in Cairo: Cinema As Secular Ritual." *Visual Anthropology* 10, nos. 2–4.

al-Gamal, Samir. 1993. *Aflam Mamnu'a wa aflam mashru'a* (Forbidden and Authorized Films). Cairo: al-Dar al-Faniyya.

Gellner, Ernest. 1995. "The Importance of Being Modular." In *Civil Society: Theory, History, Comparison,* ed. John Hall, pp. 32–55. Cambridge, Mass.: Blackwell.

Graham-Brown, Sarah. 1988. *Images of Women: The Portrayal of Women in Photography of the Middle East 1860–1950*. New York: Columbia University Press.

el-Guindy, Fadwa. 1981. "Veiling *Infitah* with Muslim Ethic." *Social Problems* 28, no. 4 (April): 465–83.

Hall, John, ed. 1995. *Civil Society: Theory, History, Comparison*. Cambridge, Mass.: Blackwell.

Hamuda, 'Adil. 1992. "Fataat Aristuqratiyya bi-'Ilbat Saga'ir" (Aristocratic Girls for the Price of a Cigarette). *Ruz al-Yusuf* 3348: 38–41.

Ibrahim, Saad Eddin. 1995. "Civil Society and Prospects for Democratization in the Arab World." In *Civil Society in the Middle East*, ed. Augustus Richard Norton, vol. 1, pp. 27–54. Leiden: E. J. Brill.

Ibrahim, Sonallah. 1997. *Sharaf* (Honor). Cairo: Dar al-Hilal.

Joseph, Suad. 1994. "Brother/Sister Relationships: Connectivity, Love, and Power in the Reproduction of Patriarchy in Lebanon." *American Ethnologist* 21, no. 1 (February): 50–73.

Lockman, Zachary. 1994. "Imagining the Working Class: Culture, Nationalism, and Class Formation in Egypt, 1899–1914." *Poetics Today* 15, no. 2 (Spring): 157–90.

Macleod, Arlene. 1991. *Accommodating Protest: Working Women, the New Veiling, and Change in Cairo*. New York: Columbia University Press.

Miller, Daniel. 1995. "Anthropology, Modernity and Consumption." In *Worlds Apart: Modernity through the Prism of the Local*, ed. Daniel Miller, pp. 1–23. New York: Routledge.

Plumb, J. H. 1973. *The Commercialisation of Leisure in Eighteenth-Century England*. Reading: University of Reading.

Rojek, Chris. 1995. *Decentring Leisure: Rethinking Leisure Theory*. London: Sage Publications.

Saad, Reem. 1998. "Shame, Reputation, and Egypt's Lovers: A Controversy over the Nation's Image." *Visual Anthropology* 10, nos. 2–4.

Stam, Robert. 1989. *Subversive Pleasures: Bakhtin, Cultural Criticism, and Film*. Baltimore: Johns Hopkins University Press.

Tester, Keith. 1992. *Civil Society*. New York: Routledge.
Turner, Bryan. 1994. *Orientalism, Postmodernism, and Globalism*. New York: Routledge.
Twitchell, James. 1992. *Carnival Culture: The Trashing of Taste in America*. New York: Columbia University Press.
Walvin, James. 1978. *Leisure and Society, 1830–1950*. New York: Longman.

FILMOGRAPHY

Head, Joanna, and Reem Saad. 1991. *Marriage Egyptian Style*. United Kingdom: BBC2.
Kamal, Husayn. 1965. *al-Mustahil* (The Impossible). Cairo: al-Sharika al-ʿAmma lil-Intag al-Sinimaʾi al-ʿArabi.
———. 1968. *al-Bustagi* (The Postman). Cairo: Sharikat al-Qahira lil-Intag al-Sinimaʾi.
———. 1969a. *Shayʾ min al-khawf* (A Bit of Fear). Cairo: al-Muʾassasa al-Misriyya al-ʿAmma lil-Sinima.
———. 1969b. *Abi foq al-shagara* (Papa's up a Tree). Cairo: Sawt al-Fann.
Karim, Salah. 1967. *al-Zawaj ʿala al-tariqa al-haditha* (Marriage the Modern Way). Cairo: Shahrazad Film.
Rida, Ali. 1962. *Ajazat nusf al-sana* (Midterm Vacation). Cairo: al-Sinimaʿiyin al-Mutahhidin.
———. 1967. al-*Gharam fi-l-karnak* (Love in Karnak). Cairo: Aflam al-Jazira.
Shahin, Yusuf. 1991. *al-Qahira munawwara bi-ahliha* (Cairo Enlightened by Its People). Cairo: Misr International.

8 /

FROM PIETY TO ROMANCE: ISLAM-ORIENTED TEXTS IN BANGLADESH

Maimuna Huq

Public protests in Bangladesh against the controversial novel *Lajja* (Shame) by the Bangladeshi feminist-secularist writer Tasleema Nasreen seemed to demonstrate the growing strength of Islamic "fundamentalism" in Bangladesh.[1] However, the furor effectively concealed the pluralistic base from which "fundamentalist" opposition to her work arose and concealed the similarities between Nasreen and many of her foes. While many among Nasreen's opponents are products of traditional religious schooling, other "fundamentalists" not only hold secular college and university degrees but are also physicians and writers, as is Nasreen. Some enjoy reading her works. Some "fundamentalists" write novels themselves—romantic ones with hard covers as "secularly" and provocatively illustrated as Nasreen's, a style and language as contemporary as hers, and plots equally laden with the sufferings of women in an unjust society. Paradoxically, the producers and readers of these novels consider them "Islamic" works, so do not deem them objectionable. While the form of these works clearly delineates the influence of new media on Muslim societies, their contents signify a shifting attitude toward Islam, and their producers and consumers constitute part of the new Muslim public sphere, primarily urban, which increasingly challenges the religious authority of traditional experts.

Most scholars of Bangladesh attribute the recent and unexpected growth in Islamic activism to "internal" efforts of the state and "external" efforts of Middle Eastern countries (Khan 1990: 50–62; Kabir 1990: 118–36; Husain

1990: 137–52). I depart from imputing such centrality to the state in explaining Islam-related developments over the last two decades and instead shift the focus from state-sponsored Islam to an Islam emerging "from below," exploring a zone of Islamic literature not dominated by the state, even though the state participates in the production of this literature through sponsorship of institutions such as the Islamic Foundation. I argue that the phenomena related to this literary zone are at least as important, if not more so, to the comprehension of the recent increase in Islamic activities in Bangladesh as the role of the state of Bangladesh or of other Muslim states, such as Saudi Arabia and Iran.

Islamic literature and Islamic activism are symbiotically related. Each field experienced new ripples as people with new qualifications began to contribute to religious discourse in Bangladesh during the late 1970s. Until then, public religious discourse in Bangladesh had been dominated by a narrow base of *madrasa*-trained specialists, a dominance facilitated by the adoption of secularism by the state from 1970 to 1975 and one that continues to be buttressed by state-sustained segregation of "religious" and "modern" education. This privatization of Islam in a society where Islam is an integral part of everyday life sustained the concentration of religious authority in the hands of traditional experts. The deliberate and sometimes scornful distancing of the secular intelligentsia from Islam-centered issues has only enhanced this process. Thus the traditional religious elite has been able to ensure that Muslim personal laws, for example, remain firmly grounded in traditional interpretations of the *shari'a*, despite the efforts of the feminist movement in Bangladesh and despite the abuse of these laws to the detriment of women. Most importantly, these traditional Islamic specialists continue to define what it means to be a "good" Muslim. The authority of these *madrasa*-trained experts has been contested in recent years by the growing number of secularly or modern-educated Islamists, even though the formal ideological core of the Islamists closely resembles the outlook of the former, especially with regard to gender ideology. It is only when the focus is shifted from the ideological terrain to that of daily practices of those "below" or on the margins of political or social authority that important differences in their approaches to Islam can be observed. One area of such practice, the emergent and seemingly apolitical domain of Islamically oriented novels, is my key concern.

Even though the successive regimes of Zia-ur-Rahman and Hussein Muhammad Ershad turned to Islam for a variety of reasons, especially to popularize their ruling bases and to garner financial support from oil-rich Middle Eastern countries, neither regime sought to challenge the entrenched authority of *madrasa*-educated religious specialists. However, the Zia regime's decision to lift the ban that the earlier government of Sheikh Mujibur Rahman had imposed on Islamist or political Islamic groups transformed the relationship between Islam and the public sphere. Along with other Islamist groups, Jamaate Islami re-entered the national stage during the late 1970s. It quickly emerged as the most powerful Islamist group in the country. A unique feature of Jamaat is its domination by those educated at secular, modern, state-run institutions of higher education as well as by those trained first at religious schools and later at secular colleges and universities. These self-styled students of Islam contribute to the fragmentation of religious authority by re-conceptualizing and disseminating discussions of religion using novel approaches evident in the compilation of political biographies, booklets, and romance novels. Indeed the domain of Islam-oriented litera-ture particularly exemplifies the changes and continuities that the public religious imagination has experienced over the last two decades in Bang-ladesh. This experience can be best grasped if considered through the junc-tures of "new media," "new people," and "new thinking" (Eickelman and Anderson, this volume).

The changing features of this literary domain from the early 1970s through the mid-1990s tell us much about how literate Bangladeshi Mus-lims conceptualize and practice Islam, blurring conventional boundaries between the religious and the secular in the cultural imagination. On the one hand, these literate Muslims are educated at largely secular state insti-tutions. On the other, they are exposed to "informal" Islamic knowledge through training in Islamist groups, through Islamist productions in print, and through exposure to audio- and videocassettes, public performances of scriptural commentary (*waaz mahfil*), and television and radio programs. The linkage between the rise of mass higher education, the globalization of media technology, and the emergence of new forms of authority in religious discourse in much of the Muslim Middle East (Eickelman 1992: 643–52) is vital for contextualizing the appearance of new genres of Islam-oriented literature in Bangladesh in recent years, especially didactic booklets and romance novels.

One way of looking at these new literary genres is to view them as profit-making projects for Islamists, who invest the money derived from the sales of romance novels with eye-catching cover illustrations in other more "serious" projects. Many would argue that these texts deceive their readers into thinking them meaningful; others see them as commodified tools of political propaganda and manipulation. However, as various arguments concerning commodification suggest, such an approach is unsatisfactory, for "things" have social lives (Appadurai 1986). I propose that a study of Bangladeshi Islamic texts, centered on the aesthetics and politics of produc-tion, allows us to trace some of the continuities and changes in the engage-ment of literate Bangladeshi Muslims with what it means to be a "true" Muslim, a "good" member of the Bangali ethnic community, and a "loyal" citizen of the Bangladeshi nation-state.

In this essay, I focus on recent transformations in this engagement, as exemplified by didactic booklets and romance novels. Such transformations are also visible in the genres of Qur'anic exegisis and *hadith* literature, the compilations of the sayings and actions of the Prophet Muhammad, although these two genres of literary space remain beyond the scope of this chapter. Here I also treat, but briefly, the continuities in Islam-oriented literature, ranging from the texts that prescribe cures and instruct in religious rituals— *mas'ala* texts—to romantic prose, can be traced back to the vast quantity of *punthi* or *dobhashi* (compositions in Bengali verse or rhymed prose heavily influenced by Arabic and Persian) literature produced by and for semi-literate Bangali Muslims during the nineteenth and early twentieth centuries (Ahmed 1974: 306–69, 1981: xvii–xxvi). Later, however, especially with the rise of Bangali nationalism in post-partition Pakistan, boundaries between the "religious" and the "secular" solidified, so that the domain of romantic love, for example, became a secular prerogative. In fact, the entire arena of creative literature came to be dominated by secular artists, and this has continued into the present decade. Whenever Islam occasionally appears in a secular novel—and this is especially true for the 1950s through the 1980s—it does so "in the form of a hypocrite *mullah* (a rural preacher with little formal Islamic education), profligate *pir* (religious leader), cohort of a reactionary political thug and the like" (Maniruzzaman 1990: 75).

Cultural, political, and material tensions between the Punjabi ruling elite based in West Pakistan (now Pakistan) and the Bangali inhabitants of East Pakistan (now Bangladesh) from the 1940s through the 1960s led to the rise of Bengali nationalism among the political and intellectual elites of East Pakistan. This nationalist spirit privileged a Bangali cultural identity over a Muslim identity and crystallized into state-sponsored secularism during the reign of Sheikh Mujibur Rahman (1971–1975), the first premier of Bangladesh (Murshid 1995: 284–360). Later governments diluted the secularist project for a number of reasons, including the continuing popular appeal of Islam as a cultural tradition. Indeed, this dilution began during the Mujib era itself (Rashiduzzaman 1996: 41–2; Kabir 1990: 46). Despite the gradual inclination of national politics toward "cultural" Islam, secular tendencies have continued to prevail in most elite national arenas, particularly that of creative literature. However, secularist hegemony in the literary arena is being increasingly contested by Islamist "micro-intellectuals," who occupy the interstices between traditionalist religious experts at one end of the intellectual spectrum and secularist intellectuals at the other.

While print culture has been shown to secularize Islamic knowledge in modern Turkey (Yavuz 1995: 2), I demonstrate that print in contemporary Bangladesh is *Islamizing* secular discourse. Islamic texts have conventionally ritualized (*mas'ala* texts) and devotionalized (biographies) religious meaning, but now they have begun to socialize, politicize, and culturalize the religious imagination. In other words, new Islamic texts—namely, polemic booklets and romance novels—attempt to introduce Islamic themes firmly into issues of cultural identity, social problems, and "national" concerns, just as new Turkish "Muslim" writings have been said to do in their setting (Meeker 1991: 203). By clarifying a unified Muslim consciousness compatible with Bangali culture, national history, scientific progress, and global modernity, these texts engender semantic spaces that provide a wide audience with common interpretative frameworks for imagining itself as a cohesive community both internally and in relation to external groups. This new approach to thinking about and presenting Islam also bears implications for older forms of religious affiliation.

Treating the market for Islamic literature as an indexical symbol, I identify it as a site of multiple intersections of the sacred and the mundane that not only "refers back to classical constructs and forward to uses in the present" (Tambiah 1993: 4) but also invents the classical or traditional through a discourse of the mandatory "Islamic state," for example, and classicizes the present by imagining it as *jaheliyat* (the Benjalized Arabic for *jahiliyya*), the pre-Islamic period in Arabia generally understood by Muslims as one of ignorance, paganism, moral depravity, and injustice.

This invention of tradition or "blurring" of temporal, cultural, and conceptual frames, implicit in Tambiah, is explicitly discussed by Eickelman and Piscatori (1996: 22–45) as an integral aspect of current Muslim politics. They criticize modernization theory for its rigid delimitation of tradition from modernity, which oversimplifies the complex interaction of tradition and religion with modern conditions and leads to serious misperceptions of Muslim societies and politics. "Since values take on symbolic form, the parameters of culture appear to remain intact while the renewal and transformation of values are in fact taking place" (Eickelman and Piscatori 1996: 28). A consideration of the interaction between tradition and context is crucial to a grasp of the complex and seemingly inconsistent ways in which Islamic activism manifests itself in Bangladesh. A good example of such heterogenous manifestation is the claim that female Islamists lay to an ideological struggle for the re-establishment of the seventh-century "golden age of Islam," even as some of these women study at unisex universities, work in offices alongside men, stay out late to participate in religious activities in defiance of parental and spousal authority, watch romantic Bangla, Hindi, and English films, and read romantic novels, including those by Western writers. An awareness of the ongoing fusion and diffusion of religion, politics, and socio-economic processes is pivotal to the illumination of the peculiarity embodied in the writing of a love story interspersed with discussions of the Qur'an and *hadith*.

While most books in the market for Islamic literature are generally within the financial reach of the middle class, one can segment this market from a "literary-economic" perspective, for this uncovers the partial link between educational level/type and purchasing power. For example, *mas'ala* texts have persisted in Bangladesh for decades because of a pragmatic and strategic convergence of economic, educational, and stylistic elements. While the

writing style often appeals to only the *madrasa*-educated, the type of knowledge provided—advice on worldly problems—is accessible to both the
madrasa-educated and the secularly educated. Furthermore, the pricing of
mas'ala texts covers a broad range, transcending economic boundaries. Although larger volumes are usually more expensive than smaller ones, they
provide formulas for treating numerous mundane concerns. Members of
the lower middle-class, especially those who have had some *madrasa* education, sometimes purchase these relatively expensive volumes as "investments"
to spare them medical fees and long trips to religious experts or saints. This
"literary-economic" perspective is useful for tracking the emergence of new
literatures and the persistence of older literary forms.

MAS'ALA TEXTS

These texts provide detailed and specific information on how to
benefit from Qur'anic verses in various aspects of life—health, intellectual
ability, socio-economic well-being, family affairs, and the attainment of
greater virtue or *sawab* for success in the Life After Death. They prescribe
religious formulas for curing illnesses, improving performance at work, en-
hancing eyesight, securing jobs, outwitting adversaries, and passing exami-
nations. They also discuss many Islamic principles, performances, and laws.
Most of the Islamic literature produced between 1971 and 1975 focused on *mas'ala*. Such texts made up one of the largest segments of Muslim Bengali literature during the nineteenth and early twentieth centuries
(Ahmed 1974: 324), and it remains one of the largest categories of religious
writings in Bangladesh today. The books enjoy wide popularity, although
both Islamic and secular activists tend to look down on them. *Mas'ala* texts,
Islamists believe, limit Islam to rituals and hinder the growth of a revolutionary or reformist consciousness. To many secularists, they embody backwardness, rusticity, and superstition. *Mas'ala* texts include translated works
of Islamic scholars and are produced in hard-cover editions with flowery
and geometric patterns or mosque domes, minarets, and the Qur'an on the
dust jackets. Since none refer to politics and few to socio-cultural concerns,
they were compatible with the socialist-secularist character of the Mujib
regime, which promoted the idea of Islam as a "religion" limited to one's
personal life. During this period, while other forms of religious literature
and public religious activities waned, publishers such as Ashrafia, Emdadia,
Nomania, Osmania, and Rahmania produced *mas'ala* texts in abundance
(Maniruzzaman 1990: 76).
Demand for this type of text also reflected the profound influence of
those Sufis whose preaching played a central role in the spread of Islam in
Bengal as early as the seventh century (Haq 1975). More importantly, it
reflected the significant difference in cultural imagination between the secularist political elite and the greater public even at a time when the nation

had just emerged from its struggle for independence from the Islamic state of Pakistan. Many Bangladeshis (then East Pakistanis), especially the political elite, felt that the Pakistani state had used Islam to oppress East Pakistanis, to exploit them economically, and to denigrate their culture. After his ascension to power following the independence war, Sheikh Mujib, with his party (Awami League) ideology of Bangali nationalism, appointed a Commission on Education to reform the educational structure on the basis of the four fundamental principles of the constitution—nationalism, democracy, secularism, and socialism (Maniruzzaman 1990: 71).

The commission submitted an interim report in May 1973, which recommended a complete separation of religion and education. Nonetheless, responses to questionnaires circulated by the commission showed that about 71 percent of the respondents, most of whom were secular-educated, advocated modernized religious education (as opposed to the *madrasa* type) as an integral part of general education. This revealed a significant gap between the worldview of the educated Bangladeshi public and that of the dominant political elite, even during the heyday of secularism.

> The Commission could not neglect the decisive opinion of the respondents. While they did not include religious education in the syllabi for classes i to iv, they reluctantly recommended religious instruction as an alternative to ethical studies in classes vi to viii and as an elective subject in classes ix to xi only for those in the humanities. (Maniruzzaman 1990: 73)

Indicative of how deeply rooted Islam is in the popular Bangladeshi imagination as a guide for daily living, *mas'ala* texts are as abundant today as ever. Alongside new *mas'ala* texts are new editions of old and popular ones, such as Shamsul Haq's *Neyamul Qor'an*. It was first published in 1937; the eleventh edition appeared in 1989. A certain Kitabul Molla, whose review was reproduced in the seventh edition (1960), claimed that the primary reason for the popularity of this text was that people benefited directly from the formulas it contained. He suggested that the most important prerequisite was complete faith in the efficacy of the text. And, since *Neyamul Qor'an* explains the "spiritual, philosophical, inherent, and *scientific* principles of the formulas it contains, this feature enhances the reader's faith in these formulas" (Haq 1989: 8; emphasis added).

In *Islame Halal-Haramer Bidhan* (1984, 1994), the Bangla translation of an Arabic text written by Yusuf al-Karzavi, the translator, Muhammad Abdur Rahim, writes that the text responds to "inquiries of the *modern* mind" (emphasis added) in the Muslim world. The topics in this book are discussed at many "centers of Islamic thought worldwide," Rahim explains, but the "*scientific* way" in which the author presents "high quality and comprehensive principles and information-based research in this text makes it unique" (al-Karzavi 1994: 8; emphasis added). More recent *mas'ala* texts imagine a "worldwide" Islamic consciousness. These attempt to enhance linkages between religion and science/modernity. Indeed, this enhanced objectification is reflected in the very forms of these texts. For example, *Islame Halal-Haramer Bidhan* is more systematically structured than older texts like *Neyamul Qor'an*.

Mas'ala texts play a significant role in shaping public consciousness of Islam by encouraging a ritual-based piety in readers. The content of the books spreads quickly by word of mouth, especially in the densely packed middle-class and lower-middle-class neighborhoods, foregrounding Islam and the Qur'an in daily practice, even if the texts do not encourage explanations. More like handbooks than discursive formations, *mas'ala* texts appeal to a majority of the *madrasa*-educated. Their pragmatic, "how-to" approach also appeals to many secularly educated Muslims—those who perceive Islam as a "religious system" (as opposed to a "code of life," which is precisely what Islam is to many Islamic activists) clearly demarcated from the political.

It has been argued that modern mass higher education in the Muslim Middle East facilitates the conceptualization of religious beliefs as "objective systems" (Eickelman 1992: 646–47), a premise easily transposed to South Asia. The view of Islam as an objective system is one that secularists and Islamists in Bangladesh share. However, while Islam represents to Islamists a system of thinking, acting, and living—socially, politically, and economically—it symbolizes an apolitical system of personal values to secularists. Both Islamists and secularists are therefore vehement in their claim to know the "real," or legitimate, concerns of Islam.

In Bangladesh, the slow but steady spread of modern/secular higher education appears to be eroding the privileged position of traditionally educated religious scholars, as is the case in several Arab countries (Eickelman 1992: 646). However, in Bangladesh, this erosion is due at least as much to the secularist activism of non-governmental organizations in rural areas as to the spread of modern/secular higher education. While a majority of Bangladeshis continue to live in rural areas, modern/secular higher education is available primarily to urban regions (Chaudhury and Ahmed 1987: 39). *Mas'ala* texts appear to further diminish the roles of traditional religious experts. By exposing the secularly educated Bengali Muslims to specific, practice-based, Qur'anic knowledge compiled by various authors, these texts allow readers to play off one authority against another and reduce the necessity for face-to-face interaction with traditional specialists.

On the other hand, these texts reassert the importance of traditional religious education, perceived as the basis for religious cures. They also enhance the dependence of secularly educated Muslims on the traditionally trained, since the former are not likely to engage in the public production of *mas'ala* discourse. This dependence is occasioned by people's need for private assistance—in the case of illness or childlessness, for instance. The language of the texts, *sadhu* or classical Bangla, is unattractive to many modern-educated persons and hard for them to emulate; knowledge required for writing *mas'ala* texts must be acquired primarily from traditional religious training.

Lacking in secular modalities for meaningful renderings of sacred phenomena, *mas'ala* texts fail to engage a majority of the modern-educated, who are reluctant to perceive a text as authoritative and interesting simply because it is full of Qur'anic verses and *hadith*. They demand that citations be explained, contextualized, and buttressed by references to shared ideas, common-sense examples, scientific evidence, or corroboration by recognized scholars. Such challenges, in turn, indicate how Islam is becoming increasingly objectified in the consciousness of many of its believers: "What is my religion? Why is it important to my life? and, How do my beliefs guide my conduct?" (Eickelman 1992: 643). While the newer *mas'ala* texts respond to shifting criteria for persuasiveness more effectively than older ones, they do not compete well with more recent booklets and novels in attracting readers in a society with rising levels of modern/secular higher education, especially readers from influential circles.

BIOGRAPHIES

Like *mas'ala* texts, biographies are an old literary form, one that constituted a very popular category of Muslim Bengali literature during the nineteenth and early twentieth centuries (Ahmed 1974: 352–53). They are one of the few types of Islamic literature available in general bookstores, probably because of their apolitical nature, easy-read style, and suitability for both adults and children. Like most *mas'ala* texts, biographies have bright-colored hard-cover designs in floral and geometric patterns, and the writing style is similar—*sadhu* Bangla with a fair amount of rhymed prose (characteristic of nineteenth-century *punthi* literature), dialogue, and monologues assigned to Allah, prophets, angels, and saintly characters. They seem to inspire piety by narrativizing the religious devotion of other characters.

A significant break in the tradition of biographical texts occurred in the late 1980s (although the older tradition remains dominant), but the new biographies are not yet visible because the project is still nascent and because new texts entail higher production costs due to their more sophisticated appearance—such as high-quality paper and print—and the qualifications of their producers, who are often the recipients of higher education in both traditional and modern state-run systems. Prices and style of presentation indicate that the audience for the new biographies is growing, but it is still a small literary-economic one—primarily members of the middle and upper-middle classes with modern higher education or higher education in both modern and religious schools. The texts are primarily sold at stores affiliated with Islamist groups and located around group headquarters or mosques that tend to be Islamist strongholds, such as the Kantaban Mosque in Dhaka. These sites are usually removed from general bookstore locations.

One example of the new biographies is *Sirate Ibne Hisham*, translated from Arabic into Bangla by Akram Farooq and first published in 1988 (re-published in 1990 and again in 1992). With a somber-colored and simply illustrated hard cover, this biography of the Prophet Muhammad is much longer and of a more "authoritative" or "serious" appearance than most popular biographies. Also, since it is a translation of an Arabic text, authored by an Egyptian named 'Abd al Salam Harun and based on Ibne Hisham's work in 1953, its organization of material and its writing style differ from those of traditional Bangladeshi biographies. For instance, the work includes a comprehensive introduction and notes. It is aimed at a wide audience, especially recipients of secular higher education.

Another instance of divergence is *Rasulullahr Biplabi Jiban* (The Revolutionary Life of the Messenger of Allah), a translated text based on a work by the Indian writer Abu Salim Muhammad Abdul Hai. A considerable amount of material has been added to the original, including a chapter entitled "The Role of Female Companions in the Preaching of Islam." According to Muhammad Habibur Rahman, translator and editor of this new-style biography, "Muslims today see the life doctrine of the world Prophet in segments, as the life of a mere preacher of religion." Consequently, they fail to grasp the "revolutionary significance" of his existence and hence do not see the need to reform their problem-ridden states and societies (1993: preface). This text claims to enable the reader to "see the *entire form* of [the Prophet's] life" (preface; emphasis added). Such emphasis on the wholeness of form resonates with the increasing perception of "religion as system and object" (Eickelman 1992: 646–47). This is one of the few biographical texts in the Bangladeshi Islamic market that attempt to objectify Islam for readers through a contemporary Islamic activist vocabulary—"Islamic movement," "Islamic state," "Islamic society," "establishment of Islam," and "training of the faithful."

It is noteworthy that translation, compilation, publication, and distribution of both *Sirate Ibne Hisham* and *Rasulullahr Biplabi Jiban* have been undertaken by Jamaate Islami. Jamaat has also contributed significantly to the new genre of Islamic literature in Bangladesh that I call "booklets," and it is to these that we now turn.

BOOKLETS

Booklets started to appear in noticeable numbers in the late 1970s. As far as the basic nature of their contents is concerned, of course, they can be traced to "social" and "political" works of nineteenth- and early-twentieth-

century *punthi* literature (Ahmed 1974: 341–52, 359–69). Current booklets are cheap and readable because they adhere closely to colloquial Bangla
and treat specific issues. They are not usually eye-catching in appearance,
probably to keep costs to a minimum and to insure accessibility to a larger
readership. Another reason might be to communicate the seriousness of the
contents. Many producers of booklets and most producers of the new-style,
austerely illustrated biographies are often affiliated with the same Islamist
group, Jamaate Islami, while *mas'ala* texts tend to be produced and purchased by those attracted to either orthodox or non-radical modes of Islam,
such as that advocated by Tablighi Jamaat. Potential recruits to Jamaate
Islami and its offshoot groups are sometimes introduced to Islamist literature through translations of the works by Maudoodi, which are often produced in booklet form (Huq 1994). In fact, these are the works through
which Jamaat launched its literary campaign following its re-entrance into
national politics in the late 1970s.

Booklet writers in Bangladesh, like those in Turkey described by Meeker
(1991: 91), "have adopted a style and stance that has no exact precedent."
They address wide-ranging issues, from broad Islamic principles to particular historical and current socio-political concerns, such as the women's
movement (Nizami 1991), secularism (Rashid 1993), and freedom of expression (Gofran 1989). Booklets Islamize what has been conventionally
regarded as secular knowledge, and, as in Turkey (Yavuz 1995: 14), play a
pivotal role in the formation and dissemination of Islam-centered discourse.
Many booklets go through five or six editions.

As mentioned above, Jamaate Islami "flooded" (Maniruzzaman 1990:
77) the market with booklets upon its return to national politics nearly two
decades ago. As it turns out, this booklet production could not have been
more opportune. While Islam has always been integral to popular culture,
its political image had just begun to recover from the severe blow suffered
in 1971. At the same time, modern schools were turning out significant
numbers of men and women who had been the recipients of higher education. Only 1,210 students were enrolled in 1968 in modern high schools;
513,835 were enrolled in colleges throughout the country in 1975 (Chaudhury and Ahmed 1987: 43, 45). These numbers are not significant in relation to the total population in 1975, but the point is that there was virtually
no Islamic literature in the mid- and late 1970s that could appeal to these
educated readers. Furthermore, these young graduates developed an interest in national and religious identities, boosted in part by the Zia government's
advocacy of "Bangladeshi nationalism" (Rashiduzzaman 1996: 42), which
departed from Mujib's "Bengali nationalism" in re-integrating Islam as an
important component of national identity and in refusing to privilege ethnic
identity over a religious one. *Mas'ala* and biographical texts, which were
practically the only types of religious literature available at the time, did not
employ modern writing styles; neither did they address elements of identity

politics. But booklets—or rather their producer, Jamaate Islami—rose to the occasion.

The production of most *mas'ala* and traditional biographical texts is not directly connected to Islamic activism, but most authors, publishers, and readers of booklets are affiliated with various Islamic groups. Jamaat-affiliated publishing agencies and distribution centers or bookstores, complete with Jamaat-connected authors, editors, translators, cover designers, and computer experts, currently dominate booklet literature. Therefore, while some booklets may be seen as formulating a new type of Islamic knowledge that is "abstract, reflective, and universal," as Yavuz argues is the case for Turkey, such information is not "context free." Islamic knowledge is not "freed from its narrative base" (Yavuz 1995: 3). Rather, it is uprooted from its more conventional bases to be resituated in a culture where modalities of secular education are increasingly dominant. Where a booklet is sold and by whom it is written, published, and read tell a great deal about the "narrative base" or social location of this Islamic discourse.

The sorts of literature discussed so far do not, however, attract the majority of the literate, who are increasingly those secularly educated at state schools, with a taste for modern styles and non-religious, non-political topics; they hold aspirations for secular, "modern" jobs and careers. Islamic literature does not entertain or help obtain well-paying positions, or facilitate peer talk on campuses, many of which continue to be secularist strongholds. Some Jamaat-affiliated publishers complain that "Islamic publishing centers, critically limited by economic factors in their productions, are unable to satisfy demands of the Muslim mind. Therefore secularists, with formidable financial resources, are taking over the literary arena empty of Islamic literature" (interview, December 24, 1994).

While booklets employ more contemporary styles of argumentation, providing a voice "flexible enough to address anyone from small shop owners to university professors," as Yavuz suggests is true for contemporary magazines in Turkey (1995: 8), they lack the right physical look and depth of discussion for the secularly educated, who lay claim to higher social and intellectual status through *enacting* sophistication. But booklets target the working middle and lower-middle classes, even though they are written primarily by degree holders from secular state universities.

Furthermore, for graduates of secular universities, the political messages of booklets arouse suspicion. Many Bangladeshis today find political propaganda unattractive, and those advocating political Islam are seen as having collaborated with the enemy in 1971. As electoral patterns and Razia Akhter Banu's (1992: 163–68) study have shown, most contemporary Bangladeshis would prefer to separate religious and political authority, even though the government is expected to uphold Muslim tenets. All these factors financially undermine the production of both existing booklets and new ones, especially ones more likely to appeal to the growing numbers of better-educated, middle-class Muslims.

NOVELS

What complaining publishers do *not* tell us is that, unable to compete with secularist literature in quantity, Islamist litterateurs are turning to novels in an attempt at diversification. The format of novels, especially romance novels, attracts an audience from active followers of political leaders—high school, college, and university students—and provides the Islamic-minded with alternatives to secular literary entertainment. Romance novels with their vividly illustrated covers have been a stronghold of secular literature, one that Islamists could not have imagined as appropriate, at least not for the purpose of Islamization, even a decade ago.

It is not difficult to see how Islamists, looking for alternative national visions, could have moved from a *mas'ala*-text-dominated market to one of booklet production in which the Islamic principles discussed in *mas'ala* texts become related to specific social, cultural, and political issues. This shift obliges readers to move from an awareness of principles to a realization of how society might be transformed. It is challenging, however, to imagine linkages between Islamic teachings and stories of romance that involve not only married couples but unmarried ones as well. Yet, when one considers the popularity of the romantic novel, particularly among the youth of Bangladesh, one can see why Islamists might have adopted this genre to move the audience toward a particular brand of Islam. Readers are persuaded to Islamically imagine various aspects of their lives and the lives of others around them. I see this adaptation of the project of Islamization to the medium of the romantic novel as a pragmatic attempt to extend and redefine the boundaries of the Islamic imagination and to create a platform for Islamist critiques of secular ideologies and practices. Since romance is well grounded in popular culture, it is strategically more effective to give a negative portrayal of certain aspects of a romantic relationship than to denounce it wholesale.

Where the interplay of cultural symbols is so layered and cacophonic that any overarching agenda the master narrative might have tends to be lost, one encounters in Bangladeshi fiction an illusion of incoherence and purposelessness. However, this style lends authenticity to the stories. In a culture where political themes threaten to eclipse all else, fiction is a welcome respite. Novels therefore become more than genres of creative writing by their performativeness, where, in the reader's imagination, ordinary individuals become performers of domination, opposition, nationhood, and culture. They have voices, desires, strengths, and weaknesses that readers can ally with (Ghosh 1993; Combs-Schilling 1996).

These developments are not unique to Bangladesh. In other Muslim-majority countries as well, the "Islamic" novel constitutes the latest mode of articulation within the broadening zone of religious discourses and symbolizes a turn to "discursive practice" and away from "didacticism," as

Meeker (1991: 214) notes for Turkey. Montgomery (1991) highlights the place of story poems in the modernization and secularization of Uzbekistan's Islamic community during the transition toward sovietization in the 1930s. Bowen (1993: 632), on the other hand, describes the use of poetry in modernist Islamic reform among the Gayo in Indonesia from the 1930s through the 1950s. Yavuz (1995: 15) and Meeker (1991: 206) mention the role of novels in the production of Islamic thought in modern Turkey, and Banks (1990) discusses the role of Malay novelists in the invention of Malay rural culture in the context of "resurgent Islam."

While some Islamic activists do not accept novels as "Islamic" literature (interviews, December 1994), the novels I am concerned with here are sold exclusively in Islamic bookstores. Some Islamic publishers see novels becoming the most popular form of Islamic writing in the near future (interview, December 24, 1994). Their popularity stems in part from the fact that novels are simply more fun to read and in part from the apparent distance between the intimately social Islam of the novels and the rhetorical Islam of propagandist literature such as booklets and newspapers, and this is refreshing for readers of Islamic materials. Most importantly, perhaps, these novels bridge the gap between the types of romantic novels written by Tasleema Nasreen and Humayun Azad, who advocate transcendence of all social mores and attack religious values, and normative Islamic literature, which is preoccupied with reaffirming Islamic principles, purifying society, and decrying the moral depravity of various Bengali cultural practices.

Such bold appropriation of the distinctively modern and secular genre of the romantic novel to disseminate ideas about Islam is unprecedented in Bangladesh. These novelists seek not only to redraw the boundaries of an Islamic imagination but also to chart new ways of *acting* (Meeker 1991: 197). More pragmatically, Bangladeshi writers and publishers use the novel to attract young readers who are not particularly enthused about religious discussions. These novels do not constitute just an Islamist space; they give voice to the large segment of "middle roaders" (Maniruzzaman 1990: 89) to whom Islam is important but who do not support the radical societal visions of either Islamists or secularists.

Although Islamic novels began to appear in Bangladesh only in the 1980s, historical novels by an Urdu writer, Nasim Hejazi, were translated into Bangla and published as early as the 1960s. Hejazi's novels are quite popular among Islamic activists. Produced in grim hard covers, these novels retain numerous Urdu words, but the writing style is dated and the progression of events slow in comparison to current Islamic and secular novels. Slightly colored with romance, Hejazi's works emphasize Islamic history. The current publisher of Hejazi's works in translation is Bangladesh Co-operative Book Society Ltd., whose chairman hails Hejazi for proving that novels can become popular in Bangladesh without being sex-oriented (Prologue, Hejazi 1988). The translator of Hejazi's *Khun Ranga Path* (Blood-Colored Path)

(1988) writes that the novels are *"inspired* by Islamic thoughts and sentiments" (emphasis added). The spaces between this Islamic intentionality and the stories told are often pregnant with the politics of ambiguity and with the potential for attracting a broad audience, for whom the same event might convey different morals.

Among more contemporary Islamic novels are series of paperback thrillers such as *Typhoon* and *Saimoom*, which closely resemble secular series like *Masud Rana* (Anwar Hossen 1994) and *Western* (Shawkat Hossen 1994) in both appearance and writing style. *Saimoom* creatively enmeshes Islamic doctrines and history in plots involving romance, adventure, and local as well as global socio-political issues. The first *Saimoom* story appeared in 1987 as *Operation Tel-Aviv—1*. Novels by Qasem Abubakar began to appear at about the same time, followed by the works of Abdus Salam Mitul in 1994. Both writers' works are similar to secular social novels such as those by Humayun Ahmed and Imdadul Haq Milan. Other novelists, writing in similar styles, began to make their presence felt during 1995 and 1996. Works by some of them are virtually indistinguishable from secular novels, since Islam does not appear in them at all. Yet they are regarded by distributors and publishers as "Islamic" and "decent" (interviews, August 1996).

Ahmed Musa, the principal character of the *Saimoom* series, is a Muslim driven from his homeland in Central Asia by Communists. He is now an international Islamic revolutionary, the leader of an international Islamic group called Saimoom. Musa travels from one part of the world to another to help Muslims in trouble. *Operation Tel-Aviv* finds him in Israel, helping Palestinians establish a state of their own. It contains fairly interesting discussions of Islamic principles, history, and organization and Muslim nationalism. The plot proceeds through strategies and counterstrategies, attacks and revenge, torture and betrayal, martyrdom and organizational loyalty, and a romance that ends in marriage between a Palestinian Islamist and an Israeli woman. Detailed descriptions of places, events, groups, and individuals, clearly as much a product of the imagination as of research, contribute to the persuasiveness of the story.

Abubakar's and Mitul's writings, on the other hand, are social novels. Both writers claim to show that novels can be entertaining without being "indecent" and casually inform readers about various aspects of Islam. According to Mitul, "In the current world of novels, a group of writers with distorted taste do not seem to be able to write novels without sexual appeal and amorous male-female interactions." He tries to show that "love is sacred and how this sacredness turns people's lives toward principles, productivity, and fear of Allah" (1994). Mitul urges readers not to weep over the pain of his main characters but to "try to accept their principles" (*Golaper Kanta* [Rose Thorn] 1994). Abubakar sketches images of urban and rural societies in *Pratikhkha* (Waiting) (1992). He hopes that the reader might

"attain some religious knowledge from [the novel] and be inspired by it."
However, while political Islam has a favorable presence in Mitul's work, it
is altogether absent in Abubakar's.

The "Islamic" nature of these novels cannot be deduced from their appearance. For instance, Abubakar's *Basar Rat* (Wedding Night) (1993) has
a glossy hard cover with a bride and groom sitting on a bed. Mitul's *Golaper
Kanta* has a glossy cover of a woman's face with a rose placed sensuously
across it (Fig. 8.1). In terms of graphics, the novels are indistinguishable
from secular novels such as those by Tasleema Nasreen and Imdadul Haq
Milan.

Despite the remarkable similarities between secular and Islamic novels
in Bangladesh, the Islamic character of the latter is quite clear in some cases.
In the case of Nasir Helal's *Obanchito Kalanka* (Undeserved Disgrace)
(1996), for example, the narrative itself contains strong Islamist overtones.
In the case of works by Abdus Salam Mitul, on the other hand, Islam is
latent in the story, but appears clearly in the preface. In his introduction to
Borkha Pora Sei Meyeti (That Veil-clad Woman) (1994), Mitul thanks Allah profusely for enabling him to write this novel. Then he recites *dorud* (a
set of Qur'anic verses in which God is implored to bless Muhammad and
his family) "hundreds of tens of million times," referring to the Prophet
Muhammad as "the great messenger of the liberation of humankind" and
"director of the liberation of the exploited, oppressed, and tortured peoples."
Abubakar, somewhat less enthusiastic, often begins "in the name of Allah,
the Extremely Merciful."

Mitul's and Abubakar's support of Islam in their novels does not mean
that their works are perceived in the same light by everyone. Group affiliations
and differences in Islamic attitudes play a key role. While the affiliations of
Asad (*Saimoom*) and Mitul with Jamaate Islami are quite clear (Asad is a
prominent Jamaat activist; Mitul's publisher, Al-Falah Publications, is Ja-
maat-linked), it is not clear to which group—if any—Abubakar is connected.
That Abubakar has no Jamaat connections is clear from the comments of a
Jamaat-affiliated publisher and salesman: "Qasem Bin Abubakar's books
do not create an interest in readers concerning the Islamic movement and
render readers suspicious towards Islamic regulations through weak and
out-of-contextual usage of the Qur'an and Hadith." He further remarked
that "seeing nudity and dirtiness alongside the Qur'an and hadith, it would
not be ridiculous to speculate that Qasem has begun to compose so-called
religious literature with a commercial outlook" (interview, December 25,
1994).

Yet Abubakar's works are stocked at this Islamist's store. One could
venture that this is because Abubakar's books sell well. But if profit is the
key factor, why not keep some popular secular works as well, especially
those without "nudity and dirtiness"? Besides the commodification of Islamic literature, we see a tolerance for literature averse to one's own taste,

Figure 8.1. It is difficult to distinguish Mitul's Islamic novel *Golaper Kanta* (Rose Thorn), above, from Nasreen's secular novel *Fera* (Returning), on the right, by appearance.

as long as there is some "Islamicness" present, a tolerance influenced perhaps by the scarcity of Islamic novels at a time when, according to this publisher, novels show the potential for becoming the most sought-after literary items among young Islam-oriented readers (interview, December 25, 1994). Such tolerance and flexibility are further produced by the educational and cultural "habitus" the producers and audiences have in common.

The fact that Abubakar's and Mitul's works sometimes have the same publisher attests to this fluidity. Publishers' personal knowledge of an author and familiarity with her/his "basic" values, regardless of whether the author actually uses Islam in his/her work, plays an important role in the publication of Islamic novels. This sort of trust goes beyond writer-publisher relations to affect writer-reader relations and relations among the audience. Particularly in the case of Islamic novels where Islam is not mentioned directly, Islamicness is imagined and becomes objectified through the book's association with an author or publisher known for her/his religiosity or knowledgeability about Islam or with a specific Islamic place such as an Islamic bookstore or fair.

Furthermore, Islamist publishers gain by publishing works of writers not affiliated with Islamic activism, for the credibility of a novel then increases for a broader audience. Two examples are works by Al Mahmud and Razia Majid. Both are known well as writers, but little is known about their political inclinations. Conventionally, their works have been published by various agencies. Razia Majid's latest novel was published by Preeti Prokashon, an Islamist publishing house. There is a color photograph of the writer at the back of the novel's glossy dust jacket, along with a blurb on her earlier publications. The photograph depicts a bespectacled female scholar with very short hair who wears make-up and fashionable clothing. In other words, it is clear that the author is among those least likely to have sympathies for Islamism.

The publisher went out of his way to violate the basic Islamist principle that a Muslim woman should carefully conceal her physical appearance from public gaze by veiling. The publisher's transgression becomes meaningful when one realizes that this novel effectively problematizes the secularist depiction of the 1971 war of the independence of Bangladesh. The controversial role that Islamists played in this war continues to haunt Islamist attempts today to popularize Islam as a political ideology.

While ambiguity as to the Islamic credentials of a novelist endows a novel with additional political innocence for a broader audience, a novel's physical location among other Islamic books tints it with the authority and propriety of more explicit Islamic books such as *mas'ala* texts, booklets, and exegetical works on the Qur'an and *hadith*. In other words, Islamic novels "become components of a 'paradigmatic' series" (Tambiah 1993: 263). Even though the *Saimoom* series contains romantic exchanges of which pious adults would disapprove, young Islamic activists can cite the name of the author of the series, Abul Asad, a prominent Islamic activist. In the imagination of an Islam-oriented audience diverse in age, educational background, and degree of religiosity, Asad's ideological commitment is stamped onto the novels he writes and serves as a guarantor for the goodness of the work.

Despite some Jamaat-affiliated publishers' approval of work by writers like Mitul, political Islam—and more accurately Jamaate Islami—does not play as prominent a role in Mitul's work as in the novels of Mosharraf Hosain Shagar. In *Abujh Ridoy* (Uncomprehending Heart) (1st ed. August 1995; 2nd ed. January 1996), for instance, Shagar describes how the main character becomes an Islamic activist and advances from one cadre to the next in an Islamic group called *Islami Mukti Sangha* (Islamic Liberation Association) (Fig. 8.2). Anyone familiar with the internal workings of Jamaat or its student groups will easily recognize the group Shagar is talking about. Malti-Douglas argues, in contrast, that in an Iraqi novel entitled *al-Ayyam al-Tawila* (The Long Days) by 'Abd al Amir Mu'alla, "a partly fictionalized account of a period in Saddam Husayn's life," this "semidisguise permits Mu'alla to take whatever liberties he wishes with the life of his protagonist, while permitting the identification with the historical personage essential to the latter's legitimation" (Malti-Douglas 1994: 47). The Bangladeshi novelist Shagar, however, takes little or no liberty with the organizational facts of the movement he deals with, yet the poor disguise is essential for legitimizing the fictional form he is using.

The fictional form itself is crucial for the contemporary Islamic activist agenda of Islamizing national culture and history, not only through didactic works and speeches but through entertainment. Islamist novelists rely heavily on readers to subscribe to the "language of politics" approach, while they use the "politics of language" approach. The former assumes that "language carries intrinsic authority that is largely independent of the political circumstances in which it is used" (Piscatori 1990: 770). The latter assumes that "language acquires authority according to usage and has primarily tactical value" (Piscatori 1990: 771). Islamic novelists' perception of the role of secular novels in contemporary society also plays a key role in their fiction. One of Shagar's goals in writing, for instance, is to counter writers who, "in the name of writing novels," are ruining "national ideology, tradition and culture and youth character" and trying to "distance young men from Islam" by "distorting the great objective and real spirit of the liberation war of 1971." Thus Islamic novelists see themselves as not only sustaining national identity but also writing national history as it "really" took place.

A decade ago, Islamic activists either avoided the issue of the independence war or became defensive when charged with betraying the Bangladeshi nation by secularists who wrote enthusiastically about this war. This secularist-Islamist split can be traced to the early twentieth century, the twi-

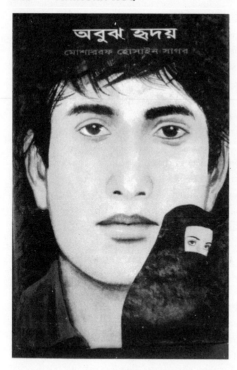

Figure 8.2. In his Islamic novel *Abujh Ridoy* (Uncomprehending Heart), Shagar makes little attempt to conceal the real identity of the Islamist group at the heart of his narrative.

light of British colonial rule in India (Murshid 1995: 120–68). For Bangladeshi secularists, the 1971 war demonstrated that the Islamic bond could not supersede cultural differences between West and East Pakistan and that embroiling Islam in politics could only lead to exploitation and disaster (284–360). For Islamists, this war was the product of the unjust rule by the military dictator of Pakistan and the efforts of Hindu-ruled India to break up Muslim-ruled Pakistan. It therefore bore no connection to "real" Islam (Asad 1990). Some Islamists collaborated with the Pakistani army in eliminating fellow Bengalis who either supported or fought for independence (Ahmad 1991: 501). An inability to adequately justify or refute charges of collaboration has prompted Islamists to shy away from the topic of the war. These charges also constitute a serious obstacle to the popularization of Islamism in present Bangladesh, for they can be and have been effectively used by opposition groups to whip up popular emotions against the Islamists.

Yet young Islamic novelists are entering previously forbidden terrain by boldly incorporating the 1971 war into their narratives for the purpose of popularizing Islamist ideologies. They employ the war as a strategy for retelling national history and for historicizing the marginalized discourse of political Islam. Challenging the negative linkage between the war and Islam in dominant secularist discourse, these Islam-oriented novelists attempt to show how good Muslims (whether affiliated with Islamic activism or not) were persecuted by both the Pakistani army and Bengali secularists. They also delineate the violence unleashed by Bengalis on Urdu-speaking or non-Bengali residents of East Pakistan as a consequence of the war. An example of such a novel is *Judhdho O Bhalobasha* (War and Love) (1996) by a female novelist named Razia Majid. As with many Islam-oriented romantic novels, it is impossible to know this book as Islamic from its cover illustration or even from the contents, for Islam appears only sporadically within the body of the text. But this is precisely why the book is effective. While distancing itself from Islamic activism, it complicates the glory and clarity of meaning that secularists assign to the war, thereby destabilizing the sharp boundaries drawn between friend and foe in the dominant literature on the war. In effect, the writer manages to accomplish what seasoned Islamist writers have not been able to before, either through booklets or through more scholarly works such as Abul Asad's *Kalo Ponchisher Age* (Prior to the Dark Twenty-fifth). This book is certainly more "historical" in appearance, style, and scope—footnoted to the hilt—but high school and college students are much more likely to pick up Majid's narrative of love and loss.

The fictional form frees authors from the need to provide concrete evidence for their claims. It also provides an element of unpredictability and distance from political motifs. While a booklet with a title suggesting the independence war immediately politicizes what is to come—and booklet titles have to be specific—fictional dialogue, especially an entertaining romance, has enabled Islamic writers to enter one of the most powerful arenas of nationalist discourse, that of the liberation war, with a voice that is not easily dismissed as political propaganda. It is the abstract and artificial engagement with reality that fiction allows that Bangladeshi Islamic intellectuals find useful for laying claim to cultural and political spaces conventionally guarded by secular intellectuals.

Most important, romantic fiction, as a popular performative genre and emblem, is a powerful pathway to the heart of the national imagination. Bangladeshi society is remarkably heterogeneous in its perceptions of a variety of national, cultural, and religious formulations. A key source of this heterogeneity is the informational arena, which consists of state and private religious schools, state and private Bengali-medium schools, a growing number of private English-medium schools, books written for these different audiences, television, movie theaters, songs on audiotapes, Hindi and Western films on videotapes, and the satellite dish. In each of these arenas, romance is envisioned somewhat differently. However, the significant presence of romance in each of these spheres, along with the wide range of meanings it encompasses, forms a thread of "national" commonality that cuts across educational and socio-economic boundaries.

Speaking in general terms, *madrasa* students tend to read romantic novels by Islam-oriented writers; Bengali-medium students read novels by secu-larly oriented writers (however, most Jamaat activists are educated at Bengali-medium schools and therefore tend to read both secular and Is-lamic novels); English-medium students read English novels such as the Mills and Boon series, the Harlequin series, the Sweet Valley High series, and novels by Danielle Steele, Barbara Cartland, and Sydney Sheldon. Many Bengali-medium and English-medium students are familiar with romantic Hindi songs and movies, and *madrasa* students are at least familiar with Bangla romantic films and drama through theater and television.

Discussions of real romantic encounters and of romantic drama and films, as well as exchanges of romantic novels, are widespread. Brightly illustrated covers of romantic novels are there for everyone to gaze on in marketplaces and at fairs, as are brightly illustrated graphic posters adver-tising new films in the theater. *Madrasa* students watch romantic Bengali films, often modeled after Hindi ones, in the theater without their parents' knowledge. Many Islamic activists continue to engage in interests that be-gan before their participation in Islamic activism, and such interests often include Bengali and Hindi romantic films and secular romantic novels such as those by Humayun Ahmed.

An example of such textured continuation is an event organized by a group of student Islamic activists, a showing of the Hindi film *Bombay*, which featured a romance and subsequent marriage between a Hindu man and a Muslim woman where the Muslim woman does not convert to her husband's religion. The movie ends with horrifying scenes from the Bombay commu-nal riots. The organizers of this event convinced their supervisors that the movie would provide an excellent opportunity for "learning about religious communalism in India." The supervisors agreed only on the condition that one of them be present to ensure its propriety. The activist assigned the task of supervision was not particularly interested in the movie and spent most of her time outside the room where the movie was being shown. Scenes of physical intimacy were quietly watched in the absence of the supervisor and fast-forwarded diligently whenever the supervisor walked into the room (Huq field notes, Dhaka, July 1997). This spilling of specific kinds of the romantic imagination across formal borders further facilitates the produc-tion of romance as a popular discourse; everyone partly knows what every-one else is talking about where romance is concerned.

Since Islamic activists are now trying to appeal not only to the Islamically inclined but also to the secularly inclined, what better icon to employ than that of the romantic novel? Such a text can discuss the blissful irresistibility of romance and its destructive potentialities, loyalty to one's Islamic organi-zation and competing loyalty to one's lover, the necessity of family life and its increasing impossibility in a fast-moving world. In these novels, registers of piety shift from praying to preying upon oppressors, from making the pilgrimage to Mecca to traveling around the globe like a true transnational revolutionary, from giving *zakat* to embracing martyrdom for a noble cause, from enjoining fasting to reforming the government.

The popularity of Islamist novels like *Saimoom* lies not in ideological coherence or consistency but in effective symbolic constancy of form-oriented closeness to a conventionally popular secular thriller series like *Masud Rana*. It is virtually impossible to distinguish between *Saimoom* and *Masud Rana* through either outer appearance or inner style. Both series use a graphic imagery of heroism, romance, sci-fi techniques, organizational conspiracies, and violence. At the same time, the heroes and heroines of *Saimoom* have a very specific kind of Islamic mission; they are upholders of a specific kind of goodness. But this ideological difference between *Saimoom* and *Masud Rana* gets muted through "emblematic constancy" (Combs-Schilling 1996: 12), through the sort of broad-banded whimsicality that is a regular feature of thriller fiction. Islamic novels attempt to become part of popular literature by having an audience that is very much a product of national education—the young Islamic activists of today—and that can easily spread the word about these novels to non-Islamic activist classmates, friends, and relatives.

Here we see an objectification of Islam different in texture from that discussed for booklets where the words impinge directly on the reader's intellect; where Islam becomes a body of clearly delimited compartments, and where authority emanates from specificity. In the case of novels, on the other hand, awareness is meant to develop through the diffuse transformation of consciousness; authority is effective because its form may not be easily recognized. This becomes clearer in looking at those novels that, despite being perceived as Islamic, do not apparently draw on Islam. Abul Khayer Muslehuddin's *Medhabi Meye* (Brilliant Girl) (1996) (Fig. 8.3) does not mention Islam but deals with the peer pressure that young women feel to acquire boyfriends and the ways that young women are seduced through false promises of marriage and then abandoned at the first sign of pregnancy. The woman becomes a social outcast, her aspirations to higher education and a career are cut short. Firoz Ashraf's *Deep Jele Jai* (I Go On Kindling the Light) (1st ed. 1993; 2nd ed. 1994; 3rd ed. 1995) treats the social problems of how men deceive women, how young women are forced into prostitution, and how women are not consulted about choice of marriage partner. The reader is entertained, but if the romance does not end in marriage or leads to physical intimacy outside marriage, it is indicted.

Reading between the lines in such novels where Islam is barely perceptible, one could perhaps see in them certain implicit Islamic messages, such as the ills of extra-marital sexual relations and of free mixing, and the need to uproot prostitution. However, such views are also fully consonant with popular Bengali cultural ideology. Instead of relying on Islam for legitimizing a particular social value, as earlier generations of Islamists in the region tended to do, contemporary Islamic novelists draw on the authority of popular notions of "cultural decency."

Figure 8.3. Islam is never evoked directly in Muslehuddin's *Medhabi Meye* (Brilliant Girl).

CONCLUSION

It remains difficult to define "Islamic" literature, especially since there is little consensus among readers: "Islamic" is a volatile signifier. When a bookseller at the Islamic Book Fair in Dhaka in August 1996 showed me a novel by Shukumar Rai entitled *Pagla Dashu* (Mad Dashu), I exclaimed, "But he is a non-Muslim writer!" The salesman smiled benignly and said, "Yes, he is a Brahmin. However, he is not anti-Islamic. There is a big difference, you know. Muslims can be anti-Islamic while non-Muslims can be tolerant. This guy brings up Islam in his work but does not attack or ridicule it—he treats it quite respectfully."

But if Islam encompasses every aspect of life and is as tidily packaged as many Islamic activists would have it, how can an Islamist read an "in-between" novel and encourage others to read it? Given the hostilities between Muslims and Hindus in India, for a well-known Indian Brahmin writer to write well of Islam not only adds to Islam's prestige but also shames those secularist Muslims who are perceived as denigrating Islam in their works.

When I asked a salesman why some Islamic activists do not consider Abubakar's work as particularly Islamic, he replied, "Well, it may not be fully Islamic, but it's certainly pro-Islamic and by no means anti-Islamic." Thus, as long as a novel does not support ideas and imagery in direct conflict with Islamic principles and is acceptable in terms of "Bengali cultural decency," it is regarded as possessing a *degree* of Islamicness and therefore suitable for Muslims. As such, it may be considered part of "Islamic literature."

This willingness to widen the boundaries of the Islamic resonates with the position of the noted Indonesian scholar Ibrahim Hosen on Islamic legal interpretations. Hosen insists that "all types of laws and rules are to be valued as Islamic (or Muslim) laws as long as they are not in opposition to the intent and spirit of *shari'a*, even if contradictory to the surface (*harfiah*) meaning" (cited in Bowen, this volume). A similar privileging of "intent and spirit" over literality enables Islamist publishers to publish non-Islamic novels.

Some Islamic activists assert that fictitious literature, even when written from Islamic perspectives, does not count as Islamic literature since it deals with the "imagined," while Islam is real. Sometimes this literature includes "romance between unmarried men and women," which cannot be a part of Islam (personal communication, December 1994). A high-school Islamist did not hesitate to challenge the Islamic nature of the thriller series *Saimoom*, even though she is an avid *Saimoom* reader and particularly appreciative of the agency granted women in this series, where women often engage in combat, espionage, and defiance of male authorities. Referring to the main character of *Saimoom*, Ahmed Musa, she commented, "I've no idea where Abul Asad (the well-known Islamist author of *Saimoom*) is going with his macho character. He refuses to let Ahmed Musa get married and kills off every woman who comes into his life. This is not Islamic, is it? Not only are marriage, family, and home important in Islam, but this endless number of romantic affairs, with occasional physical contact as well, is really a bit too much."

The issue of what role novels play in Islamic literature in Bangladesh resists closure at this time. But looking at different kinds of Islamic literature tells us several things. First, *mas'ala* texts, biographies, and booklets exemplify an "objectification" of the Muslim consciousness—codification, principles, citations from the Qur'an and *hadith*, and recognizable forms of authority (Eickelman and Piscatori 1996: 37–45). Such crystallization of Islam as a system among other systems is a product of mass higher education. It attains the effectiveness it does because of rising literacy. Booklets as well as subtle changes within *mas'ala* and biographical formats indicate changes in forms of authority in religious discourse closely linked to the increase in numbers among the secularly educated.

Second, novels depict a different type of objectification: Islam is objectified not through apparent systematicity, coherence, organization, and the positing of clear-cut differences but through the openness of cultural symbols and shared local notions, the presence of non-Islamic elements like premarital romance, the voicelessness of religious authority, and the absence of particularity. The fact that the ideas of the new Turkish Muslim intellectual Ismet Özel are not necessarily consistent with popular Muslim opinion lends his works "an atmosphere of frankness and sincerity" (Meeker 1991: 214). Likewise, the projected distance between regular political Islamic rhetoric and romantic novels creates new spaces for interest, empathy, and understanding. This projection is perfected in those novels where the Islamic credentials of the writer are purposefully rendered ambiguous. However, even as Islamic novelists seek to draw readers to their view of Islam, their reliance on the fictional form, which has traditionally been considered as secular, enhances the ambiguity of their messages and significantly dilutes their projects.

Third, variety in Islamic literature, even within a specific category such as the novel, reflects a pluralistic view of Islam, ranging from an Islam hinged on political power and organizational training to one based on shared understandings of cultural decency and goodness malleable to symbolic manipulation and semantic fluidity. While sharp differences may exist between past and present carriers of Islamic culture in certain Muslim-majority countries, such as Turkey (Yavuz 1995: 5–6), I submit that older styles of Islamic knowledge coexist with newer ones in Bangladesh, as they do in Middle Eastern countries such as Oman (Eickelman 1992: 648).

Fourth, types of literature such as thrillers and romantic novels indicate attempts to talk about religion in ways that undercut either "secularist" or "fundamentalist" approaches to Islam. Through the signifier/signified disjuncture built into their narrative forms, such Islamic writings facilitate the entrance of new voices into delicate debates over the place of religion in local culture, history, politics, and the formation of a personal identity, voices that probably could not have participated otherwise, either because secularist publishers found them "tedious" or because Islamist publishers regarded them as "indecent."

Fifth, closeness in form between secular and Islamic writing styles, as is evident in the novel, reflects complex interactions between formal, secular, higher education and informal religious training, especially in the case of writers affiliated with political Islam. Such an interaction allows those interested in Islamic discourse to rework their particular notions of what is Islamic and what is not into a "locally effective discursive form" (Bowen 1993: 629). This heterogeneity in educational imagination opens young Islamic activists to using popular cultural human imagery on book covers, considering them "acceptable," and dwelling on romance while confidently citing the Qur'an and *hadith* in appropriate places.

Last, while the recent varieties of Islamic literature do not have massive audiences, they are often aimed at and read by those from the prestigious circle of upwardly mobile professionals, the powerful communities of high school, college, and university students, and the influential associations of small and big businessmen. These are the groups out of which the national leadership arises and which serve as the conduits between the local and the global, for they are able to forge transnational connections via international conferences, business networks, study-abroad programs, and, of course, the revolutionary information superhighway. These groups, even though they constitute a small percentage of the total Bangladeshi population, grow every day, as thousands of young men and women graduate from public and private institutions of higher education throughout the country and enter the work arena.

NOTES

In transliterating Bangla words, I have preferred to go by the pronunciation rather than follow the conventional system, which treats Bangla words as though they were Sanskrit. With regard to Arabized and Persianized Bangla words or "Musulmani Bangla" such as the book title *Neyamul Qor'an*, I have transliterated them as they are printed and pronounced in Bangla. Hence the Arabic word "Qur'an" appears as "Qor'an" in the book title.

1. "Bangladeshi" denotes the national identity of the people of the nation-state of Bangladesh. "Bangali" refers to the ethnic identity based on the language "Bangla." The ethnicity of the majority of Bangladeshis is Bangali. Most inhabitants of West Bengal in India are ethnically Bangalis as well. "Bangali" is both a noun (e.g., "She is a Bangali") and an adjective (e.g., "This aspect of Bangali culture must be preserved"). "Bengali" is the anglicized term for both "Bangali" and "Bangla."

WORKS CITED

Abubakar, Qasem Bin. 1992. *Pratikhkha* (Waiting). Dhaka: Tarafdar Prokashoni.
———. 1993. *Basar Rat* (Wedding Night). Dhaka: Onubhob Prokas hon.
Ahmad, Mumtaz. 1991. "Islamic Fundamentalism in South Asia: The Jama'at-i-Islami and the Tablighi Jama'at of South Asia." In *The Fundamentalist Project*, vol. 1, *Fundamentalisms Observed*, ed. R. Scott Appleby and Martin E. Marty, pp. 457–530. Chicago: University of Chicago Press.
Ahmed, Rafiuddin. 1981 (1988). *The Bengal Muslims 1871–1906, A Quest for Identity*. New Delhi: Oxford University Press.
Ahmed, Sufia. 1974. *The Muslim Community in Bengal, 1884–1912*. Dhaka: Oxford University Press.
Appadurai, Arjun. 1992. [1986] "Introduction: Commodities and the Politics of Value." In *The Social Life of Things: Commodities in Cultural Perspective*, ed. Arjun Appadurai, pp. 3–63. New York: Cambridge University Press.
Asad, Abul. 1987. *Saimoom: Operation Tel-Aviv 1*. Dhaka: Bangla Sahitta Parishad.

————. 1990. *Kalo Ponchisher Age* (Prior to the Dark Twenty-fifth). Dhaka: Itihas Parishad.

Ashraf, Firoz. 1995. *Deep Jele Jai* (I Go On Kindling the Light). Dhaka: Shireen Publications.

Banks, David J. 1990. "Resurgent Islam and Malay Rural Culture: Malay Novelists and the Invention of Culture." *American Ethnologist* 17, no. 3 (August): 531–48.

Banu, U. A. B. Razia Akter. 1992. *Islam in Bangladesh*. Leiden: E. J. Brill.

Bowen, John R. 1993. "A Modernist Muslim Poetic: Irony and Social Critique in Gayo Islamic Verse." *The Journal of Asian Studies* 52, no. 3 (August): 629–46.

Chaudhury, Rafiqul Huda, and Nilufer Raihan Ahmed. 1987) *Female Status in Bangladesh*. Dhaka: Bangladesh Institute of Development Studies.

Combs-Schilling, Elaine. 1996. "Casablanca 1993: Negotiating Gender and Nation in Performative Space." *Journal of Ritual Studies* 10, no. 3 (Summer): 1-35.

Eickelman, Dale F. 1992. "Mass Higher Education and the Religious Imagination in Contemporary Arab Societies." *American Ethnologist* 19, no. 4 (November): 643-55.

Eickelman, Dale F., and James Piscatori. 1996. *Muslim Politics*. Princeton: Princeton University Press.

Ghosh, Amitav. 1993. "Dancing in Cambodia." *Granta* 44: 127–69.

Gofran, Sharif Abdul, ed. 1989. *Satanic Verses Banam Lekhar Sadhinata* (Satanic Verses versus Freedom of Writing). Dhaka: Shatadal Prokashoni Limited.

Hai, Abu Salim Muhammad Abdul. 1993. *Rasulullahr Biplabi Jiban* (The Revolutionary Life of the Messenger of God), ed. and trans. Muhammad Habibur Rahman. Dhaka:Khairun Prokashoni.

Haq, M. E. 1975. *A History of Sufism in Bengal*. Dhaka: Asiatic Society of Bangladesh.

Haq, Shamsul. 1989. *Neyamul Qor'an*. Dhaka: Kazi Anisur Rahman and Zaman Brothers.

Hejazi, Nasim. 1988. *Khun Ranga Path* (Blood-Colored Path). Dhaka: Bangladesh Co-operative Book Society.

Helal, Nasir. 1996. Obanchito Kalanka (Undeserved Disgrace). Dhaka: Tashfeen Fahad.

Huq, Maimuna. 1994. Old Boundaries, New Visions: Women's Islamic Activism in Bangladesh. Unpublished Senior Fellowship Program Thesis, Dartmouth College.

————. 1997 [July]. Field Notes, Dhaka.

Husain, Syed Anwar. 1990. "Islamic Fundamentalism in Bangladesh: Internal Variables and External Inputs." In *Religion, Nationalism and Politics in Bangladesh*, ed. Rafiuddin Ahmed, pp. 137–52. New Delhi: South Asian Publishers.

Kabir, M. G. 1990. "Religion, Language and Nationalism in Bangladesh." In *Religion, Nationalism and Politics in Bangladesh*, ed. Rafiuddin Ahmed, pp. 35–49. New Delhi: South Asian Publishers.

al-Karzavi, Yusuf. 1994 (1984). *Islame Halal-Haramer Bidhan*, trans. into Bengali by Muhammad Abdur Rahim. Dhaka: Khairun Prokashoni.

Khan, Zillur R. 1990. "From Mujib to Zia: Elite Politics in Bangladesh." In *Religion, Nationalism and Politics in Bangladesh*, ed. Rafiuddin Ahmed, pp. 50–62. New Delhi: South Asian Publishers.

Majid, Razia. 1996. *Judhdho O Bhalobasha* (War and Love). Dhaka: Preeti Prokashon.

Malti-Douglas, Fedwa, and Allen Douglas. 1994. *Arab Comic Strips: Politics of an Emerging Mass Culture*. Bloomington: Indiana University Press.

Maniruzzaman, Talukder. 1990. "Bangladesh Politics: Secular and Islamic Trends." In *Religion, Nationalism and Politics in Bangladesh*, ed. Rafiuddin Ahmed, pp. 63-93. New Delhi: South Asian Publishers.

Meeker, Michael E. 1991. "The New Muslim Intellectuals in the Republic of Turkey." In *Islam in Modern Turkey: Religion, Politics and Literature in a Secular State*, ed. Richard Tapper, pp. 189–219. New York: I. B. Tauris.

Mitul, Abdus Salam. 1994. *Golaper Kanta* (Rose Thorn). Dhaka: Tarafdar Prokashoni.

———. 1994. *Borkha Pora Sei Meveti* (That Veil-Clad Woman). Dhaka: Tarafdar Prokashoni.

Montgomery, David C. 1991. "Zaynab and Aman: Love and Women's Liberation in the 1930s, a Story Poem by Hamid Alimjan." In *Change and Continuity in Central Asia*, ed. Shirin Akiner, pp. 1–13. New York: Kegan Paul International.

Murshid, Tazeen Mahnaz. 1995. *The Sacred and the Secular: Bengal Muslim Discourses, 1871–1977*. Calcutta: Oxford University Press.

Muslehuddin, Abul Khayer. 1996. *Medhabi Meye* (Brilliant Girl). Dhaka: Bud Publications.

Nizami, Shamsunnahar. 1991. *Nari Mukti Andolon* (The Women's Liberation Movement). Dhaka: Al-Hera Prokashoni.

Piscatori, James. 1990. "The Rushdie Affair and the Politics of Ambiguity." *International Affairs* 66, no. 4 (Fall): 767–89.

Rashid, Harunur. 1993. *Khola Chiti* (Open Letter). Dhaka: Itihas Parishad.

Rashiduzzaman, M. 1996. "Islam, Muslim Identity and Nationalism in Bangladesh." *Journal of South Asian and Middle Eastern Studies* 18, no. 1 (Fall): 36-60.

Tambiah, Stanley J. 1993 (1984). *The Buddhist Saints of the Forest and the Cult of Amulets*. New York: Cambridge University Press.

Yavuz, Hakan. 1995. "The Role of Print and Media in the Islamic Movement: The Case of Turkey." Paper presented at conference on "Print Islam and Civic Pluralism" in Bellagio, Italy, March 25–27.

9 /

CIVIC PLURALISM DENIED?
THE NEW MEDIA AND
JIHADI VIOLENCE IN INDONESIA

Robert W. Hefner

It is a truism of modern democratic theory that prospects for democratization increase with the development of multiple centers of power
and a plurality of public discourses in society. Classical statements of this
so-called pluralist theme in political theory (Dahl 1971, Held 1987: 186–
220) emphasize that a multiplicity of ideas and authorities makes it difficult
for any single group to win a clear monopoly of power. The frustration of
monopolistic aspirations has the unintended consequence of increasing the
chances of parties to the political process agreeing to some kind of power-
sharing compromise. In other words, if incapable of capturing the whole,
actors are more likely to put aside their totalizing ambitions. If this really is
a key to democracy's possibility, of course, it means that democratization is
less the product of ancient civilizational dispositions than it is the contingent and creative outcome of contemporary pluralist impasses (*cf*. Przeworski
1988).

One commonly cited antecedent for the pluralist model of democratization is Max Weber's and Marc Bloch's description of the four-cornered contest between kings, feudal lords, town dwellers, and the Church in Western
Europe from the eleventh to the fourteenth centuries (Bloch 1961, Weber
1978: 1082–88). These models explain that by the late medieval period no
single estate was capable of effectively dominating the others. The resulting

standoff led to the great compromise embodied in the *Ständestaat* ("state of estates"), whereby the aristocracy, the bourgeoisie, and the Church pledged allegiance to the monarchy in exchange for being granted powers and liberties of their own. These included a degree of autonomy in one's own affairs and limited representation in a jointly managed, but not yet truly democratic, government (Poggi 1990: 9–51, *cf.* Lipset 1960: 88–89).

Writing on the dynamics of European democratization in a different historical period, Jürgen Habermas (1989 [1962]) has largely accepted the premises of the pluralist model. But he has also emphasized that, in addition to structural countervalences and great political compromises, democratization needs something more specifically cultural. In particular, it requires a public sphere and a participatory culture that encourage citizen participation in discussions of matters of shared interest. In the eighteenth century, Habermas observes, Western Europeans used coffee houses, newspapers, literary clubs, and other social forums to develop an incipient sense of themselves as a public with a right to speak about common concerns. Over the course of the nineteenth and twentieth centuries, these civic precedents were scaled up into general frameworks for citizen participation in state and society.

As has been widely observed (Calhoun 1992), the Habermasian model overlooked the extensive restrictions placed on the access of certain groups (women, the poor, ethnic and religious minorities) to the public sphere in this early period. The model was also silent on the way in which European frameworks of civility and participation periodically broke down, giving rise to the class and religious violence with which modern European history has been blighted. Despite these omissions, literature on the public sphere has provided a useful reminder that the social preconditions for democratization include not just countervailing powers (although these are important too), but a culture that embraces pluralism and elaborates the terms for public participation. This insight in turn points toward another; namely, that it is too simple to equate democracy with majority rule alone. Democracy involves not just the relationship of a dominant majority to a subordinate minority, but civil and non-coercive mechanisms for engaging the full variety of identities and interests present in all modern societies (*cf.* Lijphart 1977, Parekh 2000).

There is another way of stating this conclusion more immediately related to the present book's concerns with new media, new leaders, and the prospects for civic pluralism in the contemporary Muslim world. It is that civil society and democratization require not merely the growth of *plurality* in religion and society, but a commitment to engaging that plurality in a civic and pluralist manner. A society or tradition is *plural* where it has developed a high measure of social and cultural differentiation, not least of all as regards ethnicity, religion, gender, ideology, and class. A society or association can be described as *civic pluralist,* however, only where its members renounce any intention of repressing this pluralism, and respond to its challenge in a peaceful and participatory manner (Casanova 1994, Hefner 1998, 2001).

There is nothing inevitable about the transition from a structure of plurality to a culture of civic pluralism. European history provides numerous painful reminders of the fact that a plurality of groupings and interests can give rise not to democratic pluralism but to struggles to capture the state and unleash programs of ethno-cultural cleansing. New technologies of communication have a similarly double-edged potential. In his famous essay on the origins of nationalism, Benedict Anderson observed that newspaper reading among nineteenth-century Europeans helped to foster a sense of simultaneity and, ultimately, nationhood (1991: 37–46). In this case, then, new media promoted symmetrical patterns of participation and identification. However, far more than Anderson was aware (*cf.* van der Veer 1994), modern communications and associations can also be used to exclude minorities and promote public cultures that are anything but civil democratic (*cf.* Hefner 2001, Keane 1996: 10).

It is just such a contest over pluralism and the terms of public participation that is raging in the Muslim world today. As Eickelman and Piscatori (1996) have observed, in the 1970s and 1980s mass education and urbanization combined with new communications and organizations to pluralize religious authority and heighten contests over the meaning and social relevance of Islam. The seeds of pluralization and contestation had been sown earlier with the great movements of religious reformation that swept the Muslim world in the nineteenth and early twentieth centuries. However, in the 1970s and 1980s the process took a new turn. As Jon Anderson has put it (this volume), drawing on Eickelman's work, in those years new technologies of communications intersected with "the rising curve of expanded education . . . giving unprecedented access to the texts of Islam and opening interpretation to techniques outside the traditional frameworks of *madrasa* training." The classically educated scholars (*'ulama*), who long dominated the religious tradition, awoke to face a host of new challengers, including secularly educated new Muslim intellectuals, independent preachers, Internet Islamists, and other beneficiaries of new technologies and organizations.

The question these events pose, and which the present chapter addresses, concerns the prospects that this growing *plurality* of groupings might give rise to a *civic pluralism* that accepts and legitimates this diversity and, from there, goes on to develop public institutions for its peaceful regulation. Clearly, the fragmentation of religious authority in the Muslim world is creating "multiple centers of power and contenders for authority" and an "intricate politics of compromise and give-and-take" (Eickelman and Piscatori 1996: 132, 134). What remains to be seen is whether the new plurality can be "scaled up" (Evans 1996, Hefner 2001) into a stable and inclusive pluralism.

The case through which I want to explore this question is that of the *Laskar Jihad* or Jihad paramilitaries in contemporary Indonesia. The Laskar Jihad is or, as of October 15, 2002, *was* the paramilitary wing of a larger *jihadi* organization known as the Communication Forum of the Followers of the Sunna and the Community of the Prophet or FKAWJ (*Forum Komunikasi Ahlu Sunnah wal-Jamaah*). Founded in Solo, Central Java, on February 14, 1998, just prior to the collapse of the Suharto regime (1966–May 1998), the FKAWJ burst into national prominence in early 2000, when it defied Indonesia's president and sent *jihadi* paramilitaries to fight against Christians in the troubled provinces of Maluku and North Maluku in eastern Indonesia. From early 2000 to October 2002, the paramilitary fielded some 10,000 armed fighters in Maluku and on the nearby island of Sulawesi. At its peak, the FKAWJ claimed 40,000 members and several hundred thousand supporters. These and other activities eventually led the U.S. State Department to charge that the Laskar Jihad had ties to Osama bin Laden's al-Qaʿida. When terrorists blew up a nightclub for foreign tourists in Kuta, Bali, on October 12, 2002, killing some 200 people, analysts were quick to point the finger of suspicion at the Laskar Jihad.

The Laskar Jihad leadership has consistently denied any connection to al-Qaʿida and insisted that its political concerns were exclusively domestic. Muslims make up 88 percent of Indonesia's 215 million people; Christians comprise about 9 percent. In the Maluku region, however, Muslims and Christians are roughly equal in number. In the late 1990s fighting between the two communities gave rise to horrifying incidents of mass slaughter. In 1999, Muslim civilians were on the receiving end of some of the worst of this violence. The FKAWJ claimed at the time that its aim in establishing the Laskar Jihad paramilitary was to defend Muslims from Christian paramilitaries that the government seemed unable to contain.

In interviews I conducted in July–August 2000 and 2001, however, FKAWJ leaders openly admitted that their paramilitary had an additional aim: to drive President Abdurrahman Wahid from power. Before becoming president in October 1999, Wahid was known as a pro-democracy Muslim and the leader of the world's largest Muslim association, the Nahdlatul Ulama ("renaissance of religious scholars"; see Barton 2002, Feillard 1995). The FKAWJ and Laskar Jihad bitterly opposed Wahid's tenure as president, however, on the grounds that he refused to implement Islamic law, had proposed to lift the ban on the Communist Party, and was considering establishing diplomatic relations with Israel. In the eyes of the Laskar Jihad leadership, these actions marked Wahid as no less than an apostate and communist.

From the perspective of new media and the Muslim world's public sphere, the Laskar Jihad is of special interest for several reasons. First, the Laskar Jihad relied heavily on new communications technologies that became broadly available across Indonesia in the 1990s. This began with the fax machine and new software programs for desktop publishing in the early 1990s, but quickly came to include the Internet, which was introduced into large Indonesian cities in late 1997 and early 1998. No mass organization in Indonesia has relied more heavily on these technologies to coordinate its operations.

Second, the Laskar Jihad utilized these new technologies in combination with conventional media to overcome the disadvantages it faced relative to Indonesia's larger and more moderate Muslim groupings. As in Jenny B. White's (1999) discussion of Turkish Islamists, the combination of abstract, electronic communication with face-to-face mobilization extended the Laskar Jihad's appeals well beyond what would have been possible using web-based or face-to-face communication alone.

Finally, the Laskar Jihad phenomenon illustrates that the growing plurality in Muslim society does not necessarily guarantee civic pluralism or democracy. Indeed, the example suggests that the new media may at times work to the benefit of absolutist *jihadis* more than moderates. In the Indonesian case, the country's huge, mainstream Muslim associations, the Nahdlatul Ulama (35 million members) and the Muhammdiyah (25 million), were slow to take advantage of the new communications technologies. Part of the reason for the lag is political. Both bodies are, first and foremost, social-welfare and educational organizations, not ideologically cohesive parties dedicated to the transformation of Indonesian society. By contrast, the Laskar Jihad was a vanguard organization dedicated to specific political goals and willing to use whatever was required to achieve them.

Notwithstanding its media savvy and mobilizational skills, the Laskar Jihad suffered from a critical vulnerability, one that became glaringly apparent in the aftermath of the Bali bombings in October 2002. Three days after the bombings, the Laskar Jihad was suddenly and unceremoniously dissolved. Its parent organization, the FKAWJ, survives, but its future is cloudy. This unexpected outcome reminds us that, to understand the impact of new media on Muslim (or any other) politics, we have to situate them in a broader political economy of alliance, mobilization, and countervailing powers. Having done so, we can then assess the capacity of different groupings to "scale up" their influence into "solidary ties and social action on a scale that is politically and economically efficacious," not least of all against political rivals (Evans 1996: 1124). The transformative alliances that result from these initiatives are a key to understanding the impact of new media on pluralism and civility in the Muslim world.

PLURALIZATION AND CONTESTATION

Although the Communication Forum of the Followers of the Sunna and the Community of the Prophet (FKAWJ) was officially established only in February 1998, its origins go back to the great pluralization and contestation in the Muslim community during the final years of President Suharto's "New Order" regime (1966–1998). Over the course of the New Order period, Indonesia's urban population grew from less than 20 percent of the population to 35 percent today. Between 1965 and the early 1990s, the number of young adults in Indonesia with basic literacy skills rose from 40 percent to 90 percent (Jones and Manning 1992). The increase in the numbers of people completing senior high school was equally dramatic, rising from 4 percent in 1970 to more than 30 percent in 1990 (Hull and Jones 1994). This educational expansion was accompanied by the development of a new, urban, Muslim middle class. Comprising about 15 percent of the total population, the new middle class became the trendsetter in new religious media, new styles of religious education, and new ideas on Islam, state, and society.

New religious organizations and mobilizations were, of course, common across the Muslim world in the 1970s and 1980s (Eickelman and Piscatori 1996: 71, Kepel 2002). What was unusual about the development in Indonesia, however, was that the dominant streams in the resurgence were moderate, not politically radical. Several of the most distinguished new Muslim leaders were educated in the United States. In addition, the two most prominent Muslim leaders of the 1980s and early 1990s, Nurcholish Madjid (a former leader of the Muslim Students Association, or HMI) and Abdurrahman Wahid of the traditionalist Nahdlatul Ulama (NU; see Barton 2002, Hefner 2000), were outspoken supporters of religious pluralism, Western-style democracy, and heightened participation by women. The combination of higher education, a growing middle class, economic expansion, and—not insignificantly—state controls on radical Islamism seemed to give a comparative advantage to moderate Muslims.

Over time, however, the Suharto regime responded to the resurgence in a way that weakened the influence of moderates and worked to the advantage of hard-line conservatives. Since coming to power in early 1966, the New Order regime had strictly enforced regulations requiring that all citizens profess one of five state-sanctioned religions (Islam, Protestantism, Catholicism, Hinduism, or Buddhism). Students received two hours of religious instruction weekly from grade school up through their college years. State-sponsored programs of mosque building and religious proselytization (known from the Arabic as *dakwah*, or "appeal") introduced Islamic activities into neighborhoods previously indifferent or even hostile to Islamic piety. In its early years the New Order regime hoped to use these programs to inoculate the public from the perceived threats of Marxism and Western liberalism. The Suharto regime was determined that these *cultural* programs did not lead to the revival of an Islamic *political* movement. But its policies on Islam were soon to have unintended effects.

By the mid-1980s, ethnographic reports made clear that many former bastions of secular nationalism, especially in Java, which has half of the country's population, were being swept by the Islamic revival (Hefner 1987).

In the 1950s, secular nationalists, Western-style democrats, army techno-crats, and socialists were united in their opposition to any form of Islamic governance. From the late 1980s on, however, the popularity of secular nationalist ideals among the political and military elite declined significantly. Although, along with Turkey (see Göle 1996), Indonesia once had the larg-est movement for a secular or multiconfessional politics within the Muslim world, after the political violence of 1965–1966, Indonesia's conservative nationalist elite was uninterested in creating a mass-based movement com-parable to Turkey's Kemalism. Their reluctance reflected their internal ideo-logical divisions and the fact that they were more interested in containing civil society than they were in promoting any form of popular mobilization, even if conservative.

As the Islamic resurgence gathered momentum, the Suharto regime responded by changing tack, moving from its earlier policy of repression to systematic co-optation. The target of the regime's outreach changed over time. At first the regime attempted to co-opt moderate Muslims like Abdur-rahman Wahid of Nahdlatul Ulama and Amien Rais of the Muhammadi-yah. When these leaders continued to demand political reforms, however, the regime directed its appeals to the radical margins. From 1993 to 1995, Suharto intermediaries conducted a series of secret meetings with the lead-ership of the hard-line wing of the modernist Islamic community, in particu-lar with groups regarded as the ancestors of today's radical groupings: the Indonesian Council for Islamic Predication (DDII) and the Indonesian Com-mittee for Solidarity with the Islamic World (KISDI). The DDII leadership had once figured among Suharto's fiercest critics; the KISDI leadership had always been more accommodating. By 1994–1995, however, the DDII had moved from the ranks of the regime's critics to join with KISDI and became one of its most ardent defenders (Hefner 2000).

It was during these years, too, that regime spokespersons and their con-servative Islamist allies began to speak jointly of an international conspiracy of Christians and Jews against Indonesia. It was alleged that European and American criticism of Indonesia's human rights record in the occupied prov-ince of East Timor was all part of this anti-Islamic master plan; so too was Indonesia's growing democracy movement (Hefner 2000). The message was soon to be embraced by others once marginal to the Muslim mainstream.

JAFAR UMAR THALIB AND RADICAL SALAFISM

The Communication Forum of the Followers of the Sunna and the Community of the Prophet (FKAWJ) and its paramilitary wing, the Laskar Jihad, have their roots in a theologically conservative movement founded in the early 1990s by a young (born December 1961) Indonesian of Hadrami-

Arab and Madurese parentage, Jafar Umar Thalib. Thalib identifies his followers as "Salafy" (in Arabic, *Salafiya*), a reference to a long-established movement that aims to purify Islam by taking as its model the first generations of followers of the Prophet Muhammad (Shahin 1995). However, in the form promoted by Thalib, the movement is better described as neo-Salafy, because it emphasizes extreme political views not associated with earlier variants of Salafism, including those still popular in Saudi Arabia. One such emphasis is the firm belief that the United States and Israel are leading a worldwide conspiracy to destroy Islam, and that the response by Muslims to this effort must be armed *jihad*.

Thalib began his career studying in a conservative modernist religious school in Bangil, East Java, in 1981. Upset by Suharto policies on Islam and impatient with the apolitical nature of his instruction, he soon traveled to Jakarta to study at the Saudi-sponsored Institute for Islamic and Arabic Studies. In the capital, Thalib became active in student groups opposed to Suharto policies, which at that time included efforts to force all Muslim groups to accept the state's "Five Principles" (*Pancasila*) rather than Islam as their ideological foundation. Awarded a scholarship by the Indonesian Council for Islamic Predication (DDII), Jafar traveled in 1986 to Saudi Arabia to study with, among others, two well-known Wahhabi scholars, Muhammad Nasr al-Din al-Albani and 'Abd al-'Aziz 'Abd Allah bin Baz (Hasan 2001: 6). The DDII was formerly the official representative in Indonesia of the Saudi-based Muslim World League (Rabitat al-'Alam al-Islami, founded 1962). In my interviews with him, Thalib acknowledged that, though he took his education seriously, he was restless because his lessons kept him from other Muslim struggles. It was not long before he left for Afghanistan in 1987, once again under the auspices of the Saudi-sponsored Muslim World League. In Afghanistan, he met briefly with Osama bin Laden. However, Thalib opted to join with a faction of the *mujahidin* with ties to a strict Salafy organization known as the Jam'at al-Da'wa ila al-Qur'an wa-Ahl-i Hadith. This Saudi-based organization is famous for, among other things, instructing its followers that rulers who fail to implement Islamic law are apostates and must be overthrown.

In 1989, Thalib returned to Indonesia, accepting a teaching post at a Salafy school in Salatiga, central Java, a two-hour car drive northeast of Yogyakarta. Eager to further his Salafy education, he traveled back to Yemen in 1990, where he studied with a Yemeni teacher, Muqbil ibn Hadi al-Wad'i, well known for his ties to Wahhabi conservatives in Saudi Arabia. In 1993, Thalib came back to Indonesia. Now, for the first time, he directed his attention away from small-town religious schools to student circles in the nearby university town of Yogyakarta. In 1994 he founded a religious school for young adults known as the Jama'ah Ihya al-Sunnah, twelve miles north of Yogyakarta in the subdistrict of Kaliurang. According to Muslim activists I interviewed in 1999, the land on which Thalib founded his religious school was donated to his organization by a prominent army retiree, who had settled in the Yogyakarta region in the late 1980s. According to these reports, the officer met in 1993 with several other military retirees residing in the province in an attempt to bolster the efforts of conservative Islamists against what they described as growing "communist" influences in Yogyakarta's Muslim community. In an interview with me in August 2001, Thalib denied that military retirees had helped him to acquire the land for his school. Nonetheless, he acknowledged that one of his school's aims was indeed to combat "secular," "liberal," and "communist" influences among Yogyakarta's Muslims.

During these early years, however, Thalib was better known for his emphasis on the re-Islamization of society rather than any direct effort at political mobilization. He made a point of distancing himself from activists associated with the Islamic State of Indonesia (NII) movement, many of whom had recently relocated from West Java to Yogyakarta. Although Thalib criticized the democracy movement as "Christian-dominated" and "un-Islamic," he and his followers saw their primary mission as the re-Islamization of society from below. By 1996, when I first encountered members of the group, Thalib's followers were famous throughout the city for their distinctive garb and exclusive social behavior. Although women are underrepresented in the organization, they attract special attention when out in public because of their full-bodied black *hijab* and facial veil (which may or may not have slits for the eyes). As with the patriarchal Islamists whom Olivier Roy calls "neofundamentalist" (1994: 75–89), women are barred from leadership roles in the movement and, once married, are discouraged from working outside the home. Even at home, any socializing with unrelated males is strictly forbidden. Women offer snacks to their husband's male guests by handing both items to their husband while otherwise remaining behind thick cloth curtains. Male associates grow long beards, and wear white turbans, loose-fitting tunics, and baggy trousers of a broadly South Asian variety. Males, but not women, are enjoined to perform all five daily prayers in congregation.

In these early years, what was most distinctive about Thalib's proselytization was that it was aimed not at the whole Muslim community but at university students in the exact sciences, computer science, and professions. Many were at first recruited from among the discussion groups or *halaqah* popular among students in these disciplines. Students from these fields, Thalib told me, are better able to appreciate the "precision" of Islamic law than are those in the social sciences and humanities. Education in the latter fields leaves individuals "only more confused." For this reason, Thalib insisted that it is best to avoid taking courses in these topics entirely. From the beginning of his career, Thalib's proselytization was also distinctive in the way in which it combined face-to-face preaching with the new and more anonymous technologies of electronic publishing and, from late 1997 on, the Internet.

In his sermons and public lectures, Thalib decries the failures of secular nationalism and the perfidy of infidels (especially Christians), and calls repeatedly and passionately for Muslims to wage unceasing *jihad* against the infidel. For Thalib and other neo-Salafis, *jihad* is understood in a literal military sense, and is regarded as a duty as incumbent on male Muslims as the annual fast or daily prayers. The purpose of *jihad* is to cleanse society of un-Islamic influences and to bring God's law into daily life. *Jihad* also insures that unbelievers understand that their proper status in society must be that of protected minorities (*dhimmi*). A concept from classical Islamic politics (An-Na'im 1990: 88–91), dhimmihood stipulates that non-Muslims not be allowed to exercise authority over Muslims in any field. Unlike the great majority of Indonesia's Muslim leaders, then, Thalib emphasizes that the equal citizenship upheld by the constitution is antithetical to Islam. So too is the idea of democracy, which Thalib told me is a Western import intended to destroy Islam from within.

MEDIA ISLAM

More than anything else, Thalib's reliance on new communications technologies allowed him to establish a foothold in Yogyakarta's highly competitive Islamic religious market and, from there, catapult himself into a position of national leadership. Although Yogyakarta is regarded as Indonesia's leading university town and has a relatively liberal atmosphere, the city's Muslim organizations have long had a reputation for resisting out-of-town interlopers. The two largest organizations are the Muhammadiyah and the Nahdlatul Ulama. With some 25 million followers, the Muhammadiyah has one of its two national headquarters in the city, where it was founded in 1912 (Peacock 1978). The association is modernist in theological orientation, and well known for its efficiently run and centrally coordinated social-welfare activities. Although it claims 35 million followers, the Nahdlatul Ulama is a more loosely organized and fractious federation, theologically "traditionalist" in its commitment to the schools of Islamic law and canonical commentaries (Feillard 1995).

However much they might differ on questions of theology, the Muhammadiyah and Nahdlatul Ulama have long agreed in their commitment to the ideals of Indonesian nationalism. This spirit of nationalism made most of their membership resistant to Thalib's appeals for the imposition of Islamic law and the assertion of Muslim hegemony over non-Muslims. In fact, in the 1990s, Muhammadiyah and NU leaders in Yogyakarta had been at the forefront of those insisting that Islam is compatible with democracy. Some had even openly urged Muslims to join the struggle against Suharto's New Order regime.

The one portion of Yogyakarta's religious scene not dominated by these two great organizations is the city's thirty-plus colleges and universities. Since the late 1980s, Yogyakarta's universities had spawned several of Indonesia's most famous new Islamic movements. Some have been theologically conservative, but others have been pluralist and democratic (see Abdul Aziz et al. 1989). The many university-based Islamic study groups (*halaqah*) active in the city offered Thalib a means to outflank Yogyakarta's Muslim establishment and promote a vision of Islam at variance with that of the moderate mainstream. Thalib gathered a small circle of *halaqah* students around him shortly after his arrival in Yogyakarta in 1993. With the regular turnover in the student population, however, Thalib's following remained small. His Salafy school in Kaliurang had less than 100 students, minuscule by comparison with the NU-linked *pesantren* found to the south of Yogyakarta, which have thousands of students. As one of Thalib's followers told me in 1999, "the problem was that once we left the university, most of us could not stay on near the Ihya al-Sunnah school, because we had to make a living. So after graduation many of our friends would return to their home communities and lose their way, coming under the influence of unbelievers (*kafir*)."

To combat this chronic problem of membership defection and to disseminate his message more broadly, Thalib turned to the new religious media. A year after the founding of the Ihya al-Sunnah school, several of his media-proficient students got together to create *Salafy,* an inexpensive, glossy-covered monthly dedicated to Thalib's militant Salafism. Taking advantage of new desktop-publishing technologies, the staff of *Salafy* did most of the editorial and layout work at their homes or at the Ihya al-Sunnah school. Printing was then out-sourced to a shop in the nearby town of Klaten. After the establishment of the FKAWJ in February 1998, *Salafy* became its official organ.

The establishment of the FKAWJ coincided with two important shifts in Thalib's broader political strategy. First, the move reflected a heightened commitment to political activism, prompted by the crisis of governance into which Indonesia was rapidly descending. As a result of the Asian economic crisis, in late 1997 Indonesia went into severe recession, the worst since the economic ravages of the early 1960s. The economic tumult was soon compounded by a political crisis, putting new wind into the sails of the anti-Suharto democracy movement. Yogyakarta quickly became a stronghold of democratic activism, with a rank-and-file famous for including Christians, Hindus, and Buddhists alongside the Muslim majority. In interviews with me in July–August 2000 and 2001, Laskar Jihad leaders, including Thalib, explained that they felt compelled to become involved in public politics because of what they regarded as the left-wing and secularist bias of the democracy movement. Although Thalib was critical of many Suharto policies, he said that he feared that the president's ouster would usher in a government dominated by Christians, communists, and secularists. Activists close to the FKAWJ told me that military officials had also made contact with Thalib at this time, encouraging him to take action against the political left. Thalib vigorously denies that his actions had anything to do with these visits, although he acknowledges that meetings took place.

The other event with which the formation of the FKAWJ coincided was the movement's increasing reliance on the Internet. It was only in late 1997 that commercial servers made the Internet broadly available in major cities in Java and Sumatra. The net was then extended to urban centers in Kalimantan, Sulawesi, and eastern Indonesia in late 1998. The FKAWJ leadership immediately recognized the mobilizational potential of the new medium. The Internet allowed the *Salafy* staff to maintain editorial and layout operations at the Ihya al-Sunnah school outside Yogyakarta, while more than tripling their staff to include writers from around the country. As Internet technologies became more widely available, the FKAWJ established branch offices in other cities, using the Internet, telephones, and fax machines to coordinate operations.

It was only with the establishment of the Laskar Jihad paramilitary in February 2000, however, that Thalib's followers began to take full advantage of the new communications technology. The founding of the paramilitary was catalyzed by an escalation in fighting between Christians and Muslims in the eastern provinces of Maluku and north Maluku in early 1999. Maluku had been a center of conflict almost two generations earlier, when, during the war for independence (1945–1949), some in the—at that time—predominantly Christian province tried to declare their independence from the majority-Muslim republic. With the great economic shifts of the New Order era, immigration transformed the province's demographic profile. Muslims came to comprise half of the population, and the hardworking immigrants quickly dominated the economy. Combined with Suharto's shift toward a pro-Islamist policy, these changes caused deep unrest among Maluku's once dominant Christian population.

Some political analysts have argued that the violence in Maluku was deliberately inflamed by *ancien régime* provocateurs determined to use ethno-religious violence to scuttle the democracy movement, undermine Christian-Muslim unity, and turn back calls to remove the armed forces from politics (Aditjondro 2000). While acts of provocation by outsiders do indeed appear to have contributed to the violence (ICG 2002a), the fact remains that Christian Malukans, especially those from the criminal gangs known as *preman,* were responsible for some of the worst violence during the conflict's first year (1999–2000). Alarmed by Muslim losses, hard-liners in Jakarta called for a *jihad,* claiming the fighting was a Western conspiracy to dismember Indonesia. The radicals' appeals were quickly silenced by mainstream Muslims, however, who demanded that the conflict be resolved in accordance with nationalist principles and the rule of law.

With the election of Abdurrahman Wahid to the presidency in October 1999, however, the campaign for *jihad* in Maluku gained new momentum.

Wahid was deeply unpopular among the armed forces leadership because of his support for efforts to curb military power. As Wahid told me in an interview in November 1999, he was concerned that some in the armed forces might use the Maluku violence to reassert the military's right to involve itself in politics. Faced with a hostile military command, Wahid appealed to Christians and Muslims in Maluku to settle their differences peacefully and on their own. The fact that the Christian forces in 1999 still had the upper hand and had committed atrocities against Muslim civilians, however, convinced hard-line Muslims that the real reason for Wahid's reluctance to commit troops was his sympathy for the Christian side.

SCALING UNCIVIL SOCIETY

It was in this context of growing violence and disunity among political elites (national and local) that the FKAWJ established its paramilitary wing, the Laskar Jihad, in February 2000. Although Thalib has repeatedly denied the claim, two men once active in his organization told me in July 2000 that Thalib, before establishing the paramilitary, held secret meetings with representatives from a faction of the armed forces unhappy with the Wahid presidency and determined to use the Malukan crisis to drive him from power. Western intelligence reports claim that army officers transferred $9.3 million to the militant group during 2000 (Huang 2002). In interviews with me in August 2001, Thalib explained that he felt compelled to act because President Wahid was an apostate and a "communist." Earlier, in late 1999 and early 2000, Thalib had secured legal pronouncements (*fatwas*) from Salafy *muftis* in Saudi Arabia and Yemen sanctioning *jihad* in Maluku. In April 2000, a leading Salafy *mufti* in Medina, Muhammad ibn Hadi al-Madkhali, also issued a *fatwa* declaring that President Wahid's prohibition of *jihad* in Maluku was contrary to Islamic law (Hasan 2001: 17).

With these resources in hand, the Laskar Jihad leadership combined conventional mobilization techniques with new communications technology to catapult their once-fringe movement to national prominence. In April 2000, Laskar Jihad supporters marched outside the presidential palace, brandishing swords and appealing to able-bodied males to join the *jihad* in Maluku. This brazen show of force encountered no opposition from security officials. A few weeks later, the Laskar Jihad force traveled to the port city of Surabaya in eastern Java. Despite the fact that the president, the minister of defense, and the governor of Maluku all appealed to security officials to stop the militia from coming, the convoy did not encounter a single security checkpoint. Indeed, the militants were given military escorts along portions of their route. In the port of Surabaya, the fighters boarded state-owned ferries for Maluku. According to interviews I conducted with Laskar Jihad volunteers from Yogyakarta, upon their arrival in Maluku, the recruits were taken into the city and given weapons by soldiers under the command of anti-Wahid army officers. Interviews that I conducted with student activists involved in the Maluku mobilization during July 2000 indicated that a Jakarta businessman with close ties to ex-president Suharto coordinated a vast flow of funds and arms to the *jihad* forces. The flow of aid had a powerful impact. By August 2000, the Christian paramilitaries in Maluku were suffering severe losses, including the mass slaughter of 500 Christian villagers in a portion of north Maluku where atrocities had earlier been committed against Muslims (Tomagola 2000).

Coincident with the *jihad* campaign in Maluku, the Laskar Jihad established a web site at <www.laskarjihad.org>, featuring photo galleries of alleged Christian atrocities, daily news reports on the fighting, and Indonesian- and English-language commentaries on the religious significance of *jihad*. During its first year-and-a-half of operation, <www.laskarjihad.org> also featured stories and links to the web sites of other *jihadi* groups around the world, including those in Chechnya, Kashmir, and Afghanistan. Curiously, however, after September 11, 2001, and U.S. administration accusations that the Laskar Jihad had ties to al-Qaʿida, these international links were quietly removed from the site.

Another change in the content of the Laskar Jihad web site occurred after the organization's first national congress in Jakarta, on May 13–19, 2002. Up to this time, the site had featured articles describing the Maluku conflict as having been instigated by Jews, Christians, and the United States. After May 2002, accusations of international conspiracy did not disappear entirely from the web site. But the message was featured far less prominently than reports that—in a language that mimicked armed forces' appeals for national unity—accused the Christian Malukans of wanting to destroy the unity and integrity (*persatuan dan kesatuan*) of Indonesia by establishing a Republic of South Maluku. These changes provided at least suggestive confirmation of reports I was receiving from Muslim activists in Yogyakarta: that elite supporters of the Laskar Jihad were pressuring the paramilitary to sever its ties to international *jihadis* and tone down its attacks on the United States.

Since the organization was first established, the Laskar Jihad leadership demonstrated great skill at linking its Internet resources to other communications media. It used the Internet to send daily reports on the Maluku violence to each of some 24 Laskar Jihad branch offices around the country. Each bureau downloaded the messages, which were already laid out in a desktop-publishing format. These were then printed out on a single, two-sided sheet of paper, to create a bulletin with the masthead "Maluku Today" (*Maluku Hari Ini*). The Laskar Jihad emblem, with its open-paged Qur'an set above two crossed swords is featured to the left of the masthead. Information on the Laskar Jihad web site, e-mail address, bank account (for donations), and local branch address are featured on the bottom of the back page. At the height of their operation, Laskar Jihad officials in branch offices gave young male volunteers thousands of copies of the bulletin to distribute to the public. Clad in the *jihadis'* trademark tunic, trousers, and turban, the volunteers positioned themselves at stoplights in cities across Indonesia. They distributed the bulletin for free, but with the understanding (conveyed in a none-too-subtle fashion by passing a bucket in front of car windows) that donations to the Maluku campaign were welcome. The more senior among the volunteers also sold copies of the monthly *Salafy,* as well as a large, sixteen-page weekly known simply as *Buletin Laskar Jihad Ahlus Sunnah wal Jama'ah.* Unlike *Maluku Today,* the large-layout *Buletin* features color photos and advertisements.

Although the largest of the groups sponsoring *jihadi* fighters in Maluku, Laskar Jihad was not alone in the effort. Other hard-line groups, including most notably the Islamic Defenders Front (*Front Pembela Islam* or FPI) and the Indonesian Council of Jihad Fighters (*Majelis Mujahidin Indonesia*) dispatched fighters too. The Laskar Jihad contingent in Maluku, however, was ten times the size of its nearest competitor, the Council of Jihad Fighters—a fact that Council members acknowledged in interviews during July 2001. For most of 2000 and 2001, the Laskar Jihad stationed 2000 fighters in the field, rotating individuals out of the province every four to six months. While in the field, all but the senior command lived in the homes of ordinary Muslims, an arrangement intended to facilitate Salafy proselytization. According to interviews I conducted in 2000 and 2001 with Muslim Malukans residing in Yogyakarta, the military support provided by the Laskar Jihad was at first well received. Local Muslims recognized that the outsiders helped to shift the balance of the war in the Muslim favor. However, Malukan Muslims have long been famous for being casual about daily prayer, fasting, and the consumption of alcohol. Laskar Jihad opposition to these infractions led to widespread tensions and, on a few occasions, physical clashes.

The success of the Laskar's military campaign eventually revealed a critical tactical vulnerability. In March 2001, a Laskar Jihad officer in Maluku was accused of having sex outside marriage. The condemned man acknowledged his guilt and accepted the sentence Thalib pronounced against him, death by stoning (*rajam*). The death sentence was carried out. A few weeks later, Thalib was arrested by the police on charges of incitement to violence and murder. Three weeks later, after conservative Muslim politicians rallied to his defense, Thalib was released from custody, although the charges against him were never resolved.

By March of 2002, momentum for a peace accord in Maluku was growing. A report released by the Brussels-based International Crisis Group (ICG 2002a) stated that there were indications that some in the armed forces were attempting to prolong the conflict because of the lucrative income it generated. In late July 2001, however, President Wahid had been removed from power, and the new president, Megawati Sukarnoputri, was known to have cordial ties with the senior military command. Megawati made clear that she had no interest in supporting further investigations into alleged human rights abuses by the military. With Wahid out of the way, pressures for a peace deal in Maluku grew, and Christian and Muslim leaders signed an accord in April 2002.

Thalib showed that, whatever his ties, he was no simple puppet of the military, and quickly went public with his opposition to the peace plan. In early May 2002, he called on his supporters to defy the government and continue the *jihad* against "Christian separatists." In the months preceding this declaration, Thalib had also worked furiously to extend the reach of his paramilitary to new fronts. In August 2001, he dispatched 1000 fighters to Poso, Central Sulawesi, an area where, like Maluku, a native Christian population had done battle with Muslim immigrants. In December 2001, Thalib sent a smaller team of Laskar Jihad trainers to the province of West Papua, where some of the local population, which is non-Muslim, was militating for independence. On February 14, 2002, Thalib traveled to Aceh, another province plagued by secessionist violence, where he formalized the opening of a branch of the FKAWJ. Even conservative Muslim leaders in the troubled province denounced Thalib as a proxy for hard-line elements in the armed forces.

In mid-May 2002, Thalib was again arrested and charged with incitement to violence. Police officials explained that Thalib's arrest was sparked by a speech he gave on a Muslim-owned radio station in Maluku, in which he appealed to Muslims to defy the peace accord and continue the battle against Christians. Thalib's arrest provoked a flurry of demonstrations by his supporters across the country. Conservative Islamists, and some independent journalists, accused the government of arresting Thalib so as to create the impression that it supported the U.S.-led campaign against terrorism. A religious conservative and the leader of the country's largest Muslim party, Vice President Hamzah Haz defied President Megawati and visited Thalib in prison, declaring that he too felt the arrest was politically motivated.

The legal case against Thalib was still unresolved when, on October 12, 2002, someone planted two bombs outside a popular tourist nightspot in Kuta, Bali, killing 200 people, most of them young foreigners. Some in the conservative Muslim press denounced the attack as a provocation instigated by the United States to discredit Indonesia as a haven for international terrorism. A week later (and at the time of this writing), however, the climate of opinion in the mainstream Muslim community seemed to be shifting. Like many of their non-Muslim counterparts, most Muslims in Indonesia are bitterly opposed to the American administration's policies with regard to Israel-Palestine and Iraq. However, mainstream Muslims were also shocked by the slaughter in Bali and by the idea that such actions might have any place in Islam. They were also concerned that the calamity might send the country into even deeper political and economic crisis. Spurred by this sentiment, on October 19 the government announced stern measures against organizations and individuals suspected of ties to international terrorism.

Three days after the bombing and before the government put these new regulations into effect, Laskar Jihad officials dissolved their paramilitary, shut down their offices, and closed their site on the World Wide Web. The leadership claimed that the measures had been planned since September and were in no way related to the bombing in Bali. My Muslim contacts in Yogyakarta confirmed that the dissolution of the paramilitary had indeed been under discussion in early September. However, these reports add that many Laskar Jihad officers were actually opposed to dissolving their organization, but were overruled by Thalib, who was said to be under great pressure from former supporters in the military and among military retirees.

The irony to Laskar Jihad's dissolution is that, of the two domestic organizations identified as possible suspects in the Bali bombings, the Laskar Jihad is the least likely to have been in any way involved. Although when I first interviewed high ranking Laskar Jihad leaders in August 2000 they expressed sympathy for Osama bin Laden, Thalib himself was more cautious. In an interview, he reminded me that he had opted not to work with bin Laden's forces when in Afghanistan in the 1980s. He also expressed disdain for bin Laden's understanding of Islam, and took exception to bin Laden's effort to overthrow the Saudi government.

By contrast, Abu Bakar Ba'asyir, the spiritual leader of the other *jihadi* grouping regarded as a possible suspect in the Bali bombings (the Council of Indonesian Jihad fighters, a group with ties to the *Jemaah Islamiyah* and, possibly, al-Qa'ida; see ICG 2002b), has expressed strong support for bin Laden and the attacks on the United States. He did so once again in the course of a long-distance interview he granted me (conducted with the help of a local field assistant) on May 19, 2002. Although Ba'asyir denied involvement in any acts of violence, he acknowledged, with a beguiling smile, that some among his students have been "naughty" (*nakal*) and may have had something to do with "certain actions" in Malaysia and the Philippines. These and other comments provide no indication one way or another of Abu Bakar Ba'syir's involvement in the Bali bombings. Leaving the question of the bombings aside, however, Ba'asyir's statements and his international ties place him under a darker cloud of suspicion than Jafar Umar Thalib.

Unlike Thalib's Laskar Jihad, Ba'asyir's Council of Jihad Fighters had always kept its distance from armed forces officials, and does not appear to have enjoyed the support of either active or retired members of the military. Indeed, in Yogyakarta, it is an open secret that police and army officials despise the Council, which they associate with the Darul Islam, an Islamist movement against which the military did battle in the 1950s (van Dijk 1981).

In our discussions, Thalib was always careful to distinguish his organization from Ba'asyir's Council. Just like many in the armed forces, Thalib characterized the latter as a Darul Islam front, and described Darul Islam itself as a rebellion that had betrayed the Indonesian nation.

The irony here is that it is precisely because the Laskar Jihad enjoyed a close relationship with some active and retired army officials that, when pressure grew on the Indonesian government to take action against Islamist radicals, the organization was more vulnerable than the rival Council of Jihad Fighters. Elite support and the skillful use of new media technologies had allowed the Laskar Jihad to outflank Indonesia's mainstream Muslim organizations. In so doing, the Laskar Jihad had challenged their moral vision and scaled up a militantly anti-Christian and anti-pluralist interpretation of Islam. Unfortunately for the Laskar Jihad, their radical message, dispersed organization, and, perhaps most important, ties to elite supporters, made them all the more vulnerable to the changing winds of elite politics. Media savvy alone could not save them when some in the shadowy coalition of which they had been a part concluded that the Laskar Jihad had become a political liability.

CONCLUSION

In the last half of the Suharto era, the expansion of education, new media, and a new Muslim leadership brought about a remarkable pluralization of the country's Muslim community. Indonesia also witnessed a movement for a civic-pluralist reorientation of Muslim politics that, after contemporary Iran, was arguably the Muslim world's most vibrant. The democracy movement that toppled President Suharto in May 1998 was a multireligious coalition that included Christians and secular nationalists as well as Muslims in its ranks. Among its core theorists, however, was a diverse group of intellectuals interested in devising Islamic grounds for pluralism, democracy, and civil tolerance (see Abdillah 1997, Barton 2002, Hefner 2000).

Although secular-minded theorists may not recognize its importance, a key feature of Muslim politics is that political initiatives must be justified in relation to divine injunctions and religious commentaries. The role of Qur'an and Sunna-based rationales in Muslim politics is so decisive that the scaling up required to develop a civic-pluralist politics must involve not only countervailing powers and a social capital of civil society groupings, but a sustained enunciation of the religious grounds for pluralism and democracy. Indonesia in the 1990s was unusual in that it had an efflorescence of such discourses. Moreover, unlike related efforts in Egypt, Morocco, or Syria, the reorientation of Muslim politics wasn't just the work of a few intellectuals or tiny civil society organizations. On the contrary, the initiative showed one of the key features that political theorists like O'Donnell and Schmitter identify as necessary for a transition from authoritarian rule: a coalitional structure linking "exemplary individuals" to mass-based organizations in society (1986: 48–56). By these twin measures of intellectual vitality and mass base, Indonesia in the late 1990s was one of the most vibrant centers for new Muslim political thinking the modern world has seen.

Sadly, Indonesian Muslims may never get credit for this achievement because their movement to create a civic-pluralist Muslim politics was quickly overtaken by events on the ground. The ethnic and religious violence in Maluku, in particular, dealt a major blow to their efforts. Part, but only one part, of the answer to the question of how this came to be lies in the fact that the new media and technologies of communication that swept Indonesia in the 1990s were more skillfully exploited by *jihadi* hard-liners than they were civic pluralists. The example provides a sobering reminder that, although new media and mass education are agents of pluralization, they alone cannot guarantee a transition to civic pluralism or democracy.

Just why this is so, just why new media and social pluralism cannot alone generate a culture of civic pluralism, recalls an insight into transitions from authoritarian rule offered a few years ago by the California political sociologist Peter Evans (1996). Evans observed that for a transition to succeed it is not enough that there be a vibrant civil society or reform-minded citizenry. For a transition to move forward, civil and democratic precedents in society have to be scaled up into state institutions capable of amplifying and solidifying civil trends in society. When Evans talks of scaling up, the primary thing he has in mind is the social capital of civic associations and citizen networks. As the Indonesian case shows, however, the scaling up to create a civic-pluralist Islam must be cultural and discursive as well. It requires a cultural capital that legitimates pluralism and civility in Islamic terms, and provides religious grounds for challenging those who would deny the plurality of the modern world through the imposition of a totalizing and repressive unitarianism.

As has been the case with pluralism and democratization in the modern West, there is nothing inevitable about the outcome of this transition. The chances of success are greatly enhanced, however, with the development of new media, mass education, and a participatory and plural public sphere. But the process is made even more secure if the broader political economy creates a multiplicity of social powers, making it difficult for any single class, party, ethnicity, or status group to impose its will on the whole. These pluralizing developments in society remain vulnerable, however, if they are not also accompanied by efforts to implement pluralism-defending structures in the state. It is this scaling up from society to the state that has proved especially difficult for Indonesia's moderate Muslims. Their task has been complicated by the preference of some in the political elite, local and national, for making common cause with violent radicals rather than with quietistic moderates.

As the aftermath of the Bali bombings has shown, however, the contest between *jihadi* and moderate Muslims is far from over. Perhaps the greatest advantage enjoyed by the moderates is not simply their numbers, but the depth of their moral opposition to those who would use cruelty and violence in the name of Islam.

WORKS CITED

Abdillah, Masykuri. 1997. *Responses of Indonesian Muslim Intellectuals to the Concept of Democracy (1966–1993)*. Hamburg: Abera Verlag Meyer and Co.

Aditjondro, George. 2000. "The Political Economy of Violence in Maluku Indonesia." *Mundindo* February 27: 1–20.

Anderson, Benedict. 1991. *Imagined Communities: Reflections on the Origin and Spread of Nationalism*. 2nd ed. London: Verso.

An-Na'im, Abdullahi Ahmed. 1990. *Toward an Islamic Reformation: Civil Liberties, Human Rights, and International Law*. Syracuse: Syracuse University Press.

Aziz, Abdul, Imam Tholkhah, and Soetarman, eds. 1989. *Gerakan Islam Kontemporer di Indonesia* (Contemporary Islamic movements in Indonesia). Jakarta: Pustaka Firdaus.

Barton, Greg. 2002. *Gus Dur: The Authorized Biography of Abdurrahman Wahid*. Singapore: Equinox Publishing.

Bloch, Marc. 1961. *Feudal Society*. Chicago: University of Chicago Press.

Calhoun, Craig, ed. 1992. *Habermas and the Public Sphere*. Cambridge, Mass.: MIT Press.

Casanova, José. 1994. *Public Religions in the Modern World*. Chicago: University of Chicago Press.

Dahl, Robert A. 1971. *Polyarchy: Participation and Opposition*. New Haven: Yale University Press.

Dijk, C. van. 1981. *Rebellion Under the Banner of Islam: The Darul Islam in Indonesia*. The Hague: Martinus Nijhoff.

Eickelman, Dale F. 1992. "The Art of Memory: Islamic Education and Its Social Reproduction." In *Comparing Muslim Societies: Knowledge and the State in a World Civilization*, ed. Juan R. I. Cole, pp. 97–132. Ann Arbor: University of Michigan Press.

Eickelman, Dale F., and James Piscatori. 1996. *Muslim Politics*. Princeton: Princeton University Press.

Evans, Peter. 1996. "Government Action, Social Capital and Development: Reviewing the Evidence on Synergy." *World Development* 24 no. 6: 1119–1132.

Feillard, Andrée. 1995. *L'Islam et armée dans l'indonésie contemporaine*. Paris: Cahier d'Archipel 28, Éditions L'Harmattan.

Göle, Nilüfer. 1996. "Authoritarian Secularism and Islamist Politics: The Case of Turkey." In *Civil Society in the Middle East*, vol. 2, ed. Augustus Richard Norton, pp. 17–43. Leiden: E. J. Brill.

Habermas, Jürgen. 1989 (orig. 1962). *The Structural Transformation of the Public Sphere: An Inquiry into a Category of Bourgeois Society*, trans. T. Burger. Cambridge, Mass.: MIT Press.

Hasan, Noorhaidi. 2001. "Between Faith and Politics: The Rise of the Laskar Jihad in the Political Arena of Indonesia." Paper presented at the Third European-Southeast Asian Studies Conference, London, U.K., September 7.

Hefner, Robert W. 1987. "Islamizing Java? Religion and Politics in Rural East Java." *Journal of Asian Studies* 46 no. 3: 533–54.

————. 1998. "On the History and Cross-Cultural Possibility of a Democratic Ideal." In *Democratic Civility: The History and Cross-Cultural Possibility of a Modern Political Ideal,* ed. Robert W. Hefner, pp. 3–49. New Brunswick: Transaction Publishers.

————. 2000. *Civil Islam: Muslims and Democratization in Indonesia.* Princeton: Princeton University Press.

————. 2001. "Introduction: Multiculturalism and Citizenship in Malaysia, Singapore, and Indonesia." In *The Politics of Multiculturalism: Pluralism and Citizenship in Malaysia, Singapore, and Indonesia,* ed. Robert W. Hefner, pp. 3–58. Honolulu: University of Hawaii Press.

Held, David. 1987. *Models of Democracy.* Stanford: Stanford University Press.

Huang, Reyko. 2002. *In the Spotlight: Laskar Jihad.* Washington, D.C.: Center for Defense Information.

Hull, Terence H., and Gavin W. Jones. 1994. "Demographic Perspectives." In *Indonesia's New Order: The Dynamics of Socio-Economic Transformation,* ed. Hall Hill, pp. 123–78. Honolulu: University of Hawaii Press.

ICG. 2002a. "Indonesia: The Search for Peace in Maluku." Brussels: Asia Report no. 31, International Crisis Group.

ICG. 2002b. "Al-Qaeda in Southeast Asia: The Case of the 'Ngruki Network' in Indonesia." Brussels: ICG Asia Briefing, August 8.

Jones, Gavin W., and Chris Manning. 1992. "Labour Force and Employment during the 1980s." In *The Oil Boom and After: Indonesian Economic Policy and Performance in the Suharto Era,* ed. Ann Booth, pp. 363–410. Kuala Lumpur: Oxford University Press.

Keane, John. 1996. *Reflections on Violence.* London: Verso.

Kepel, Gilles. 2002. *Jihad: The Trail of Political Islam.* Cambridge, Mass.: Harvard University Press.

Lijphart, Arend. 1977. *Democracy in Plural Societies: A Comparative Exploration.* New Haven: Yale University Press.

Lipset, Seymour Martin. 1960. *Political Man: The Social Bases of Politics.* Garden City: Doubleday.

O'Donnell, Guillermo, and Philippe C. Schmitter. 1986. *Transitions from Authoritarian Rule: Tentative Conclusions about Uncertain Democracies.* Baltimore: Johns Hopkins University Press.

Parekh, Bhikhu. 2000. *Rethinking Multiculturalism: Cultural Diversity and Political Theory.* Cambridge, Mass.: Harvard University Press.

Peacock, James L. 1978. *Muslim Puritans: Reformist Psychology in Southeast Asian Islam.* Berkeley: University of California Press.

Poggi, Gianfranco. 1990. *The State: Its Nature, Development, and Prospects.* Stanford: Stanford University Press.

Przeworski, Adam. 1988. "Democracy as a Contingent Outcome of Conflicts." In *Constitutionalism and Democracy,* ed. John Elster and Rune Slagstad, pp. 58–80. Cambridge, U.K.: Cambridge University Press.

Roy, Olivier. 1994. *The Failure of Political Islam,* trans. Carol Volk. Cambridge, Mass.: Harvard University Press.

Shahin, Emad Eldin. 1995. "Salafiyah." In *The Oxford Encyclopedia of the Modern Islamic World,* ed. John L. Esposito, vol. 3, pp. 463–69. New York: Oxford University Press.

Tomagola, Tamrin Amal. 2000. "The Bleeding Halmahera of North Moluccas." In *Political Violence: Indonesia and India in Comparative Perspective,* ed. Olle Tornquist, pp. 21–29. Oslo: SUM Report no. 9, Center for Development and the Environment, University of Oslo.

van der Veer, Peter. 1994. *Religious Nationalism: Hindus and Muslims in India.* Berkeley: University of California Press.

Weber, Max. 1978. *Economy and Society,* ed. Guenther Roth and Claus Wittich. Berkeley: University of California Press.

White, Jenny B. 1999. "Amplifying Trust: Community and Communication in Turkey." In *New Media in the Muslim World: The Emerging Public Sphere,* 1st ed., ed. Dale F. Eickelman and Jon W. Anderson, pp. 162–79. Bloomington: Indiana University Press.

10 /

MEDIA IDENTITIES FOR

ALEVIS AND KURDS IN TURKEY

M. Hakan Yavuz

The assertion of identity among Turkey's diverse religious (Alevi, Nurcu, and Nakşibendi) and ethnic (Kurdish, Bosniak, Albanian, and Cherkes) groups since the 1980s has taken on new dimensions through expanding communication channels, expansion of the higher education system, and political and economic liberalization. New communication networks have aided the struggles of Alevi and Kurdish groups for public recognition.[1] These networks provide a means for framing socio-political issues, contesting and accommodating different conceptions of identity, and "globalizing" local identities. With the help of new communications technology, for example, Alevis and Kurds frame their local views in terms of universal concepts of human rights, democracy, and self-determination. Even the everyday imaginations of "authentic" and "autonomous" identity are shaped by this synthesis in the expanded public sphere facilitated by a burgeoning of new media (Eickelman and Piscatori 1996: 37–42).

COMMUNICATION NETWORKS
AS A SPACE FOR IDENTITY CREATION

Turkey is one of the most media-saturated Muslim countries in the world. It has 10 national newspapers; 20 national, 35 regional, and 350 local television stations; 41 national, 120 regional, and 1234 local radio stations—numbers that far exceed those of any other Muslim country (Sönmez 1996; *The Economist* 1996).[2] A private television channel, Star One, brought formerly taboo subjects to the public airwaves, and by 1992 Show TV, Kanal 6, Flash TV, HBB, ATV, and TGRT joined the television market.[3] These new communication networks mix and cross-fertilize ideas from ethics to fashion to religion in Turkey. More important, the media outlets—private television and radio stations, newspapers, and magazines—offer new avenues for ethno-religious entrepreneurs to enter the public domain by inventing, legitimizing, disseminating, and shaping national histories and charts of identities (Aziz 1991).

The recent proliferation of television, radio, periodicals, and newspapers has provided a habitat for the evolution of native intellectuals. Through these media outlets, "organic" intellectuals become pivotal in identity-seeking movements. Broad and long-term shifts from an oral to a print culture, based on the spread of mass education, diminish the significance of traditional religious scholars (*ulema* for Sunni Muslims, *dede* for Alevis) in favor of urbanized intellectuals better adjusted to new media outlets. Local mechanisms of socialization through neighborhood Qur'anic seminaries or *dede*-based teaching have gradually lost their authority, leading to searches for new ways of building authority to challenge, articulate, and participate in the formation of identities and ideas on a national scale. The new communications networks promote such shifts in the production and control of knowledge by offering new avenues for the introduction of more abstract and flexible frames of reference to cope with the evolving socio-political landscape. Identity makers, cultural entrepreneurs, and opinion makers all struggle to carve out a space for themselves in these new media by bringing sensitive issues into the public debate.

These new communication networks also bring "hidden others" and "distant others" into the household. Private television channels have offered debates on Alevi practices, homosexuality, feminism, Kurdish nationalism, and other formerly taboo issues. For example, the *Siyaset Meydanı* (Political Forum) of Ali Kırca became a main arena for airing hitherto suppressed ideas and positions in public, hosting an open debate on Alevism on September 24, 1994. Such issues are also discussed increasingly in the press.

GLOBALIZATION THROUGH NEW COMMUNI- CATION NETWORKS AND PRIVATIZATION

The new communications channels have combined with a wave of Islamic movements to promote sectarian and ethnic minority consciousness by a fusion of local and global identities. Interaction between the state-centered national Turkish culture and Kurdish or Alevi culture has been marked by resistance, acculturation, and borrowing. While modern mass media have promoted a state-centered and territorial Turkish identity, contemporary Alevi and Kurdish identities have been, to a substantial degree, constructed in Berlin, Brussels, Köln, London, and Paris and projected into Turkey via communications networks such as Kurdish MED-TV and Alevi Alcanlar TV based in Berlin. But the impact of all this media is conditioned by the contexts within which messages are embedded, the availability of local idioms to express global ideas, and the institutional rules that regulate the functioning of the media.

In the context of Turkish experience, new communication networks join themes for articulating proper conduct within society and the image of the good life. Besides providing arenas for exploring such questions, their pluralization and privatization contribute to constestation over the definition of identities and to their objectification as commercialization of television networks has shifted their main function of education and state-sanctioned information in service of secular nation-building to entertainment and alternative life-styles. Even self-styled Islamist television channels, such as Kanal 7, Samanyolu television, and TGRT, which helped objectify Islam, now offer diverse Islamic frames of references, and wrap those in a commercial context.

To attract an audience, for instance, talk shows bring together a variety of perspectives, including Islamist and Alevi. For issues as diverse as the environment and pop music, these shows use scholars to present the "Islamist" or the "Alevi" view (Öncü 1995). Moreover, Islamist television stations and Alevi radio stations compete within a larger common market. In this way, the "new" Islam—what Fethullah Gülen (1995) refers to as the "Islam of Turkey" as opposed to a Turkish (i.e., national) Islam—and Alevi identity are made and sold on television, in newspapers, and on radio. This introduces the competition-based logic of the marketplace into the identity debate and thus, in turn, into the fragmentation of identity.

Privatization of the media has accompanied a shift from passive reception or one-way transmission to active engagement with communicative networks and expanding political rights. One of the popular radio stations, AKRA-Radio, belongs to a Nakşibendi Sufi order led by Sheikh Esad Coşan. Listeners can call the sheikh and raise questions that might be seen as outside traditional protocol. The station's programming appears to be directed primarily to supporters of the order. Similarly, Alevi Mozaik Radio also deals with such sensitive issues as Sunni views of women, sex, and alcohol to mold the identity of its listeners.[4]

Cultural solidarity associations, with their financial resources and skills, even more than profit-oriented individuals, can use the new communications networks not only to talk to their audience but also to seek recognition in the public domain. Amir Hassanpour argues that MED-TV "empowered the stateless people to communicate with each other for the first time by disregarding the international borders that have divided them. Many

Kurds felt that the independent body in the sky was a historical step toward sovereignty on earth" (1995: 16). Although new communication networks address a common Kurdish culture in the sky, they also highlight linguistic, religious, and class-based differences within the Kurdish community.

SHIFTING IDENTITIES AND THE FORMATION OF COMMUNICATIVE SPACES

Perhaps most striking, new communication networks combined with economic and political liberalization led to a new debate over identity and citizenship. A popular expression in Erzurum, a conservative town in eastern Turkey, says that "Muslims were forced to change their *kıble* [the direction one faces for prayer] three times during the last century." Likewise, citizens of Turkey had to change *kıble*s three times within a generation. National identity in Turkey has been framed first by religion (Islam), then by language (Turkish), and more recently by territory (of the state).

In the Ottoman Empire (prior to 1923), Sultan Abdülhamid II (r. 1876–1908) created institutions to formalize the union of the Muslim nation (*millet*) and the state (Yavuz 1993: 184–90). This union of Muslim state and nation was swept away with declaration of the republican state that made language, rather than religion, the unifying factor for constructing a Turkish nation-state. From the 1920s through the 1940s, the republican state treated ethno-religious diversity as a threat to its project of nation building, and it used every means at its disposal to eliminate the causes and consequences of differences (Beşikci, 1990).[5] The state closely organized and monitored the public sphere as national and secular arena to exclude Alevi, Kurdish, and Islamic identities. This, in turn, transformed Islam into an oppositional identity; even Kurdish identity was contained within this oppositional Islamic identity. There were more than a dozen rebellions between 1924 and 1938. Not until the 1950s did the availability of limited communication networks under a multi-party system enable social groups to articulate their concerns publicly vis-à-vis the center. However, the communications explosion that began in 1980 shattered state-built homogeneity and brought "diversity" to the forefront as an issue. Increased news coverage and the airing of suppressed collective memory and history are regarded with some skepticism by supporters of the state ideology, but this has not prevented ethnic (Kurdish) and religious (Alevi, Nurcu, Nakşibendi) groups from publishing their own magazines and newspapers. Nurcu publishes *Zaman*, a newspaper that is also available on a web site (http://www.zaman.com), and it owns the (national) Samanyolu television station. The Nakşibendi own radio stations, periodicals, and web sites that they use to shape public opinion. According to Esad Coşan, leader of the Iskenderpaşa Nakşibendi order, the new site of *jihad* for the faith is the media, and the new frontiers of evangelizing are the radio waves (Coşan 1993: 31–32). The Alevi community in Ankara has opened seven radio stations: Mozaik, Cankaya, Cağdaş, Arkadaş Ezgim, Imaj, and Gerçek.[6] Radio Mozaik, has become a national station, and the Alevi Cankaya television beams signals to several regions of Turkey.

THE ALEVIS: FROM CO-OPTED ALLY TO IMAGINED ENEMY

The Alevis make up 11 to 30 percent of Turkey's total population (Andrews 1989: 48, 57; Üzüm 1997: 11) and have several identities, such as ethnic, regional, and family, stressing one identity over another in any given situation. Alevis are a syncretic religious group whose practices vary from one region to another. Generally, they emphasize inner spirituality and call on members to internalize faith. The Alevi belief is expressed in narratives, poems, songs, legends and popular sayings. In daily practice, Turkish Alevis speak Turkish, and Kurdish Alevis speak Zaza or Kirmanji (dialects of Kurdish); but for both, the liturgy is in Turkish (van Bruinessen 1996b). Scholars such as Nur Yalman and David Shankland essentialize the confessional and communal boundary between the Alevis and Sunni Muslims by reducing it to different interpretations of the five pillars of Islam (Yalman 1969: 53; Shankland 1994); but this approach does not explain how, when, and which cultural differences are politicized. Neither religious- nor descent-based essentialism fully explains the malleability of Alevi identity.

The marking of the boundaries of the Alevi community goes back to the sixteenth and seventeenth centuries, when the Ottoman state viewed the Alevis as a fifth column of Safavid Iran and treated the Alevis as blasphemers and heretics (Imber 1979). The Alevis were targets of frequent massacres by the central government, which forced them into small communities in the mountainous areas of Turkey. Isolation played a key role in maintaining the boundaries of the community, and dissimulation was one way of overcoming Sunni prejudices. This experience of oppression at the hands of the Ottoman state made the Alevi community a supporter of Kemalist reforms, which aimed at instituting a more secular polity. As a multi-party electoral system emerged, the Alevi community supported the Democratic Party (DP) against the Ismet Inönü (r. 1938–1950) government in the 1950 national election. When the DP adopted pro-Islamic (Sunni) positions, the Alevis shifted their support in the 1957 elections to the Republican People's Party (RPP). In October 1966, a group of Alevis formed the Alevi Union Party of Turkey (Türkiye Birlik Partisi), which failed to gain a seat in Parliament until 1969.[7]

Expansion of education and urbanization in the 1960s and 1970s led to geographic and social mobility and increased interaction between the Sunni and Alevi communities and heightened the Alevi consciousness. The first urban-born generation of Alevis, those whose parents moved to the squatter towns of major metropolitan areas in the late 1950s and the early 1960s and supported more revolutionary socialist ideas, dominated the identity debate because its members were literate and switched easily between local idioms and universal concepts.

The state and various left-leaning groups saw the Alevis as a group susceptible to secular-progressive or Marxist ideas (Atalay 1991; Coşkun 1990: 104-06; Mardin 1982). The heterodox practices of the Alevis and their collective suffering were articulated in folk music and poetry that became associated with left-wing ideas. This association provided an opportunity for conservative Sunni groups to charge that the Alevis were "Communist."[8] Martin van Bruinessen (1996a: 8), a leading authority on the Alevi and Kurdish minorities, argues that "the radical left, construing the Alevi rebellions of the past as proto-communist movements, considered the Alevis natural allies." Thus, the Alevi community moved in the late 1970s from being the ally of secular forces to being a "communist threat." This, in turn, made the Alevis a target of communal pogroms in 1978–1979.

The leaders of the 1980 coup introduced an Islamization of Turkish nationalism as a move against Kurdish assertiveness, and further alienated the Turkish Alevi community from the state. This state ideology, known as the Turkish-Islamic synthesis, turned the Alevi community into an oppositional minority, and the Alevi community became more isolated and insecure. To overcome this sense of insecurity, many Alevis organized around regional associations and supported specific magazines so as to benefit from the new wave of political and economic liberalization of the late 1980s. With the collapse of socialist ideology and the rise of a Sunni Islamic movement, the Alevi community, using new communication networks, has subsequently transformed syncretic religious practices into communal boundary markers for the purpose of political mobilization.

Alevi assertiveness presents a paradox: modern Alevi identities, objectified by commercial and communicative means, are subjectively rooted in "ancient" histories. These identities have the power to mobilize, but they are prone to fragmentation along differences of class, region, and dialect in the flourishing publication and broadcast media outlet. In the 1990s, different versions of Alevism competed for control of community symbols. A major conflict took place on July 2, 1993, when the Pir Sultan Cultural Association gathered left-wing Alevi intellectuals in Sivas to commemorate the Alevi saint Pir Sultan Abdal (Coşkun 1990). The gathering included the late Aziz Nesin, one of Turkey's leading atheist Sunni writers, who had translated extracts of Salman Rushdie's *Satanic Verses*. A mob, mobilized by pro-Welfare Party (Refah) activists, attacked the hotel where the meeting was taking place, and many of the intellectuals were killed. The incident was filmed by the city police force and the video was leaked to private television channels, where (like the film of the Rodney King beating in Los Angeles) it was rebroadcast continuously for almost a week. The film showed the police making little attempt to disperse the mob.

The government's response to the attack was a turning point for the Alevi community. The film heightened their security concerns and catalyzed their mobilization and organization. A parliamentary investigative committee blamed Nesin's inflammatory statements for the conflict, and the police blamed the Alevi association for holding the meeting in a conservative Sunni town (*TBMM* 1993). Although a court originally sentenced 26 people to fifteen years' imprisonment and 60 more to three years' imprisonment, the Alevi community was not placated. Citing state complicity in the Sivas incident and the statements of Erdal İnönü, then a deputy prime minister in the coalition government, Alevi intellectuals made use of the wide availability of diverse communications networks to reject Kemalist secularism as a "surrogate identity" for Alevis and to articulate a more autonomous Alevi identity.

As Alevi magazines, publications, and radio stations became active arenas for political mobilization, the Sunni-Islamist magazine *İzlenim*, presented the articulation of Alevi identity in public space as the impulse of a community that seeks to "come out from the underground" (Kanber 1993). Subsequently, Turkey's major newspapers have competed with one another through series of articles on the question of Alevi identity. In 1995, the Kemalist newspaper *Cumhuriyet* published a week-long series on "What do Alevis want?" (Engin 1995). This practical question brings forth other questions: "Who are the Alevis?" and "How and who will speak for the Alevis?" The media also offer images and concepts from similar cases around the globe for adaptation, borrowing, and participation (Yavuz and Indeoğlu 1996).

At the same time, Alevi folk culture has become increasingly intellectualized and politicized through media exposure. Media are spaces for cultural elites to articulate and redefine subcultures and to carve a space for themselves in the cultural and political arenas. New private communications channels such as television, radio, and satellite expand the public domain and move global discourses on human rights and self-determination downward while pulling local identities and prejudices upward. When Güner Ümit, a leading talk-show personality, expressed a common stereotype among Sunnis, that Alevis practice incest, the Alevi community in Istanbul launched a massive demonstration in front of Interstar television on 9 January 1995, and Ümit was forced to resign. This event illustrates how new media outlets promote an open discussion of historical prejudices (see also Yaman and Güner 1995). However, an Islamist magazine, *İzlenim*, ran an article about an Alevi ritual service in which the reporter claimed, "When I heard the Alevi *dede* [spiritual leader], Hüseyin Orhon, saying to his flock 'do not come to the ritual ceremony (*cemayini*) without *gusul*' [Islamic ritual ablution after sexual intercourse], my conviction that the Alevis do not take *gusul* was shattered" (Kanber 1993: 13). The media can also dispel deeply rooted pejorative images that circulate unchallenged in other channels.

Modern media provide avenues to connect Alevis with Turkey's national culture and with the global community, too. For example, there are eleven new web sites on the Alevi identity and community. To Alevi youth, the enlarged public space for them allows the options both of belonging to and of feeling free of their community. Through the media, Alevi youth unite the symbols of Ali and Atatürk in their demonstrations. Underneath Ali's picture, for example, often is written "Guide" (*Rehber*), and under Atatürk "Leader" (*Önder*): *Ali Rehber, Ata Önder*. This cultural reimagination fuses the religious and secular, local and universal, traditional and modern within the modalities brought about by new communication networks and in an environment in which Alevi intellectuals are more dominant than traditional *dedes*.

THE SHIFT OF AUTHORITY FROM *DEDE* TO ALEVI INTELLECTUALS AND *DERGAH* TO MAGAZINES

Due to the Ottoman state oppression, the Alevi community institutionalized its religious authority through genealogical origins. The *dede* has been central to Alevi identity. These itinerant holy men, who controlled esoteric religious knowledge and often claimed descent from the Prophet Muhammad, were "living libraries" who tightly controlled religious knowledge and selectively shared it with their followers. Thus *dedes* formed a well-functioning network of information throughout the country by belonging to a holy lineage, known as a heart (*oçak*). This kin-based religious leadership remained at the center of Alevi practices until print-culture became the dominant medium for constructing knowledge. The role of the *dedes* has been under challenge for some time, and a new class of intellectuals now leads the community. Nejat Birdoğan, for example, a popular writer on Alevi issues, openly challenged the hereditary nature of the institution of the *dede* and argued that "since Alevism is outside Islam, these *dedes* cannot be coming from Prophet Muhammad's lineage" (Birdoğan 1994b: 19–20). Some Alevis reacted sharply to Birdoğan's interpretation of Alevism as a Turkish "faith system" outside Islam (Aktüel 1994); under this interpretation, *dedes* have almost no role in the new codification of Alevi culture and beliefs. Print media has replaced *dedes* with journals.

These new forms of journal-based religious authority emerge around people with modern university degrees who have become commanding authorities. For example, in the 1990s the debate over Alevi identity began with the formation of media outlets (*Cumhuriyet* 1991), and Alevi periodicals such as *Cem, Nefes, Genç Erenler, Asura, Kervan, Çağdaş Zülfikar* became forums for debate. New communication networks not only led the shift of authority to modern intellectuals but also decentered the construction of Alevi identity from Istanbul to Köln and Berlin (Mandel 1990). The Federation of European Alevi Union, with 140 associations and 150,000 members, plays an active role in the internationalization of the Alevi identity. Major financial support comes from Europe, where the Alevi community is well organized and where Alevis own local television stations and publish journals that play a prominent role in Turkey's political life. The Alevi community in Berlin, for example, publishes a magazine called *Algül* and owns both an Alcanlar radio station and an Alcanlar television station which broadcast four hours a week (Zaptcioğlu 1995).

The second major impact of these new media outlets is an historicization of Alevi identity (Bender 1991; Bozkurt 1990). Writings about the historical roots of Alevi culture increasingly deploy a Manichean dualism of good and evil, justice and injustice, freedom and oppression through the narrative of Caliph Ali's sons Hasan and Hüseyin and the Ummayad ruler Yezid. Good is represented in the persons of Ali and Hüseyin and by Hacı Bektaşi Veli and Pir Sultan Abdal, who was executed by Hızır Pasha. Yezid and Hızır Pasha are presented as the personifications of injustice. Significantly, Kemal Atatürk is treated as a "liberator from Sunni hegemony." The myth of collective suffering at the hands of Sunni rulers because of their beliefs and practices has been a mobilizing force in Alevi assertiveness (Eral 1993), popularized through the printed word in a more systematized way than would have been possible through oral tradition. There has been a veritable explosion of books and journals on Alevi culture and practices. Karin Vorhoff, a leading scholar on modern Alevis in Turkey, notes that

> At the turn of 1989 to 1990 a press campaign and a deluge of books on Anatolian Alevism not only put an end to the silence that had reigned on Alevi beliefs and practices, but also to the process of dissolution that had grasped the Alevi community and their religious system as a result of secularization, modernization, wide-ranging migration, and the severing of political conflict in the 1970s. (1995: 7)

The debate and literature around the great historic Alevi figure of Hacı Bektaşi Veli (d.1290?) indicates several versions of Hacı Bektaşi Veli in formation. Some scholars (e.g., Sener 1991) represent Hacı Bektaşi Veli as the revolutionary leader of a suppressed community. In this representation, they construct a vision of Alevi culture that reinterprets oral tradition within a global idiom of human rights, democracy, tolerance, and freedom (Zelyut

1992). This process of blending local folk beliefs and global culture or reading religious culture in secular terms facilitates standardization. Abidin Özgünay, editor of the prominent Alevi magazine *Cem*, argues that "secularism, democracy, the rule of law, and modernity are integral parts of Alevism" (1993: 13). This case indicates how moving communication to a more global context breaks down barriers and reframes integral, local figures in more universalist terms that fragment local frames.

A third major result of new communication networks has been the contestation and pluralization of Alevi identity. Two separate Alevi identities have been presented by two competing Alevi journals. The first revolves around *Cem*, a magazine funded by affluent Alevis in 1991 with a circulation of about 5,000. *Cem* is pro-state and pro-Turkish nationalism. To a great extent, it propagates the views of Turkish scholars (Ersöz 1977; Fığlalı 1994) that the Alevi understanding of Islam originates in a Turkic, semi-nomadic conceptualization. *Cem*'s editorial board champions a liberal economic order and demands official recognition of Alevism. It is dominated by Turkish Alevis, who present Alevism as the "essence of Islam." Articles in *Cem* situate Alevism in the Qur'an and the Turkic culture of Ahmed Yasevi and Hacı Bektaşi Veli (Noyan 1995: 84). These magazines stress secularism, modernity, and human rights as integral elements of Alevi teaching. The Cem Foundation organized the first international conference on Alevism, held in Istanbul in March 1996, and demanded that the state integrate Alevism into the Directorate of Religious Affairs (Aydın 1996; Camuroğlu 1996).[9] The foundation also receives state support.

The Cem Foundation's leader, Alevi intellectual-*dede*, İzzettin Doğan, a professor of international relations at Galatasaray University, argues that "Alevi identity is a synthesis of Turkism and Islamism. This is the Turkish understanding of Islam, which is more tolerant" (Doğan, 1992). One of Doğan's goals is to introduce courses on Alevism into the schools and to produce television and radio programs explaining the Alevi belief system (Doğan 1995). Doğan also presents Alevism as a guarantor of Kemalist secularism. The mass media, major talk shows, and radio programs have made Doğan a public figure, and his profession adds to his authority: those who are part of the university system become authoritative sources of Alevism.

Some state officials also played Alevism against Kurdish nationalism and mounting Sunni Islamic political activism. In 1991, the Directorate of Religious Affairs organized a series of meetings with prominent Alevi leaders (Aygün 1991), and the semi-official Foundation of the Directorate of Religious Affairs organized a conference on Alevi belief and Islam in 1992 (Mert 1992). A group of Alevi youth formed the magazine *Genç Erenler* in 1995 to disseminate their own understanding of Alevi identity. This group, led by Tuğcu Kütahya, a sociologist at Hacettepe University, stresses the unity of the Turkish state and interprets Alevism within the dominant Sunni paradigm as a folk Turkish culture, not a belief system.

The presentation of Alevism as quintessential Turkish Islam by the Turkish state and *Cem* has been sharply criticized. Cemsid Bender, a Kurdish-Alevi (1991), argues that Alevism is a Kurdish religion.[10] Kurdish Alevis, mostly Zaza-speakers, tend to integrate Marxist terminology into Alevi discourse to express their universality. *Pir Sultan Abdal Kültür Sanat Dergisi*, a Marxist, anti-state magazine, argues that Alevism is not "rooted in Islam" but is influenced by Islam, as does Murteza Demir (1993), head of the Pir Sultan Abdal Associations.[11] These associations, which have 35,000 members, refuse to join the Directorate of Religious Affairs because they fear assimilation into the state system.

Intermediate positions between the poles represented by *Cem* and by *Pir Sultan Abdal* are associated with other associations and publications. The Hacı Bektaşi Association, for example, presents Alevi identity as anti-state and stresses traditional institutions of Alevi identity, such as the *dede*. Alevi communities in Corum and Amasya, unlike other Alevis, go regularly to mosque and represent themselves as being in accord with Shi'i understandings of Islam through their own magazine, *Aşsura* (Şahin 1995).

TURNING ALEVISM AGAINST THE STATE AND SUNNI ISLAMIC MOVEMENTS: GAZIOSMANPAŞA INCIDENT

In 1995 gunmen opened fire on Alevi tea-houses in the Gaziosmanpaşa neighborhood of Istanbul, killing two people and wounding three. The police were slow to react, and a rumor spread in the neighborhood that the local police station might have been involved in the attack. An Alevi detainee had been killed earlier while being held at the same police station, and the rumor galvanized the Alevi community. Alevis from all over Istanbul poured into the neighborhood. The presence of television cameras and journalists encouraged the demonstrators to harden their stance, and they subsequently encircled the police station, demanding justice. When a group of armed demonstrators fired on the police, the police responded in kind, and the clash ended with twenty-two deaths, all Alevis.

This conflict and the one in Sivas show how new avenues of communication, increasing literacy, and political and economic liberalism have transformed Turkish society and previously subsumed identities. By the 1990s, many in the Alevi community viewed the police as hostile. İzzettin Doğan, a prominent Alevi leader, claims that there is "open discrimination against the Alevi community[;] . . . they are not made governors or accepted into the military high schools." Doğan presents the view that "many Alevis believe that the state is preventing them from having a higher position in the civil service; they feel marginalized" (Doğan 1995). However, this shared perception did not overcome socio-cultural cleavages within the Alevi community. With opportunities opened by the media and the market, added to state policies to hinder the formation of a unified Alevi front, Alevism has become a zone of contestation among different Alevi groups. Today, more than 170 associations in Istanbul are based primarily on regions of origin. These associations have become centers for power struggles among Alevi elites, and this in turn leads to fragmentation. To reconcile the competing versions of Alevi beliefs and establish a single representative body, thirteen major Alevi associations convened in Istanbul in 1994 and formed the Assembly of Representatives of Alevi-Bektaşi (Alevi-Bektaşi Temsilciler Meclisi). (The Cem Foundation subsequently broke with the assembly and established its own independent structure.) The assembly council decided to produce a text of common Alevi rituals and practices entitled "Contemporary Anatolian Alevi Charter" (*Çağdaş Anadolu Aleviliği Buyruğu*). Unfortunately, the council itself disintegrated in internal strife and disagreement over who had the authority to codify Alevi practices and oral traditions. The second initiative for unification took place in 1996 (Demir 1996).

This move of an oral folk culture into print has created a new forum for diverse versions of Alevi identity. Because Alevis include both ethnic Turks and Kurds, the print media have become a site of contest among different ethnic, linguistic, and educational groups. Since the rise of the (Sunni) Islamist Welfare Party into the government in 1996, secular newspapers such as *Cumhuriyet, Milliyet,* and *Yeni Yüzyıl* and some state organizations present the Alevi as a natural ally. The Kemalist Republican People's Party sought to capitalize on the Alevi community's fear of the rising Sunni Islamic movements.[12] With the changing perception of threat from the left-wing movements to Islamic political movements, the Turkish state is seeking to expand its social base by meeting the demands of Alevis. After the 1995 national elections, the armed forces and the Republican People's Party regularly invoked Alevi sensibilities to garner political support, and many political commentators argued that the change of the Sivas court verdict from imprisonment to capital punishment was aimed at overcoming Alevi alienation from the state.

POLITICIZATION OF THE KURDISH LANGUAGE AND THE LAW OF 1983

A major reason for the military takeover in 1980 was to end leftist use of Alevi culture to penetrate Turkish society; a second reason was the desire to curb Kurdish ethno-nationalism in Turkey. The leaders of the 1980 coup justified their actions in a small booklet (*Türkiye'de Bölücü ve Yıkıcı Akımlar*) distributed to high-ranking officials with a stamp indicating that it was "secret and not open to public consumption." The first "divisive and destructive force" they mentioned is the Kurds, who are defined as those "who live in the mountains of eastern Turkey where there is too much snow." As stated in *Türkiye'de Bölücü ve Yıkıcı Akımlar* (1982: 43): "Those who walk on this snow create a different noise, and this noise is known as Kurd." The coup introduced several harsh measures, including a total ban on printing in Kurdish or its use in public spaces. These measures helped crystallize Kurdish identity around language.

A repressive language law, Law 2932, imposed by the military regime on October 22, 1983 (*Resmi Gazete* 1983: 28–29), gave authorities the right to curb Kurdish cultural activities, even in the private sphere. This law prohibits the "utilization of any language in the dissemination, printing, and expression of ideas which is not in the official language recognized by the Turkish state" (Article 2). It declares Turkish as the "mother tongue" of all Turkish citizens and prohibits the use of other languages as a mother tongue (Article 3). This law contributed to the promotion of the Kirmanji dialect as the "official" Kurdish language, which served as a rallying point for Kurdish ethno-nationalism. The main grievance of the Kurds shifted from underdevelopment of the Kurdish populated provinces to the issue of language and cultural rights. When Turkish state officials argued that there was no standardized Kurdish language to be recognized, Kurdish intellectuals mobilized to make the Kirmanji dialect a standardized Kurdish language. Most of the activity took place in Europe, and Sweden and Germany became the centers of standardization and publication in Kurdish.

Partly in response, Turgut Özal (1983–1991) adopted a new set of domestic and international strategies toward the Kurdish question as part of his goal of making Turkey a regional power in concert with Western strategic interests. He allowed them greater cultural freedom and, for the first time, recognized them as a distinct ethnic group; he introduced a set of bills designed to remove restrictions on the Kurdish language. In 1991 he met with the leaders of two Iraqi Kurdish factions and repealed the draconian Law 2932, in response to European Community conditions for closer European-Turkish relations. Kurds were free to sing songs in Kurdish and to publish in Kurdish, but not to use their language in public. However, military measures against the Kurds continued, and Article 89 of the 1982 Constitution remained in force: it states that "no political party may concern itself with the defense, development, or diffusion of any non-Turkish language or culture; nor may seek to create minorities within our frontiers or to destroy our national unity."[13]

The Formation of a "Literary" Kurdish

From the moment Law 2932 placed the language issue at the center of debate, Kurdish intellectuals mobilized to standardize the Kurdish language. The first Kurdish Institute was opened in Paris in 1983, a second in London in 1984, another in Brussels in 1989, and a subsequent one in Berlin in 1993. In this diasporic space, Kurdish intellectuals in Europe developed a standardized Kurdish language based on the Kirmanji dialect and introduced Kurdish language courses in many European cities. Advances in the technologies of printing and distribution assisted this diasporic "revival" of Kurdish, filtered in through new communication media from grammar books to cassettes, videos, and movies.

The language issue assumed additional dimensions when a group of Kurds in Europe established MED-TV and began to broadcast to Turkey via satellite. A Turkish official has claimed that "MED-TV threatens the security of this nation more than the guerrilla attacks of the PKK [Kurdistan Worker's Party]."[14] MED-TV programming suggests three interrelated goals: entertainment (articulating a distinct national culture and addressing a collective memory), education (teaching Kirmanji Kurdish and promulgating the antiquity of Kurdish nationhood), and information (providing news and political debates to promote ethno-linguistic political consciousness) (Hassanpour 1995).[15] The introduction of MED-TV challenges the state's attempt to promote the Turkish language and control news of ongoing conflicts in the region.

With the proliferation in Sweden, Germany, and France of Kirmanji as the standardized version of Kurdish through broadcasts and cassette distribution and on MED-TV's World Wide Web site on the Internet, a new, full-fledged Kurdish "nation" is being formed by Kurdish cultural entrepreneurs. Using every means possible to historicize the Kurdish nation, these cultural entrepreneurs claim that "MED" stands as proof that Kurds are descended from the Medes (Gürsel 1977: 77).[16] This identity is not constructed within the local space and a stable community but instead within transnational space and by expanding the boundaries of knowledge. A group of jailed Kurdish members of the Turkish parliament argue that

> MED-TV brought life to the Kurdish cultural scene the way water and a mirror reflected their reality to them. Thanks to MED-TV, the Kurdish language [Kirmanji] was coming alive, something which threatened those who wanted to suffocate it. MED-TV epitomized the hope of the Kurdish people for recognition; it was a magnet which drew the Kurds together.[17]

Between MED-TV and printed materials in Hawar (Turkicized Latin) characters, Kurmanji is becoming a "literary" language. In Iraq, official Kurdish is still the Sorani dialect, and it is the only language taught in Kurdish schools there. In Iran, Kirmanji, Sorani, and Zaza dialects are used by the Kurds, but Kirmanji has emerged as the main literary language. There are several Kurdish television and radio stations, most of which broadcast in the Kirmanji dialect.

MED-TV began to air Kurdish and Turkish programs from Europe in March 1995. Most of its programs are prepared by a Belgian communications company, ROJ N.V., while MED-TV itself received licenses from the British Independent Television Committee (ITC) to open studios in London.[18] It first used Polish TELECOM satellites to broadcast to Turkey and northern Iraq, but Turkish government diplomatic intervention prompted the Polish government to halt the broadcasting. MED-TV then rented American INTELSAT satellites for its broadcasting. Through new communications technology Kurdish nationalists have been able to circumvent the Turkish state's attempt to enforce its official ideology.

The Turkish government claims that MED-TV activities are linked to the PKK and to drug trafficking. But INTELSAT is owned by 139 governments—including Turkey—and merely broadcasts programs. According to spokesperson T. Trujillo, "INTELSAT cannot control the content of the programs" (Bozkurt 1996: 13). MED-TV employs its British company to use INTELSAT; that corporation claims that "If MED-TV promotes terrorism, then the Turkish government should pressure the British government to stop the use of the satellite" (Bozkurt 1996: 13). The British government refuses to pressure ITC on the grounds that "there is no evidence which shows direct connections between the PKK and MED-TV" (Bozkurt 1996: 13). However, Turkish government pressure forced London to conduct a massive police search of the offices of the Kurdish-language satellite station, MED-TV studios in London, and its production company, ROJ N.V., on September 18, 1996. While the investigation of MED-TV is still going on in Europe, it is the most popular TV station among Turkey's Kurds. Sahin Alpay, a journalist who recently visited the region with the help of the military, asked the government to establish its own Kurdish TV station to counter the popular MED-TV (1997).

New communications networks have simultaneously reinforced the consciousness of a shared identity and increased an awareness of difference. MED-TV, which is a powerful agent for the standardization of Kirmanji among the Sunni Kurds of Turkey, is also forcing a competing Kurdish consciousness among Zaza-speaking Alevis and Sorani-speaking Iraqi Kurds. The language of MED-TV is not spoken by most Alevi Kurds living in Turkey, who speak the Zaza dialect. Alevis increasingly refer to themselves more as Zaza than as Kurd, suggesting the emergence of a new language-based identity (van Bruinessen 1992).

Conclusion

New communications networks are reshaping political spaces and linking global discourse on human rights and the recognition of alternative ethnic and religious identities of great complexity. These networks have helped to create a new class of cultural entrepreneurs who work as editors, journalists, talk-show personalities, and fiction writers to construct and disseminate reimagined Kurdish or Alevi identities. Significantly, they have displaced older networks of communication that fitted Kurd and Alevi identity to past regimes. Upheavals of the twentieth century exchanged these oral networks for others forged by literacy and by media. Particularly with the reordering of political and economic spaces in the 1980s, Alevi identity has gradually transformed into a political "confessional" identity. The Alevi community is experiencing profound systematization of its oral doctrine, secularization and rationalization of oral Alevi practices and beliefs, and a shift of leadership to those who command the means of these processes.

These processes extend from journals, magazines, and local broadcasting to the introduction of MED-TV, which has made the Kurds the first "satellite" nation. They do not have a seat at the United Nations, but they do have a powerful television frequency with which to shape the imagination of Kurds, at the same time that "Alevi" has been recast in the commercialized environment of more mundane media from exotic marginals to "essentially Turkish." By comparison, "Zaza" identity is a counter-move that shifts the domain to linguistics, again highlighting the changing interplay of community and communication. Communication networks have simultaneously reshaped consciousness of a shared identity previously taken for granted and increased an awareness of differences. The media, by offering many opportunities for politically conscious elites to diffuse their ideas, have brought ethno-linguistic and ethno-religious identities into public space and contributed to the fragmentation of authority by multiplying not just its voices but also their subjects and, most important, their contexts. Above all, it is the multiplication of media and of media outlets that contributes to this fragmentation. On the one hand, it contributes simplification of previously complex, nuanced identities. On the other, the contribution of media to this process is what, and who, they bring together.

NOTES

I would like to thank Amir Hassanpour, Dale F. Eickelman, Eric Hooglund, Karin Vorhoff, Jon Anderson, Martin van Bruinessen, and Tayfun Atay for their comments and the MacArthur Foundation Consortium for the opportunity to present an earlier version of this paper at Stanford University, March 7–9, 1997.

1. Two major cultural cleavages in Turkey are the ethnic split into Turks and Kurds (7 to 20 percent of Turkey's population) and the religious division into Sunni (orthodox majority) and the Alevi. The Alevi make up 11 to 30 percent of the population. Ethnic and religious divisions partially overlap, and there are Alevi Turks and Alevi Kurds, Sunni Turks and Sunni Kurds.

2. According to *The Economist* (1996: 7), "at the last count there were 16 national and 15 regional stations, as well as about 300 local ones. Radio is even more extravagant: 35 national stations, 109 regional and almost 1,000 local ones." According to the Supreme Board of Radio and Television, a state watchdog that

monitors radio and television broadcasts to ensure compliance with the Kemalist principles, 260 TV stations and 1200 radio stations have an official license, and there are many more without license (*Zaman*, 25 March 1998).

3. The television revolution began in 1992, when the Magic Box Channel, Star One (a German-based Turkish company, in which President Turgut Özal's son was a partner) began beaming programs to Turkey. Article 133 of the 1982 Constitution made television and radio broadcasting the province of the state. This article has become irrelevant as a result of transnational broadcasting.

4. Mozaik Radio was established and funded by the Köln-based Federation of European Alevi Associations in 1994. For economic reasons, the Federation sold the station to Ali Haydar Veziroğlu, a prominent Alevi businessmen, in 1997.

5. Earlier state-centered studies (Lewis 1968) of Turkey celebrated the homogeneous Turkish nation and its march toward modernity. Recent scholars (for example, Andrews 1989; van Bruinessen 1992) pay attention to Turkey's diversity.

6. Gerçek, however, is in the process of closing. Almost all these stations are located in or near Ankara, which has the largest Alevi concentration. Most of the Alevis in Dikmen are Kurdish and are economically better off than the Turkish Alevis in Mamak, another Ankara neighborhood. Most political demonstrations take place in Dikmen, where Kurdish identity is expressed through Alevism. Rapidly growing cities such as Istanbul, Ankara, and Adana do not become melting pots but rather agglomerations of coexisting neighborhoods defined by ethnic, religious, and regional origins.

7. The symbol of the party, a lion, represented Ali, son-in-law of Prophet Muhammed. The party received 2.8 percent of the 1969 national vote and garnered eight seats in the parliament.

8. Ayşe Güneş Ayata (1995) argues that, since Alevi migration to urban centers was higher in the 1960s, they became blue-collar workers. She challenges the accepted notion that egalitarianism and democratic thinking are inherent in Alevi culture and argues that these characteristics have only became ensconced in the Alevi culture since the 1960s.

9. The associations and printing houses that participated in this meeting are Avrupa Alevi Birlikleri Federasyonu, Pir Sultan Abdal Kültür Dernekleri, Hacı Bektaş Veli Kültür Dernekleri, Hollanda-Alevi-Bektaşi Sosyal ve Kültür Dernekleri Federasyonu, Şahkulu Sultan Derneği, Karacaahmet Derneği, Semah Kültür ve Araştırma Vakfı, Pir Sultan Abdal Kültür Dergisi, Cem Dergisi, Can Yayınları, Yurtta Birlik Gazetesi, Gönüllerin Sesi Gazetesi, and Kervan Dergisi. Six of the thirteen groups owned either a journal or a publishing house.

10. Two magazines support the connection between Kurdish nationalism and Alevism, *Çağdas Zülfikar* (in print since 1994) and *Yeni Zülfikar* (June 1996).

11. *Pir Sultan Abdal Kültür Sanat Dergisi*, no. 17 (December 1994), p.1.

12. Ali Haydar Veziroğlu is a rich ex-parliamentarian of the Republican People's Party from Tunceli Province who formed the Democratic Peace Movement (Demokratik Baris Hareketi). Before the 1995 general election, DPM pulled out of the election to allow RPP to overcome the 10 percent hurdle (*Siyah Beyaz*, December 12, 1995). Almost all DPM candidates were Alevi (for names and provinces, see *Siyah Beyaz*, December 2, 1995). The slogan of the DPM is "Our first names are different; our last name is Turkey" (*Adlarımız farklı olabilir, soyadımız Türkiye*). DPM advertisements stressed the cultural rights of different ethno-religious groups, a non-nationalistic state, and constitutional citizenship (see *Cumhuriyet*, July 7, 1996). However, most Alevis do not support the concept of a "confessional" party.

13. M. Hakan Yavuz, "A Preamble to the Kurdish Question: The Politics of Kurdish Identity," Introduction to special issue on the Kurds, *Journal of Muslim Minority Affiars* 18, no. 1 (1998), pp. 9–18.

14. Interview with high-ranking Turkish military officers in Ankara, June 1996.

15. Hassanpour offers this breakdown of MED-TV programming for November 1995: information (news, debate, politics), 37 percent of total program; education (youth, children, culture, history, documentary, religion), 35 percent; entertainment (music, film), 35 percent.

16. The founding charter of the Kurdish Democratic Party of Turkey (Türkiye Kürdistan Demokrat Partisi) offers an example of "invented history" by claiming that Kurds derive from the Mede and Karduk civilizations. It argues that Kurds have always lived in independent empires and states.

17. Cited by the Canadian Kurdish Information Network (CKIN) in a press release condemning Turkish government policies toward MED-TV.

18. MED Broadcasting Limited is registered in England (Company Number 2960 755 and VAT Number 653 1082 60). Its current director is Hikmet Tabak, a Turkish Kurd.

WORKS CITED

"Alevilik Islam'la Özdeştir." 1994. Aktüel, no. 173: 24–25.
Alpay, Şahin. 1997. "Halkı kazanmak." Milliyet, November 27.
Andrews, Peter Alford, ed. 1989. Ethnic Groups in the Republic of Turkey. Wiesbaden: Reichert.
Atalay, Besim. 1991. Bektaşilik ve Edebıyatı, 2nd ed. Istanbul: Ant Yayınları.
Ayata, Ayşe Güneş. 1995. Cumhuriyet, April 2.
Aydın, Erdoğan. 1996. "Devletci Alevi Konferansı." Cumhuriyet, April 6.
Aygün, Hakan. 1991. "Diyanet, Alevilere Acılıyor," Cumhuriyet, December 11.
Aziz, Aysel. 1991. "Star I'nin meşrulastırılmasının Öyküsü." Medya 4, no. 9: 12-19.
Bender, Cemsid. 1991. Kürt Uygarlığında Alevilik. Istanbul: Kaynak Yayınları.
Beşikci, Ismail. 1990. Tunceli Kanunu (1935) ve Dersim jenosidi. Istanbul: Belge Yayınları.
Birdoğan, Nejat. 1994a. Anadolu'nun Gizli Kültürü: Alevilik, 2nd ed. Istanbul: Berfin.
———. 1994. "Alevi Araştırmacı Nejat Birdoğan 'Esas' Tartışmayi Baslatıyor." Aktuel, no. 172: 19-20.
Bozkurt, Fuat. 1990. Aleviliğin Toplumsal Boyutları. Istanbul: Tekin Yayınları.
Bozkurt, Abdullah. 1996. "Med-TV Neden Susturulamıyor?" Zaman, November 2.
Camuroğlu, Reha. 1992. Tarih, Heteredoksi ve Babailer. Istanbul: Metis.
———. 1996. "Din hizmetleri nasıl yapılmalı?" Milliyet, April 3.
Coşan, Esad. 1993. Yeni Dönemde Yeni Görevlerimiz. Istanbul. Seha.
Coşkun, Zeki. 1990. Aleviler, Sunniler ve Öteki Sivas. Istanbul: Iletisim Yayınları.
Demir, Murteza. 1993. Pir Sultan Abdal Dergisi, February.
———. 1996. "Örgütlenmek Hala Yasak." Yeni Yüzyıl, March 3.
Doğan, İzzettin. 1992. "Aleviler de vatandaş." Milliyet, August 9.
———. 1995a. "Ciğerciğime delik delindi." Zaman, March 19.
———. 1995b. "Hacı Bektaş'i seviyorsanız, güvercini ucurmalısınız, hem de incitmeden." Milliyet, August 17.
Eickelman, Dale F., and James Piscatori. 1996. Muslim Politics. Princeton: Princeton University Press.
Engin, Aydın. 1995. "Aleviler Ne Istiyor?" Cumhuriyet, April 2–9.
Ersöz, Mehmet. 1977. Türkiye'de Alevilik-Bektaşilik. Istanbul: Otağ Matbaacılık.
Eral, Sadik. 1993. Anadolu'da Alevi Katliamlar. Istanbul: Yalçın Yayınları.

Fığlalı, Ethem Ruhi. 1994. *Türkiye'de Alevilik Bektaşilik*. Ankara: Selcuk Yayınları.

Gülen, Fethullah. 1995. "Ufuk Turu." *Zaman*, August 23–29.

Gürsel, Ibrahim Etem. 1977. *Kürtcülük Gerçeği*. Ankara: Komen Yayınları.

Hassanpour, Amir. 1995. "MED-TV, Britain, and the Turkish State: A Stateless Nation's Quest for Sovereignty in the Sky." Paper presented at the Freie Universität Berlin, November 7, 1995.

Imber, Colin H. 1979. "Persecution of the Ottoman Shi'ites According to the Muhimme Defterleri 1565–1585." *Der Islam* 56: 245-74.

Kanber, Sükrü. 1993. "Aleviler anlaşılmak istiyor," *İzlenim* (May): 19–20.

Lewis, Bernard. 1968. *The Emergence of Modern Turkey*. London: Oxford University Press.

Mandel, Ruth. 1990. "Shifting centres and emergent identities: Turkey and Germany in the lives of Turkish *Gastarbeiter*." In *Muslim Travellers: Pilgrimage, Migration, and the Religious Imagination*, ed. Dale F. Eickelman and James Piscatori, pp. 153–74. Berkeley: University of California Press.

Mardin, Şerif. 1982. "Turkey: Islam and Westernization." In *Religions and Societies: Asia and the Middle East*, ed. Carlo Caldarola, pp. 171–98. New York: Mouton.

Mert, Hamdi. 1992. "Gündem: Alevilik." *Diyanet*, no. 12, February.

Noyan, Bedri. 1995. *Bektaşilik Alevilik Nedir?* Istanbul, Ant/Can Yayınları.

Öncü, Ayşe. 1995. "Packaging Islam: Cultural Politics on the Landscape of Turkish Commercial Television." *Public Culture* 8, no. 1 (Fall): 51–71.

Özgünay, Abidin. 1993. "Alevilik Islam'in Özgün Parcasıdır." *İzlenim*, May.

Resmi Gazete. 1983. October 22, pp. 28–29.

Şahin, Teoman. 1995. *Alevilere Söylenen Yalanlar: Bektaşilik Soruşturmsı I*. Ankara: Armağan Kitap ve Yayınevi.

Şener, Cener. 1991. *Alevilik Olayı: Toplumsal Bir Başkaldırının Kisa Tarihçesi*. Istanbul: Tekin.

Shankland, David. 1994. "Social Change and Culture: Responses to Modernization in an Alevi Village in Anatolia." In *When History Accelerates*, ed. C. Hann, pp. 238–54. London: Athlone Press.

Sönmez, Mustafa. 1996. "Türk medya sektöründe yoğunlaşma ve sonuçları." *Birikim* 92: 76–86.

TBMM Genel Kurul Görüşmeleri. 1993. Birleşim 28; Oturum 1, November 16, pp. 1–37.

"Televizyon Patladı" (TV Explosion). 1991. *Nokta* (February): 5–13.

Türkdoğan, Orhan. 1995. *Alevi-Bektaşi Kimliği: Sosyo-Antropolojik Araştırma*. Istanbul: Timas.

"Turkey: The Elusive Golden Apple." 1996. *The Economist*, June 8, p. 7.

TSK. 1982. *Türkiye'de Yıkıcı ve Bölücü Akımlar*. Ankara: Kara Kuvvetleri Komutanlığı Yayınları.

Üzüm, Ilyas. 1997. "Günümüz Alevi Örgütlenmeleri." Unpublished paper.

van Bruinessen, Martin. 1992. *Agha, Shaikh and State: The Social and Political Structures of Kurdistan*. London: Zed.

———. 1996a. "Kurds, Turks and the Alevi Revival in Turkey." *Middle East Report* 26, no. 3 (Summer): 7–10.

———. 1996b. *The Debate on the Ethnic Identity of the Kurds*. Working paper, Centre for the Study of Asia and the Middle East, Deakin University, Australia.

Vorhoff, Karin. 1995. "The 'Making of Tradition': A Case-Study of a Religious Grouping in Recent Turkey." Paper presented at the Orient-Institute Istanbul, May 5.

Yalman, Nur. 1969. "Islamic Reform and the Mystic Tradition in Eastern Turkey." *European Journal of Sociology* 10, no. 1 (May): 41–62.

Yaman, Ali, and Sadık Güner. 1995. "Basında Alevilik." *Cem* 4, no. 45 (February): 42–43.

Yavuz, M. Hakan. 1993. "Nationalism and Islam: Yusuf Akçura Üç Tarz-ı Siyaset." *Oxford Journal of Islamic Studies* 4, no. 2 (July): 175–208.

———. 1998. "A Preamble to the Kurdish Question: The Politics of Kurdish Identity." Introduction to special issue on the Kurds, *Journal of Muslim Minority Affairs* 18, no. 1 (April): 9–18.

———. 1998. "Kimlikleri Gelistires, Iletisim ve Alevilik." *Milliyet,* August 12.

Yavuz, Sevinç, and Murat Inceoğlu. 1996. "Aleviler ne istiyor?" *Yeni Yüzyıl,* March 3.

Yörükoğlu, R. 1990. *Okunacak Kitap İnsandir: Tarihten Günümüzde Alevilik.* Istanbul: Alev Yayınları.

Zaptcioğlu, Dilek. 1995. "Almanya'da Alevi rönesansi." *Yeni Yüzyıl,* April 3.

Zelyut, Rıza. 1992. *Öz Kaynaklarına Göre Alevilik.* Istanbul: Yön.

RECENT CHANGES IN TURKISH MEDIA: AN UPDATE

In April 1999, Britain's Independent Television Commission revoked the license of MED-TV, charging that the station repeatedly flouted its regulations on incitement to violence, and also for sympathizing with Turkey's Kurdish separatists. Blocked in Britain, Kurdish intellectuals in July 1999 established Medya TV and began broadcasting from Paris via satellite. The Turkish state tried to penalize viewers by, for example, firing five teachers caught listening to Medya TV broadcasts and publicizing the incident (*Politika,* February 2, 2002, <www. ozgurpolitika.org/2002/02/02/hab07.html>).

Turkey's expanding public sphere has both differentiated and unified the cultural and political aspects of Kurdish identity politics. After the 1999 arrest of Abdullah Ocala, the head of the PKK, the right to education in Kurdish became the core issue for Kurdish cultural rights, as for many others in Turkey. A hopeful step toward accommodation started with the European Union's recognition of Turkey's "candidate status" for joining the EU in December 1999. On the basis of this new status, the EU asked Ankara to reform its legal system and to recognize Kurdish cultural rights. Turkey responded by allowing "broadcasting in other mother tongues" and amended the Turkish constitution in accord with common EU criteria. Despite these legal changes, the Turkish government expelled thousands of Kurdish university students from their schools when they petitioned for education in Kurdish in 2002.

GLOSSARY

Key to abbreviations: Ar, Arabic; Ben, Bangla or Bengali;
In, bahasa Indonesia; Per, Persian; Turk, Turkish

'ada (In; orig. Ar): custom

ahkam (sing.); *hukm* (Ar): scale of religious precepts, from obligatory to
forbidden, applicable to various activities

Alevi (Turk): Shi'i religious sect found in Turkey, Iraq, Syria, and Lebanon

al-khaliq (Ar): "the Creator," one of the names of God

al-makhluqin (Ar): "the created" (pl.), those subject to God's rules

Ba'ath (Ar): populist political party, primarily in Syria and Iraq, which com-
bines doctrines of Arab nationalism and socialism

CDLR: Committee for the Defense of Legitimate Rights (*Lajnat al-Difa'
'an al-Hurur al-Shar'iyya*), an overseas Saudi oppositional group

CD-ROM: "Compact Disk Read-Only Memory," permanent storage of
computerized data

dalil (Ar): guide to interpretation provided through revelation; scriptural
proof

Da'wa (Ar): outreach, proselytizing

dede (Turk): Alevi religious leader

dobhashi: See *punthi*

dorud (Ben): a set of Qur'anic verses in which God is implored to bless
Muhammad and his family

dowreh (Per): an informal discussion circle, frequently meeting on a regular
schedule, among friends in Iran

electronic bulletin boards: See *newsgroups*

falsafa (Ar): philosophy

fatwa (Ar): religious ruling, decree, advice

fiqh (Ar): Islamic jurisprudence

galabiyya (Egyptian Ar): tunic, ankle-length outer garment

hadith (Ar): oral traditions recounting the actions and sayings of Muhammed *halaqa* (In, from Ar): circle, or study circle

hijab (Ar): the "Islamic" head-covering for women, also refers to the practice of wearing one

'Id (Ar): religious holiday or feast day holiday marked by sacrifice

ifta' (Ar): the giving of nonbinding opinions by a religious authority (*mufti*) in response to a question

ijma' (Ar): a "consensus" of scholars with respect to interpretations of Islamic law (*shari'a*)

ijtihad (Ar): striving to interpret correctly the divine path, *shari'a,* revealed through scripture

infitah (Ar): "opening"; Egypt's post-1973 "open door" economic policy

jaheliyat (Ben; orig. Ar *jahiliyya*): the pre-Islamic period in Arabia commonly understood as being one of ignorance, paganism, and injustice

jihad (Ar): an effort to achieve a determined objective, ranging from military action to solving a legal problem or attaining moral perfection

kapalı, (Turk): "closed," referring to the conservative head-covering common for women

kafir (Ar, also In): unbeliever

khatib (Ar): preacher

kıble (Turk; Ar *qibla*): the direction one faces for prayer

madrasa (Ar): mosque-university or religious school

marja' (Ar): Shi'i religious authority

mas'ala (Ben; orig. Ar): question, problem, issue

masjid (Ar): mosque

maslaha (Ar): legal doctrine of social interest or utility

Mihna (Ar): inquisition (of A.D. 833–848)

millet (Turk): nation; sectarian community under the Ottoman empire

Moro (orig. Spanish): Muslim ethno-linguistic group in the Philippines

mufti (Ar): the religious authority who delivers a legal opinion

mujahid (Ar): struggler or striver (for a religious cause)

murid (Ar): a Sufi follower or disciple

Nakşibandi (Turk): Sufi order prominent in Turkey and Central Asia

nashid (Ar): martial chant or chanted poem in praise of the Prophet

newsgroups, also *electronic bulletin boards*: Internet sites where messages and commentary on them may be posted and arranged by topic

niqab (Ar): Saudi-style face veil that covers a woman's entire head, leaving only a narrow opening for the eyes

pesantren (In, pl.): religious schools

pir (Per): a Sufi master or model

punthi or *dobhashi* (Ben): Bengali verse or rhymed prose produced by and for semi-literate Bengali Muslims during the nineteenth and early twentieth centuries

qadi (Ar): Islamic judge

ra'i (Ar, French *raï*): a hybrid of North African folk music with rock rhythms

sadhu (Ben): classical Bangla

Salafiyya: a liberal movement for reform in late-19th- and early 20th-century Egypt

salat (Ar): ritual prayers

shari'a (Ar): conventional jurisprudence interpreted by traditionally educated scholars

shura (Ar): consultation, today used for limited parliaments; upper house of the Egyptian parliament

Simay-i-Matlub (Per): "Optimal Image," Iranian government committee for programs to rival Western music videos for audience appeal

siyasa (Ar): politics; policy

Sufism: Islamic mysticism

sunna (Ar): conduct, especially that modeled on the conduct and precepts of the Prophet Muhammad

Syndicate: officially sponsored professional associations in Egypt and some other Arab countries

'ulama (Ar): Islamic men of learning. Also *ulama* (In), *ulema* (Turk)

umma (Ar): the (religious) community of believers in Islam

waaz mahfil (Ben): public performances of scriptural commentary (in Bangladesh)

waqf (Ar): pious trust, endowment for religious purpose

wila' al-umur (Ar): "legitimate rulers"

wilayat-i faqih (Per): "government of the jurist," the sovereignty of jurists over the texts they interpret

zakat (Ar): tithe, one of the five basic Islamic obligations

zawiya (Ar): Sufi religious lodge

JON W. ANDERSON is Professor of Anthropology at the Catholic University of America. From 1992 to 1997 he was editor of the *Middle East Studies Association Bulletin,* in which capacity he introduced regular coverage of Internet resources for Middle East studies. He has written several articles about the Internet in the Middle East and Muslim worlds, some of which are available on-line from the Internet Society (www.isoc.org), the U.S. Institute of Peace (www.usip.org/oc/virtual_dipl.html), the *Arab Studies Journal* (www.georgetown.edu/sfs/programs/ccas/asj/), and the *Middle East Studies Association Bulletin* (www.mesa.arizona.edu/bulletin).

WALTER ARMBRUST is the Albert Hourani Fellow of Modern Middle East Studies at St. Antony's College, University of Oxford. He is the author of *Mass Media and Modernism in Egypt* (1996), and editor of *Mass Mediations: New Approaches to Popular Culture in the Middle East and Beyond* (2000).

DALE F. EICKELMAN is Ralph and Richard Lazarus Professor of Anthropology and Human Relations at Dartmouth College. His books include *Knowledge and Power in Morocco* (1985), *Muslim Politics* (co-authored with James Piscatori, 1996), and *The Middle East and Central Asia: An Anthropological Approach,* 4th edition (2002). He is past president of the Middle East Studies Association, a 1992 Guggenheim Fellow, and a 2000–2001 fellow at the Wissenschaftskolleg zu Berlin. In 2001–2002 he co-directed (with Armando Salvatore) a summer institute for postdoctoral scholars, "The Public Sphere and Muslim Identities," for the Alexander von Humboldt Foundation.

YVES GONZALEZ-QUIJANO teaches contemporary Arabic literature at the Université Lyon II–Louis Lumières. He has worked previously for the Institut du Monde Arabe in Paris, led a translation project for UNESCO, and created a collection of contemporary Arab writings in translation for the French publishing house Actes Sud. During his academic training at the Institut d'Études Politiques de Paris, he worked with Rémy Leveau and Gilles Kepel on a research program on Maghrebi immigration to France. He is the author of *Les Gens du livre: Édition et champ intellectuel dans l'Égypte républicaine* (1998) and numerous articles on popular Arab culture and the impact of information technology on Arab societies.

ROBERT W. HEFNER is Professor of Anthropology, Associate Director of the Institute for the Study of Economic Culture, and Researcher on Religion and Democracy at the Institute on Religion and World Affairs (IRWA) at Boston University. He just completed a Ford Foundation three-year project on "Southeast Pluralisms: Social Resources for Civility and Participation" (1998–2001). He currently directs the project "Civil Democratic Islam: Prospects and Policies for a Changing Muslim World" for the Pew Charitable Trusts and IRWA. His recent books include *Civil Islam: Muslims and Democratization in Indonesia* (2000) and the edited *The Politics of Multiculturalism: Pluralism and Citizenship in Malaysia, Singapore, and Indonesia* (2001).

MAIMUNA HUQ is a Ph.D. candidate in Social Anthropology at Columbia University. She is studying contemporary Islamic activism in the Middle East and South Asia, especially Bangladesh.

AUGUSTUS RICHARD NORTON is Professor of Anthropology and International Relations at Boston University. From 1991 to 1994 he directed the Civil Society in the Middle East program at New York University, where he was also a visiting research professor. His books include *Amal and the Shi'a: Struggle for the Soul of Lebanon* (1987) and *Civil Society in the Middle East,* 2 vols. (1995, 1996), and he has written several articles on the problems of political liberalization in the Middle East. He is also the co-producer of *Quest for Change,* a documentary film on civil society in the Middle East. He and Farhad Kazemi are currently working on a book on political reform in the Middle East.

GREGORY STARRETT is Associate Professor of Anthropology at the University of North Carolina at Charlotte. A graduate of Stanford University, he has written articles on Islamic literature, ritual interpretation, public culture, and religious commodities in Egypt. He has recently published *Putting Islam to Work: Education, Politics, and Religious Transformation in Egypt* and is currently conducting research on the production and consumption of Islamic intellectual goods.

M. HAKAN YAVUZ is Assistant Professor of Political Science at the University of Utah and a research fellow at the Faculty of Political Science at Sarajevo University. He has written several articles on the Turkish Refah (Welfare) Party, nationalism, ethnicity, and democratization.

INDEX

Italicized page numbers indicate illustrations.